Palgrave Studies in Political Leadership

Series Editors
Ludger Helms
University of Innsbruck
Innsbruck, Austria

Gillian Peele
Department of Politics and International Relations
University of Oxford
Oxford, UK

Bert A. Rockman
Department of Political Science
Purdue University
West Lafayette, IN, USA

Palgrave Studies in Political Leadership seeks to gather some of the best work on political leadership broadly defined, stretching from classical areas such as executive, legislative and party leadership to understudied manifestations of political leadership beyond the state. Edited by an international board of distinguished leadership scholars from the United States, Europe and Asia, the series publishes cutting-edge research that reaches out to a global readership. The editors are gratefully supported by an advisory board comprising of: Takashi Inoguchi (University of Tokyo, Japan), R.A.W Rhodes (University of Southampton, UK) and Ferdinand Müller-Rommel (University of Luneburg, Germany).

More information about this series at
https://link.springer.com/bookseries/14602

Ferdinand Müller-Rommel
Michelangelo Vercesi • Jan Berz

Prime Ministers in Europe

Changing Career Experiences and Profiles

Ferdinand Müller-Rommel
Center for the Study of Democracy
Leuphana University Lüneburg
Lüneburg, Germany

Michelangelo Vercesi
Center for the Study of Democracy
Leuphana University Lüneburg
Lüneburg, Germany

Jan Berz
Department of Political Science
Trinity College Dublin
Dublin, Ireland

ISSN 2947-5821   ISSN 2947-583X   (electronic)
Palgrave Studies in Political Leadership
ISBN 978-3-030-90890-4   ISBN 978-3-030-90891-1   (eBook)
https://doi.org/10.1007/978-3-030-90891-1

© The Editor(s) (if applicable) and The Author(s), under exclusive licence to Springer Nature Switzerland AG 2022, corrected publication 2022
This work is subject to copyright. All rights are solely and exclusively licensed by the Publisher, whether the whole or part of the material is concerned, specifically the rights of translation, reprinting, reuse of illustrations, recitation, broadcasting, reproduction on microfilms or in any other physical way, and transmission or information storage and retrieval, electronic adaptation, computer software, or by similar or dissimilar methodology now known or hereafter developed.
The use of general descriptive names, registered names, trademarks, service marks, etc. in this publication does not imply, even in the absence of a specific statement, that such names are exempt from the relevant protective laws and regulations and therefore free for general use.
The publisher, the authors and the editors are safe to assume that the advice and information in this book are believed to be true and accurate at the date of publication. Neither the publisher nor the authors or the editors give a warranty, expressed or implied, with respect to the material contained herein or for any errors or omissions that may have been made. The publisher remains neutral with regard to jurisdictional claims in published maps and institutional affiliations.

Cover image: © Dutchy / Getty Images

This Palgrave Macmillan imprint is published by the registered company Springer Nature Switzerland AG.
The registered company address is: Gewerbestrasse 11, 6330 Cham, Switzerland

To Jean Blondel
a highly respected scholar, mentor, and friend

Foreword

Every professional or non-professional observer of political life has little doubt about the importance of prime ministers in the parliamentary or semi-presidential regimes typical of Europe (but not only). Prime ministers, their actions and declarations, their tweets are almost daily at the center of media attention. Who they are, where they come from, and how successful their conduct of government affairs is are the objects of constant discussion. It is a bit surprising therefore that political scientists have devoted much less systematic attention to these figures. Is it the fear to be not sufficiently scientific by taking a personalistic view of politics instead of adopting a more structural vision? Is it because prevailing research frameworks do not have a well-defined place for these political figures? Whatever the reason for this, there is obviously a disturbing gap in our knowledge. It is therefore good news that a book devoted entirely to the analysis of these political figures should be published. And it is also good news that the book should be based on solid and systematic empirical evidence and on a well-articulated theoretical perspective.

Ferdinand Müller-Rommel, with a long scholarly experience in the study of governments, and the two younger coauthors, Michelangelo Vercesi and Jan Berz, put straightforwardly at the center of this book the question: who are the European prime ministers? And this question, to make it even more relevant, is nested in the wider perspective of party government, the dominant although today somewhat more uncertain variant of democracy in the European context. What is then the relationship between prime ministers and parties and what prime ministers' profiles can tell us about the role of the latter in a central democratic institution as the government? By raising these questions, the three authors make this book as an important contribution not only to our knowledge about crucial policy-makers as prime ministers are but also to the ongoing scholarly debate about the decline (or transformation) of party government.

Exploiting the first systematic collection of biographical data for 350 prime ministers in 26 European countries the book cannot only provide an average profile of these political figures but also document variations across groups of countries and over time of this profile.

Throughout the chapters of the book, we come to know who the prime ministers of Europe are in terms of their gender, age when coming into office, education, occupational background, and political positions occupied in parliament, cabinet, or party office. We are led to appreciate the differences in background patterns between three main groups of European countries, those with a democratic experience dating to the first years after the Second World War, the Southern European countries who democratized in the mid-1970s, and the large Central and Eastern European set of countries who became democratic between the end of the 1980s and the beginning of the 1990s. This articulation of the analysis already provides important hints about the impact of historical periods on the shaping of prime ministerial careers; but in a following step the book, further pursuing this theme, explores variations by decades of all the main features of prime ministers.

This rich and systematic descriptive analysis provides an interesting starting point for a more theoretically articulate discussion of some important trends of political change: populism, technocracy, and presidentialization of executive office. Although the book does not directly produce a causal analysis of the relationship between these trends and the profile of prime ministers, it provides a very important starting point for developing further research along these lines.

It is fair to conclude that for all those who are convinced that prime ministers are among the most important political players in today's world this book is a must.

Florence, Italy   Maurizio Cotta

Preface

Insofar as party governments matter, prime ministers do too. They are among the best-known politicians in parliamentary and semi-presidential democracies. Their political and private lives are under constant media scrutiny. They are featured almost daily in the print and online media. Their hours worked, their regular participation in events, as well as the speeches and interviews they give seem innumerable. As a result, the large majority of voters view prime ministers as the politically most powerful government officials. This public opinion corresponds impressively with the scholarly debate about the empowerment of prime ministers in parliamentary democracies, which has come to be associated with the 'personalization' and 'presidentialization' of politics. Both concepts imply directly or indirectly that prime ministers with a technical background—rather than traditional 'partisan prime ministers'—are more likely to hold the highest executive position in parliamentary and semi-presidential governments of the twenty-first century. It therefore seems reasonable to argue that in contemporary governments, the career profiles of chief executives are slowly changing.

This book assesses how the career experiences and the career profiles of the 350 prime ministers who governed more than 400 million citizens in 26 European liberal democracies between the years 1945 and 2020 have changed over time and across countries. We want to know who these prime ministers are, what their individual background characteristics were prior to entering office, as well as when and where their career profiles shifted from partisan to technical types over the past seven decades.

This volume is a product of a close academic collaboration between three political scientists who are at different stages in their academic career. Together, they have a common interest in the study of prime ministers. The origin of this book goes back to many discussions we had with Jean Blondel who made us aware that there is—most surprisingly—very little scholarly interest in studying prime ministers from liberal democracies outside of Westminster systems. Consequently, he proposed to bring prime ministers 'back in' to the study of comparative government. Following his advice, we decided to examine the changing role of European prime ministers in times of declining party government. This book therefore provides rigorous descriptive findings about the consequences, and the implications, of declining party governments on the career patterns of prime ministers in Western, Southern, and Central-Eastern Europe.

Parts of this book have benefited greatly from the critical and constructive reflections of participants at the 'Tuesday Seminar' of the *Center for the Study of Democracy* at Leuphana University Lüneburg, as well as from attendees at the 2020 General Conference of the European Consortium of Political Research (ECPR) and the 2021 World Congress of the International Political Science Association (IPSA). In particular, we are most grateful to Annarita Criscitiello, Sebastian Jäckle, Eoin O'Malley, Elena Semenova, Ilana Shpaizman, and Gregor Zons for their stimulating intellectual feedback on our paper which covered the content from three of the chapters found in this book. We would also like to express our gratitude to Corinna Kroeber, Florian Grotz, and Thomas Poguntke for having commented on single chapters of the manuscript. Many thanks also to the two anonymous reviewers of the book proposal. Whoever you are, you provided substantive comments and valuable suggestions! Last but certainly not least, we would like to thank Aaron Martin for his thorough copyediting.

A project such as this could not have materialized without significant financial support and continuous administrative help. The data collection on prime ministers' personal background and their political careers has been financed by the German Research Foundation (*Deutsche Forschungsgemeinschaft*) within the framework of a larger project on career profiles and political performance of prime ministers (*GR3311/3-1* and *MU618/18-1*). We are also most grateful to the *Center for the Study of Democracy* at Leuphana University Lüneburg for having supported us with the necessary technical and administrative infrastructure over the course of the development of this book.

At Palgrave Macmillan we had the pleasure of working with Ambra Finotello and her colleagues, who provided guidance and continuous support throughout the entire project. We are also indebted to Ludger Helms, and the editors of the *Palgrave Studies in Political Leadership*, for having included this book in their series.

Our greatest appreciation, however, goes to Jean Blondel whose books, including *World Leaders, Government Ministers in the Contemporary World*, and *The Profession of Government Ministers in Western Europe*, as well as his personal scholarly support over many years, have greatly inspired this comparative analysis of prime ministers in the 'new' Europe. The book is therefore dedicated to him.

Lüneburg, Germany Ferdinand Müller-Rommel
Lüneburg, Germany Michelangelo Vercesi
Dublin, Ireland Jan Berz
February 2022

Contents

1 Studying Prime Ministers' Careers: An Introduction 1

2 The Background of Prime Ministers: Who They Are 29

3 Change of Prime Ministers' Careers: Theoretical Considerations 65

4 Changing Career Experiences: Less Political, More Technical 101

5 Changing Career Profiles: From Party-Agents to Party-Principals 135

6 Conclusion: What Have We Learned and What Needs to Be Done? 181

Correction to: Studying Prime Ministers' Careers: An Introduction C1

Appendix 197

Index 225

List of Figures

Fig. 3.1	From party government to prime ministers' career changes	67
Fig. 4.1	Political experiences of prime ministers by decades (aggregated share, in percent)	107
Fig. 4.2	'Insider experience' of prime ministers by region and decade (in percent)	108
Fig. 4.3	Duration of prime ministers' parliamentary experience by region and decade	112
Fig. 4.4	Duration of prime ministers' ministerial experience by region and decade	114
Fig. 4.5	Duration of prime ministers' experience as party leader by region and decade	115
Fig. 4.6	Prime ministers' subnational political experience by region and decade. (Note: The label 'local assembly' comprises all levels of government and both legislative and executive institutions)	117
Fig. 4.7	Prime ministers' experience in the European Parliament by region and decade. (Note: Thick black bars represent the quartiles and median; hollow circles represent outliers)	119
Fig. 4.8	Levels of prime ministers' technical and political experience by decade	126
Fig. 4.9	Levels of prime ministers' technical and political experience by decade and region	127
Fig. 4.10	Relationship between prime ministers' technical and political experience by decade. (Note: Dashed horizontal and vertical lines represent the average value of political and technical experiences)	130

xvi LIST OF FIGURES

Fig. 5.1	Party-agent and party-principal factor scores of individual prime ministers across Europe. (Note: Prime ministers with the highest and lowest score for each career profile type are named for each region)	143
Fig. 5.2	Distribution of factor score coefficients in the three regions. (Note: Boxplots show the median (*white line*) and the lower (25th) and upper (75th) quartiles. Whiskers represent 1.5 times IQR (interquartile range) and individual dots indicate outliers)	146
Fig. 5.3	Longitudinal developments of prime ministers' career profiles on European level. (Note: The upper panel shows the raw party-principal and party-agent values. The lower panel shows the difference between party-principal and party-agent scores as a direct test of our hypothesis ($p < 0.001$). Removing the outlier case of Prime Minister Winston Churchill leaves the results and the p-value level unchanged)	148
Fig. 5.4	Linear longitudinal change of prime ministers' career profiles by region. (Note: Linear fit between career profile scores and time in the three regions. Western Europe (WE); Central-Eastern Europe (CEE); Southern Europe (SE))	149
Fig. 5.5	Longitudinal development of prime ministers' career profiles in Western Europe by country	151
Fig. 5.6	Longitudinal development of prime ministers' career profiles in Southern Europe by country	151
Fig. 5.7	Longitudinal development of prime ministers' career profiles in Central-Eastern Europe by country	152
Fig. 5.8	Electoral volatility and prime ministers' career profiles. (Note: The left-hand panel shows the raw party-principal and party-agent scores by electoral volatility. The right-hand panel shows the difference between party-principal and party-agent scores by electoral volatility as a direct test of our hypothesis ($p < 0.01$))	155
Fig. 5.9	Prime ministers' career profiles in parliamentary and semi-presidential systems. (Note: Boxplots show the median (*white line*) and the lower (25th) and upper (75th) quartiles. Whiskers represent 1.5 times IQR and individual dots reveal outliers)	158
Fig. 5.10	Longitudinal development of prime ministers' career profiles by form of government	159
Fig. 5.11	The relationship between prime ministerial powers and prime ministers' career profiles	162

Fig. 5.12	Longitudinal development of prime ministers' career profiles by power of cabinet agenda control	163
Fig. 5.13	Relationship between presidential powers and prime ministers' career profiles	165
Fig. 5.14	Presidential powers and prime ministers' career profiles by prime ministerial agenda control	166
Fig. 5.15	Longitudinal developments of prime ministers' career profiles by party family	169
Fig. 5.16	Party-agents and party-principals in different party families. (Note: Boxplots show the median (*white line*) and the lower (25th) and upper (75th) quartiles. Whiskers represent 1.5 times IQR and individual dots reveal outliers)	170
Fig. 5.17	Distribution of party-agent and party-principal factor score coefficients between women and men. (Note: Boxplots show the median (*white line*) and the lower (25th) and upper (75th) quartiles. Whiskers represent 1.5 times IQR and individual dots reveal outliers)	172
Fig. 5.18	Development of party-agent and party-principal factor score coefficients among women and men. (Note: The linear development of party-principal and party-agent profile scores among women prime ministers is visually indistinguishable)	173
Fig. A1	Eigenvalues of the correlation matrix show only two factors with values above one	223
Fig. A2	Electoral volatility at the time of prime ministers' first investiture into office	223

List of Tables

Table 1.1	Parliamentary and semi-presidential democracies under study (*N*=26)	17
Table 2.1	Female and male prime ministers by country	33
Table 2.2	Age and seniority of prime ministers by country	35
Table 2.3	Educational background of prime ministers by country	39
Table 2.4	Occupational background of prime ministers by country N (%)	42
Table 2.5	Prime ministers by political positions in the European regions prior to entering office, N (%)	45
Table 2.6	Prime ministers by held political positions in the European countries prior to entering office, N (%)	46
Table 2.7	Prime ministers' former cabinet portfolios and opposition parliamentary party leader, N (%)	48
Table 2.8	Partisan background of prime ministers by country (when entering office for the first time), N (%)	52
Table 2.9	Prime ministers' duration and interruptions in office	57
Table 4.1	Insider and outsider experience of prime ministers	106
Table 4.2	Experience of prime ministers by political post, region, and decade (in percent)	110
Table 4.3	Prime ministers with experience in enterprises by region and decade (in percent)	121
Table 4.4	Prime ministers' technical experience in interest groups by region and decade (in percent)	122
Table 4.5	Prime ministers' technical experience as senior civil servant, diplomat, and member of international organizations by region and decade (in percent)	123
Table 4.6	Ordinal measure of technical experience and prime ministers' distribution	125

Table 4.7	Prime ministers' technical and political experiences: a typology	128
Table 5.1	Expected relationship between individual career attributes and career profiles	140
Table 5.2	Correlation of career profile factors with career attributes (principal factor method)	141
Table 5.3	Prime ministerial powers within the cabinet in Europe, 1945–2020	161

CHAPTER 1

Studying Prime Ministers' Careers: An Introduction

On May 17, 2016, the Social Democratic Party of Austria (SPÖ) appointed Christian Kern as chancellor. Kern, who remained in office until December 2017, was an unusual figure in the history of Austrian party government. After graduating with a degree in journalism and communication, Kern worked for three years as a business journalist and for another three years as assistant to the Federal Chancellery's secretary of state, Peter Kostelka. In 1994 he became the spokesman for the SPÖ's parliamentary leader. After another three years, Kern began a successful career in business for the *Verbund AG*, the largest electricity supplier in Austria. In 2009, he became a board member of the football club Austria Vienna; in 2010, he took over as CEO of the public Austrian Federal Railways (ÖBB); and, in 2014, he was appointed chairman of the Community of European Railway and Infrastructure Companies (CER). When Chancellor Faymann (SPÖ) resigned due to his party's poor performance in the 2016 Austrian presidential election, the Social Democratic Party selected Kern to be the new head of government and its party leader.

Although Christian Kern did have a party affiliation and spent part of his career in close contact with politics, his professional profile tended

---

The original version of this chapter was revised. The correction to this chapter can be found at https://doi.org/10.1007/978-3-030-90891-1_7

© The Author(s), under exclusive license to Springer Nature Switzerland AG 2022, corrected publication 2022
F. Müller-Rommel et al., *Prime Ministers in Europe*, Palgrave Studies in Political Leadership,
https://doi.org/10.1007/978-3-030-90891-1_1

toward that of a business manager at the time of his investiture. Kern neither fit the ideal-type of a technocratic prime minister, devoid of political experience, nor did he match the career model of a typical, partisan prime minister, who gained extensive experience in parliament, in cabinet, or as party head, prior to entering office. In fact, Kern was an atypical, but appealing, party member whose main professional experiences were gathered outside of politics.

What explains the nomination of Christian Kern as prime minister? We argue in this book that something new is happening in the selection of prime ministers in European liberal democracies. In the 'golden age' of party government between the 1950s and 1970s, political parties were the most influential political organizations for mobilizing and representing citizens. For about 30 years, they held a firm grasp on all aspects of the democratic process. During these years, prime ministers were mainly *Berufspolitiker* (Weber, 1919), a term later adopted in political science by King (1981) as 'career politicians', who learned the craft of politics by acquiring expertise as professional government practitioners. These politicians bring with them experiences gained from political apprenticeships and politically adjacent occupations, such as journalism, public relations, and academia. They understand the intra-party, legislative, and cabinet rules and procedures. Most of them are disposed toward compromise and are able to make convincing political judgments (Allen et al., 2020). Political parties select these career politicians as prime ministers because of their reliability as party-agents. Thereby, their previous career positions in parliament, in government, and in the political party were seen as proxies for loyalty and competence that are valuable characteristics for being selected for the prime ministerial job.

Yet, as we will see below, between the 1970s and the 1980s, things started to change: social cleavages lost relevance as sources of political division and constituencies became less cohesive and more individualized. Furthermore, party identification and membership decreased while volatility and party system fragmentation increased (Casal Bértoa & Enyedi, 2021). As a result, the conditions for a well-functioning, party government declined (Mair, 2013, p. 65). Along with the eroding model of party government, new populist and technocratic demands for representation emerged in several European countries[1] (Bertsou & Pastorella, 2017).

At the same time, the pressure from an increasing internationalization of politics, defined by global governance through intergovernmental negotiations, shifted power away from parliament and single cabinet ministers toward government and prime ministers. The increasing demand for domestic and international policy coordination, as well as the growing complexity and sectoral specialization within the center of government, has led to a substantial empowerment of prime ministers with managerial skills and a knowledge of special policy fields. Moreover, the emergence of new forms of mass communication and political participation, as well as the convergence of all major parties toward the 'ideological center' of politics, strengthened leadership-oriented party organizations, and as a result, led to a more personalized style of political representation among executives. Prime ministers not only received more political power but also became more prominent political figures within and outside of party politics, a development which scholars refer to as the 'presidentialization of politics' (Foley, 2000; Heffernan, 2005; Poguntke & Webb, 2005). Thus, the decline of party government as well as the new challenges presented by the presidentialization of politics made individual leaders more important relative to their party organizations. These new leaders transitioned from being dependent on their own party to taking over and becoming principals of their parties, exhibiting stronger leadership styles, a more prominent public image, and expertise in major policy areas.

Against this background, we argue that party demand for prime ministers' background characteristics have changed (Chap. 3) and that, over time, prime ministers have accumulated less political experience within national, party-based, political institutions and more technical experience outside of politics (Chap. 4). In addition, we claim that prime ministers' career profiles have moved from a 'party-agent' ideal-type to a 'party-principal' ideal-type (Chap. 5). These processes have affected older European democracies as well as countries in Southern and Central-Eastern Europe which democratized in the 1970s and 1990s. We wrote this book to provide empirical evidence for these conjectures.

The Political Role of Prime Ministers

The political role of prime ministers in liberal democracies has changed markedly over the past decades. In parliamentary democracies, prime ministers exercise public leadership and represent the government to citizens. Together with their cabinet ministers they are collectively responsible to the parliament, which has the power to execute a vote of no confidence between elections. Put differently, prime ministers are delegated by the assembly to lead the cabinet and its decision-making and, at the same time, they are held accountable to voters through both the parliament and the party that has nominated them. As pointed out by Strøm (2000), the prime minister lies at the crossroads of a complex institutional twine, which can be depicted like a chain of delegation with the shape of an hourglass (turned horizontal). In this chain, 'representation begins with a multitude of principals (the citizens) and ends with a large number of agents (civil servants)'; the prime minister is the neck of the hourglass, who 'connects the elected representatives of the people and the administrators of the state' (Strøm, 2000, p. 270).

Very often, the prime minister is also the head of the political party and the leading candidate in electoral campaigns. Particularly in countries with single-member district electoral systems, the prime minister leads a single-party majority cabinet, for which she chooses the ministers and has the freedom to define governmental policy. Conversely, in consensus democracies where parliamentary seats are allocated proportionally, the prime minister fronts a coalition, and in some cases even a minority cabinet, where governmental decisions need to be continuously negotiated between coalition partners and the respective party leaders (Lijphart, 2012).

The responsibilities that a prime minister bears in the government, in the party, and in the country define the 'prime ministerial job' and constitute a litmus test for assessing prime ministerial performance (Weller, 1985, 2018). The prime minister has four main *delegated tasks* (Grotz et al., 2021, pp. 1915–1916). First, she resolves cabinet conflicts when ministers drift away from the governmental policy, either because they are defending competing departmental interests or because they are promoting the interests of their own party instead of the coalitional program (Andeweg, 2000). Second, the prime minister shapes public policy, ideally in a way that respects voters' preferences (Weller, 2014, p. 495). Third, she provides solutions to exogenous crises, which usually have a significant impact on the political system. These crises require the prime minister to make policy decisions intended to maximize collective benefits and minimize collective costs (Boin et al., 2012, pp. 121–122). Fourth, the prime minister speaks for the country and represents its national interests abroad. The prime minister is indeed an 'international ambassador' who operates globally and whose 'annual diary [...] is shaped by a series of international meetings fixed long in advance' (Weller, 2014, p. 498).

In addition, the prime minister fulfills two *accountability tasks*, which include maintaining the support of the parliamentary majority and the endorsement of the political party. The risk of being 'dismissed' by one of these two entities is a powerful incentive to act responsibly toward citizens' demands (Grotz et al., 2021, p. 1911). Finally, in semi-presidential democracies, the prime minister must also cooperate with the elected president, whose term in office is fixed[2] and whose party affiliation can be either the same as the prime minister's or different (Schleiter & Morgan-Jones, 2010, pp. 1423–1424; Grotz & Kukec, 2021, pp. 409–412).

One of the most vibrant scholarly discussions on this topic focuses on how the power of the prime ministerial office has increased over time. In particular, observers recognize that, over the years, prime ministers have gained political influence and responsibility while other cabinet members, and their parties, have been marginalized. This change has, in turn, made the prime minister's actions more consequential for democratic governance. The advocates of this argument highlight that the chief executive's position has undergone an 'institutional stretch' which endows the holder with new chances to control an increasing number of political decisions. Hennessy (2012), for instance, detects a continuous concentration of duties in the hands of the prime minister in the United Kingdom with no equivalent transfer of responsibility in the opposite direction (i.e., away from the prime minister). Overall, Hennessey calculates that the number of prerogatives supervised by the prime minister increased from 12 in the 1940s up to 47 in the 1990s (Hennessy, 2012, pp. 118–131). These 47 prerogatives can be grouped into six main fields of intervention: 'constitutional and procedural (10 duties); appointments (9); conduct of cabinet and parliamentary business (8); policy strategy and communications (3); organizational and efficiency questions (3); budget and market-sensitive questions (2); national security (8); and special personal responsibilities (4)' (Weller, 2018, p. 61).

On a more comparative basis, O'Malley proposes an expert-based estimation of the prime ministerial 'influence over the policy output of the government' (2007, p. 11). His findings show that, in fact, there has been growth in the ability of prime ministers to get their 'preferred policies accepted and enacted' and that this holds for several countries. In this context, a strand of the literature also claims that parliamentary democracies have witnessed a process of presidentialization (see Chap. 3), whereby prime ministers have become relatively similar to chief executives in presidential systems. In particular, it is argued that prime ministers become more autonomous from their parties when selecting their ministerial team and running their cabinets (Poguntke & Webb, 2005; Bäck et al., 2009). Other scholars have elaborated on this, arguing that prime ministers often turn into 'personal leaders' who govern using a more direct type of popular legitimation (Musella, 2018). In sum, these changes have enhanced prime ministers' influence over policy-making and agenda-setting power.

This observation applies to both Westminster democracies and coalition-based political systems (Poguntke & Webb, 2015; Martocchia Diodati et al., 2018).

Two 'mutually reinforcing phenomena' have particularly favored this evolution: the centralization of executive decision-making and the personalization of politics (Strangio et al., 2013, p. 10). The former refers to the shift of policy authority from the cabinet to the bureaucratic and personal offices that support the prime minister and thereby to a parallel reduction of ministerial and departmental power. Personalization, in turn, increases the visibility of prime ministers, who are constantly under the public spotlight and at the forefront of the political stage (Dowding, 2013, p. 625; Strangio et al., 2013, p. 10).

The centralization of administrative structures at the prime minister's disposal has led to an increase in the coordination capacity within national executives. As Peters et al. argue 'there has been a gradual accretion of power and responsibility towards the office of the chief executive, and also some apparent waning of the powers of other institutions' (2000, p. 265). Both the number of people specialized in advising and supporting the prime minister and the sum of financial resources available to prime ministerial staff have increased over time (Müller-Rommel, 2008). For example, the number of permanently employed experts who professionally manage the prime minister's public communication through the use of mass media has increased substantially over the past decades (Musella, 2018, pp. 105–106).

At the same time, personalization has made individual political actors more prominent, while collective, political entities have declined. Three types of personalization have affected the prime minister: institutional, media, and behavioral (Rahat & Kenig, 2018, p. 118 ff). Institutional personalization applies when rules emphasize the influence of the prime minister *vis-à-vis* other political collective actors (e.g., the cabinet or the political party). For instance, granting the prime minister more power in the selection of cabinet ministers or in the overall cabinet decision-making processes is considered as a form of institutional personalization. Second, contemporary mass media cover prime ministers and individual politicians more often than collective entities, such as parties or other political groupings. For example, Karvonen (2010, p. 89) observes a growing trend in the percentage of articles covering the incumbent prime minister by name or position in the British newspaper *The Times*. Higher levels of personalization in newspapers, radios, televisions, and informational websites have become a common feature of advanced democracies (Rahat & Kenig, 2018, pp. 154–157). Third, behavioral personalization occurs when prime ministers move from being 'team players' who act together with party officials and cabinet members to 'separate politicians' with uncoordinated actions. The shift in prime ministers' behavior toward a 'centralized personalization' affects the electoral outcomes significantly because the choices of voters become increasingly driven by prime ministers' personal characteristics rather than by party politics (Garzia, 2014; Berz, 2019). Moreover, the centralized personalization of prime ministers can increase or decrease voter turnout for parliamentary elections, especially when the consumption of television is high (Ferreira da Silva et al., 2021).

In sum, the empirical evidence shows that the traditional tasks of prime ministers, that is, linking citizens' demands with governmental policy, remains the same, but their role in fulfilling these tasks, that is, their personal empowerment, changed over the past decades. The centralization of decision-making and the personalization of politics have deeply affected popular expectations about the prime ministers' role and their job in office. Prime ministers are increasingly recognized as drivers of decision-making in the heart of government and as the 'architects' of overall governmental policy. They carry out their office under the watchful eye of the citizen, who holds them accountable at the next elections. It is for this reason that prime ministers have strong personal incentives to handle their job successfully, thus enhancing their chances to stay in office for another term.

In this book, we claim that these popular expectations have a pronounced effect on the careers of prime ministers. The idea is simple: we argue that a career background in politics provides prime ministers with relevant skills and expertise to succeed while in office. If prime ministers are expected to fulfill new functions or to fulfill old functions in new institutional settings, then they need congruent experience and adequate skills. Put differently, new job descriptions require new political expertise. Thus, we expect the career experiences and profiles of prime ministers to change in times of changing job requirements, accordingly.

Why Study Prime Ministers' Careers?

Prime ministers are the most powerful and prestigious politicians in parliamentary democracies. They are major political decision-makers and administrators whose activities affect the public life of the entire country.

It is therefore not surprising that their political and private lives are under constant media observation and that the public knows more about prime ministers than any other cabinet member (Jones, 1991). Depending on the prime ministers' political performance and public reputation, national governments often bear their names (e.g., Kreisky, Thatcher, Kohl, Merkel government) rather than the name of the governing party or party family. Many prime ministers, therefore, dominate the headlines and represent the state and government to millions of citizens beyond the boundaries of their own country. Who are these prime ministers and why study their careers?

Previous research stated that the individual background characteristics of chief executives matter for their performance in office and thereby for the quality of liberal democracy. In his classic book on state politics, V.O. Key (1956, p. 10), for instance, claimed that 'the nature of the workings of government depends ultimately on the men who run it'. Ten years later, Almond and Powell (1966, p. 48) stated more precisely that 'the background of those who are recruited into political roles is bound to have some impact on their performance of these roles'. Similarly, Putnam (1976, p. IX) argued in his seminal book on political elites: 'insofar as political decisions matter, political decision makers do, too'. Most recently Krcmaric et al. (2020, pp. 135–136) pointed out that the individual biography of political leaders, including their socio-demographic background as well as their career paths, affect their political behavior in office and thereby the quality of democratic governance. A similar argument was introduced many years ago by Simon (1985) who studied the personality of chief executives. In a nutshell, he suggests that five individual characteristics matter for understanding their political behavior in office: (1) their basic beliefs and core values on politics; (2) their motivations for office-seeking and office-holding; (3) their individual leadership styles; (4) their behavior in times of political crisis; and (5) their socio-demographic composition as well as their political experiences. If we take these statements seriously and consider prime ministers as those politicians who are responsible for directing the 'fabric' of government and driving national policy-making, then we need to answer at least one crucial question: what individual and political background characteristics do European prime ministers share during their career?

Despite their changing role and their increasing relevance in party government, systematic research on prime ministers' careers is still a relatively unexplored field in comparative politics, particularly compared to the numerous theoretical and empirical studies on legislative and ministerial careers (Blondel, 1985; Blondel & Thiébault, 1991; MacKenzie & Kousser, 2014). This research deficit exists because the selection of prime ministers appears to be less transparent and linear than the career paths of parliamentary members and cabinet ministers. Moreover, the career pathways of prime ministers are more complex and depend on various personal and institutional characteristics, as well as on unpredictable historical events.

This is one of the reasons why most studies on prime ministerial careers concentrate on (anecdotical) biographies and autobiographies by journalists, historians, political scientists, and politicians themselves. The strength of these studies lies in the rich historical detail provided about the cultural and political environment that often determine a prime minister's career. The weakness of the conventional biographies, however, is that they offer information only on one politician, which does not allow for comparison between different prime ministers' careers at different points in time. In other words, biographies do not collect data on multiple prime ministers in a systematic way. Moreover, while most biographies and autobiographies on prime ministers cover aspects associated to their reasons for seeking office, their leadership style, and their behavior in cabinet decision-making, it is somewhat surprising that the socio-demographic composition and the career experiences that prime ministers bring into office have never been examined systematically neither in case studies nor in comparative analysis. This lacuna is even more striking since we know—as mentioned above—that the political behavior of prime ministers in office is strongly related to their individual background characteristics as well as their personal political experiences that they have made prior and during their professional careers (Dyson & Preston, 2006; Carnes, 2013; Alexiadou, 2015; Gift & Krcmaric, 2017; Jentleson, 2018).

Any systematic comparative study of prime ministers' careers in Europe must start with a conceptual definition and a review of the existing literature. In this book, we follow Bakema (1991, p. 71) who defined a political career as the number and type of political positions held by an individual prime minister during a certain period of time. These positions are usually ranked hierarchically in relation to their power and prestige. Every political career involves selection to office, duration in office, and exit from office. Thus, the period from prime ministers' first political appointment to their exit from the chief executive office can be regarded as the parameters of their political careers.

The literature on prime ministers' careers has focused on four distinct aspects. The first makes use of the individual social and occupational background of prime ministers, aiming to show the shared characteristics of those with successful executive careers. The second set of studies explains the selection and de-selection of prime ministers by applying the principal-agent theory. A third set of scholarly work highlights the impact of political careers on the performance of prime ministers. Finally, a share of the literature examines the political careers of female prime ministers. The major findings of these four conceptual approaches are introduced in the following section.[3]

Clues from Existing Research

The *social and occupational background* of prime ministers constitutes a first indicator for showing the impact of personal characteristics on executive careers. One of the main assumptions of this research is that people with certain characteristics are more likely to reach executive office than others (e.g., Hallerberg & Wehner, 2018). Therefore, those who become chief executives do not mirror all societal groups equally, but are characterized by exceptional social backgrounds. Heads of government, so the argument goes, are mostly drawn from an 'upper class' elite in terms of educational and occupational composition. Putnam (1976, p. 37) refers to this as the 'law of increasing disproportion'—as the level of elite status increases, the bias in the social characteristics between the elite and the remaining population expands.

Müller and Philipp (1991) provide the most extensive, cross-national investigation into the social and occupational composition of prime ministers. Their seminal work proposes a wealth of information about prime ministers in Western Europe from the aftermath of the Second World War to the 1980s. First, they find that most prime ministers are men, with high educational levels and with high-status occupations. Second, prime ministers often acquire experiences in the public sector, occupy parliamentary and ministerial positions, and hold party leadership. Third, many prime ministers hold ministerial portfolios in the most powerful and prestigious departments, such as economics, finance, justice, and foreign affairs. Finally, they observe substantial variation between the social and political background of prime ministers in Continental Europe, Scandinavia, and the Anglo-Saxon countries.

A second explanation for prime ministers' career trajectories builds on the *selection and de-selection* of politicians by political parties and other institutional gate-keepers. This approach relies conceptually on the principal-agent theory (Dowding & Dumont, 2009; Berlinski et al., 2012) and posits that some political positions are filled by principals who select prospective agents, with certain social and professional characteristics, to occupy the prime minister's post. In parliamentary democracies, for instance, voters are the principal of members of parliament, who are then the principals of prime ministers. The prime minister is the principal of line ministers, who are the principals of the civil servants in their respective ministry. To ensure that agents follow the principals' will, different accountability mechanisms can be employed. Samuels and Shugart (2010), for instance, claim that political parties select prime ministers as agents, only after having screened their political experience in advance. Since the political executive in parliamentary systems stems from the legislature (rather than from popular vote), political parties are more likely to select 'political insiders' who have a long tenure in politics and therefore a higher degree of political professionalization. These prime ministers have gained political experiences in legislative and/or executive offices, prior to entering office, which is why they are considered reliable agents by their party-principals. It is therefore not surprising that Samuels and Shugart (2010) find prime ministers with extra-parliamentary experiences ('political outsiders') to be appointed less frequently in parliamentary than in semi-presidential systems. Protsyk (2005) also argues that in semi-presidential systems, powerful presidents mostly select 'technocratic' prime ministers because they can be closer to their ideal policies than other high-ranking party officials. In a similar vein, Schleiter and Morgan-Jones (2009) suggest that in semi-presidential systems strong elected presidents are more likely to select loyal non-partisans. However, complex parliamentary bargaining environments in semi-presidential systems can increase the likelihood of having the president and the prime minister from the same party (Bucur & Cheibub, 2017).

Grotz and Weber (2017) introduced another aspect of prime ministerial selection. In their study on the role of party leadership among prime ministers in Central-Eastern Europe, they find that the selection of prime ministers is moderated by the timing of the government formation process. After elections, parties tend to select their leaders for prime ministerial offices, but if the office needs to be filled during a term, parties favor experienced cabinet members, rather than party leaders, to ensure short-term stability before the next election.

Pre-executive political careers also impact prime ministers' survival in office. Previous political experience in several posts provides prime ministers with better skills to fulfill their tasks. Prime ministers with political expertise are therefore expected to serve longer periods in office than their counterparts with less political experience. In this context, Baylis (2007, p. 91, 81) argues that prime ministers in Central-Eastern Europe are generally characterized by a 'shortage of experience in democratic politics' which is one reason that they 'appear to have been relatively weak figures'. Grotz and Weber (2017), analyzing Central-Eastern Europe, show that prime ministers who served as party leaders are more likely to survive in office than those who were only cabinet ministers. Furthermore, Byrne et al. (2017) determine that being the opposition leader is sometimes an important career step for future prime ministers in the United Kingdom, arguing that this experience supported Cameron's survival in office and his capacity to implement his policy positions in the cabinet decision-making processes.

A third sub-set of research reveals the impact of political careers on the *performance of prime ministers*. This approach promotes the argument that certain types of career trajectories are related to prime ministers' specific policy preferences. While Theakston and Gill (2006) find that expert ratings of British prime ministerial performance do not clearly correlate with their political careers, Helms (2020) clarifies that, for 'heir' prime ministers (i.e., those who get their office from a predecessor between two parliamentary elections), the relationship between political careers and governmental performance exists, albeit not in the expected direction—the best performing 'heir' prime ministers are those with less parliamentary and ministerial experience.

In a more recent study of prime ministers in Central-Eastern Europe, Grotz et al. (2021) find that political career experience helps executives succeed in office. In particular, previous experience as party leader is decisive for fulfilling the chief executive's tasks, while prior parliamentary membership substantially enhances the prime minister's capacity to secure the support of a parliamentary majority. Former ministerial experience, however, does not significantly affect the performance of prime ministers in Central-East European democracies.

A final set of literature focuses on the political careers of *female prime ministers*. Scholars have identified the scarcity of available offices as a major obstacle hindering the selection of women for the prime ministerial position (Barnes & Taylor-Robinson, 2018). The findings show that men are more likely than women to start political careers and to reach the top executive positions. However, the number of female prime ministers has increased remarkably in European cabinets over the past decades, indicating that gender parity is becoming more frequent in modern democracies. Despite some regional differences, most of the female prime ministers served during the last two decades. Scandinavian countries have provided better opportunities for females to pursue political careers than Southern Europe (Jalalzai, 2014). However, as noted above major differences regarding the socio-demographic background of prime ministers do not exist between male and female prime ministers. Although women have held only a small number of prime ministerial posts, their age, their first occupation, and their educational background characteristics are similar to their male counterparts (Müller-Rommel & Vercesi, 2017, p. 250).

In a comprehensive study on the political careers of female prime ministers, Jalalzai (2013) shows that women have higher access to executive positions in dual executives when there is a dominant, elected president (i.e., in semi-presidential systems). Institutionalized leadership selection processes, and major political transitions between political regimes, are other factors which open opportunities for women to enter government. Moreover, as the examples of Chancellor Angela Merkel in Germany as well as Prime Ministers Margaret Thatcher and Theresa May in the United Kingdom show, the availability of offices for female aspirants might increase if parties face internal leadership crises (Jensen, 2008). Building on such examples, Beckwith (2015) concludes that political scandals or electoral failures are the most beneficial preconditions for the selection of female prime ministers. Finally, 'corporatist-oriented' catch-all parties are favorable for women's executive careers (Wiliarty, 2008). Given the broad membership of these parties, they aim to promote different factions by representing female politicians in various committees and offices, thereby allowing minorities to climb the ladder toward the prime ministerial office (Jalalzai, 2011).

In sum, comparative research on prime ministers' political careers shows that, despite their increasing political relevance in times of party governmental change, comprehensive comparative studies on their personal background and their career trajectories are still a *terra incognita* in executive elite research. Put differently, we know hardly anything about the differences and similarities of prime ministers' careers from a truly cross-national and longitudinal perspective. Against this background and in order to better understand the changing careers of prime ministers in Europe, this book aims to go beyond existing research by offering a substantial theoretical and empirical contribution to the debate about the origin and the political effect of 'old' and 'new' career types of prime ministers in European parliamentary and semi-presidential systems.

Going Beyond Existing Research

Our study of prime ministers' careers builds on the comparative literature outlined above; however, it goes beyond the current state of research by providing a number of theoretical and empirical innovations. The present study provides *theoretical contributions* to three fields of research: first, it enlarges the theory of party government (Budge & Keman, 1990; Keman & Müller-Rommel, 2012) by linking prime ministers' career experiences and profiles to the debate about the decline of party government. Our argument states that the decline of the traditional party government model leads to the weakening of party organizations, in conjunction with the empowerment of prime ministers. This trend has—as we will show later in this book—severe consequences for the future of democratic representation and democratic governance in Europe.

Second, our study offers new theoretical ideas about prime ministers' career trajectories that are related to three sets of scholarly work: it suggests additional conceptual approaches to the evidence-based variation of prime ministers' careers over time and space (Blondel & Thiébault, 1991; Dowding & Dumont, 2009, 2015); it connects two streams of thought that explain different trajectories to executive office by focusing not only on the individual background characteristics of a successful prime ministerial career ('actor-oriented approach') but also on the macro-level institutional factors that explain different career choices ('context-oriented approach') (Jahr & Edinger, 2015). Moreover, it suggests general conclusions on the effect of different prime ministers' career trajectories on the prime ministers' capacity to fulfill their job and to perform well in office (Strangio et al., 2013; Grotz et al., 2021). Third, this work also enriches the 'integration theories' of the so-called New Europe, that is, studies on the 'new' democracies in Southern and Central-Eastern Europe, *vis-à-vis* the established ones in Western Europe, because it allows us to assess convergences in the careers of prime ministers between these geographical regions.

The *empirical contribution* of this study is equally innovative. It provides the field with a comprehensive and unique, comparative dataset, rich with information about the individual background characteristics and careers of 350 prime ministers in 26 European countries over the past seven decades (see Appendix). Methodologically, we provide a comparative analysis about the change of prime ministers' careers based on descriptive inference. More precisely, we present a 'grand historical narrative' approach (Elgie & Passarelli, 2019), or—as Elgie (2020) suggests in his review on methodologies in the study of political executives—an 'analytical narrative' about long-term trends in prime ministers' careers across geographical regions. Although departing from dominant standards of statistical inference, such as multivariate regression, our investigation is deductive in its essence; the 'analytical narrative' approach statistically clusters prime ministers' political and technical experiences, as well as their career profiles, using a cross-national and longitudinal perspective.

Coming from the initial vantage point of asking how the career experiences and the career profiles of prime ministers in Europe have changed, three sets of research questions lie at the heart of this study. The first set of questions addresses the individual level of prime ministerial careers by asking: *Do prime ministers follow homogeneous career patterns? How long do prime ministers survive in office? Do the prime ministerial career experiences cluster around certain career types? To what extent have 'new' career profiles developed among prime ministers?*

The second set of questions goes beyond the individual level and stresses on the impact of institutional factors on the political careers, asking: *How does the decline of party government affect prime ministers' political experiences and their career profiles? Which political institutions create opportunities for changes in prime ministerial career profiles? Which selection mechanisms influence women's chances to become prime minister?*

The third set of questions focus on the similarities and differences between prime ministers' careers across Europe and over time, asking: *Do different forms of career experience change over time and across regions? To what extent do prime ministers' career profiles differ in 'old' and 'new' European democracies?*

By answering these questions, we do not only provide new empirical findings in the comparative study of prime ministers' careers but also offer valuable information to policy advisors and engaged citizens who are interested in getting to know 'Who Governs?' (Dahl, 1961) and who has governed liberal democracies in Europe.

Prime Ministers in 26 European Democracies

The geographical focus of this study is the so-called *New Europe*, that is, the 'old' West European countries and the 'new' democracies in Southern and Central-Eastern Europe (Budge et al., 1997). These countries differ in the length of their democratic experience and in their population and territorial size. Included in our study are only developed parliamentary and semi-presidential democracies—defined as countries scoring at least 5 on the Polity V scale (Marshall et al., 2018)—with more than one million inhabitants in 2019 (see Appendix). Thus, 'small states' (Anckar, 1999) such as Iceland, Luxembourg, and Malta are omitted from the sample. Table 1.1 contains a list of the 26 democracies under study. Nearly half of these countries are geographically located in 'old' Western Europe (Austria, Belgium, Denmark, Finland, France, Germany, Ireland, Italy, Netherlands, Norway, Sweden, and the United Kingdom). The second (much smaller) group consists of Mediterranean countries that turned into democracies during the 'third wave of democratization', which started in Europe after the fall of the Greek dictatorship in 1974 (Greece, Portugal, and Spain). Finally, we include the Central-East European countries which transitioned to democracy following the collapse of the communist regimes between 1989 and the 1990s (Bulgaria, Croatia,[4] Czech Republic, Estonia, Hungary, Latvia, Lithuania, Poland, Romania, Slovakia, and Slovenia).

Because the prime ministerial post represents the zenith of a political career there is only a limited number of 350 politicians who held these positions over the past seven decades. Among them 200 in Western Europe, 115 in Central-Eastern Europe, and 35 in Southern Europe (Table 1.1).

A closer look at these countries reveals several salient *similarities.* First, all of them have adopted a fully-fledged party government system which is characterized by using elections to link popular preferences to processes of executive decision-making. This system provides power to the cabinet, to ministers, and to parliaments, and gives formally the prime minister a *primus inter pares* position within the cabinet structure. Although party governments in the 'old' and the 'new' European democracies still show some differences, these are less dramatic than is often thought. Previous research underlines that convergence, rather than divergence, of party governments has taken place in the 26 European democracies. In these countries,

1 STUDYING PRIME MINISTERS' CAREERS: AN INTRODUCTION

Table 1.1 Parliamentary and semi-presidential democracies under study ($N=26$)

Country	Prime ministers (N)	Year of first observation	Year of last observation	Observed time span (years)	Form of government
Western Europe	(200)				
Austria	14	1945	2019	74	Semi-presidential
Belgium	20	1945	2019	74	Parliamentary
Denmark	15	1945	2019	74	Parliamentary
Finland	28	1946	2019	73	Semi-presidential
France	22	1959	2017	58	Semi-presidential
Germany	8	1949	2005	56	Parliamentary
Ireland	12	1948	2017	69	Semi-presidential
Italy	29	1945	2018	73	Parliamentary
Netherlands	14	1946	2010	64	Parliamentary
Norway	14	1945	2013	68	Parliamentary
Sweden	9	1946	2014	68	Parliamentary
United Kingdom	15	1940	2019	79	Parliamentary
Central-Eastern Europe	(115)				
Bulgaria	12	1991	2014	23	Semi-presidential
Croatia	6	2000	2016	16	Semi-presidential
Czech Republic	12	1992	2017	25	Parliamentary/ semi-presidential
Estonia	9	1992	2016	24	Parliamentary
Hungary	7	1990	2009	19	Parliamentary
Latvia	14	1990	2019	29	Parliamentary
Lithuania	10	1991	2016	25	Semi-presidential
Poland	14	1991	2017	26	Semi-presidential
Romania	17	1992	2019	27	Semi-presidential
Slovakia	6	1992	2018	26	Parliamentary/ Semi-presidential
Slovenia	8	1992	2018	26	Semi-presidential
Southern Europe	(35)				
Greece	15	1980	2019	39	Parliamentary
Portugal	13	1976	2015	39	Semi-presidential
Spain	7	1976	2018	42	Parliamentary
Total	350				Form of government

Note: Slovakia introduced the direct election of the president in 1998, while Czech Republic made the same change in 2012. Although Cyprus is an EU member country, it is not included in the sample because of its pure presidential system political parties play similar roles as agents to the electorate and as principals to the government (Keman & Müller-Rommel, 2012).

Second, all countries (except of Norway and the United Kingdom)[5] are members of the European Union (EU), which guarantees certain common political and economic standards as required by the Copenhagen criteria. For instance, all EU member countries need to have stable democratic institutions, a functioning market economy, and the capacity to cope with competitive pressure and market forces within the Union. They also support the general aims of political and economic union.

Third, all 26 countries are defined by relatively strong socio-economic performance. Most people work in the industrial and in the public and private service sectors, and only a small number are occupied in agriculture, forestry, and fishing. Moreover, the majority of the population live in urban areas. Admittedly, the economies in the continental countries are in a better shape than the ones in Southern and Central-Eastern Europe, but the latter have increasingly done better over the past decades.

Fourth, although Norway and the United Kingdom (since 2020) are not EU members, they are included in our sample, because they are closely linked to the other 24 EU members, as socially homogeneous, politically stable, and economically advanced parliamentary democracies. The only other large non-EU democracy in Europe is Switzerland, which is excluded because its directorial form of government is not based on the traditional party government model of parliamentary and semi-presidential democracies; therefore, it is not comparable to the other countries in this comparative study of prime ministers' careers.

Aside from these similarities, the European countries also exhibit several cross-national *differences*. First, the population and the territorial size of the countries in our sample diverge substantially. For example, Germany is about 80 times more populous than Estonia, and four countries (Germany, France, Italy, United Kingdom) have more than half of the population of the other 22 countries combined (in 2019). The differences in the population are also reflected in the territorial size: Germany, France, Italy, and the United Kingdom are much larger than many other single countries. However, the way territorial and population size affects party governance, and in particular the careers of prime ministers, remains an open question (Corbett & Veenendaal, 2018).

Second, the 'life' of these democracies started at different times. Although several European countries were full democracies between the two World Wars, our study does not take into consideration this period. In 'old' Western Europe, the year of our first observation ranges from 1945 for most countries to 1949 for Germany. France is an exceptional case since its democratic regime was undermined for six months during the transition from the parliamentary system of the Fourth Republic (1946–1958) to the semi-presidential Fifth Republic (since 1958).[6] Because of the major differences between the two regimes and the fundamental regime crisis in 1958, only the Fifth Republic is included as a long-term democracy in our sample. In the post-fascist Mediterranean countries, the first elected heads of government in our sample were appointed in 1976 (Portugal and Spain) and 1980 (Greece). For Central-Eastern Europe, the identification of the 'first' cabinet is not straightforward. In some countries, the first free and competitive elections took place in 1990, followed by the first non-communist cabinet. Yet, all countries (except for Hungary) adopted their constitution only after the first free elections. Furthermore, several countries became independent states after the first competitive elections (e.g., Czech Republic, Estonia, Latvia, Lithuania, Slovakia, and Slovenia). Thus, in Central-Eastern Europe, the 'founding cabinets' with the 'founding prime ministers' started at different times between 1990 and 1992 (Blondel et al., 2007, p. 44). In contrast to all other post-communist countries, Croatia introduced a democratic semi-presidential system much later in 2000.

Third, although all 26 democracies share a governmental system in which a cabinet is collectively accountable to the parliament, they differ regarding the constitutional authority vested in prime ministers and heads of state. In this context, the literature usually refers to 'pure' parliamentary and 'semi-presidential' forms of government (Shugart & Carey, 1992). In the latter sub-type, the state president is directly (or quasi-directly, as in France until 1962) elected by the citizens and has more formal power than in ordinary parliamentary systems. Both forms of government are equally distributed in our sample of countries (13 parliamentary and 13 semi-presidential countries in the year of last observation). The semi-presidential countries are more widespread in the 'new' democracies than in the 'old'. Nine of the 14 'new' democracies fit the criteria of this form of government (Bulgaria, Croatia, Czech Republic since 2012, Lithuania, Poland, Portugal, Romania, Slovakia since 1998, Slovenia) while the other five are 'pure' parliamentary (Estonia, Greece, Hungary, Latvia, Spain). Among the 12 'old' democracies, there are only four with semi-presidential systems (Austria, Finland, France, Ireland) and eight that belong to the type of 'pure' parliamentary (Belgium, Denmark, Germany, Italy, Netherlands,

Norway, Sweden, United Kingdom). Austria is the only country in Europe where the cabinet is formally accountable to both the president and the parliament.

Our study covers prime ministers who were appointed in these countries from 1945 until December 2019 (see Appendix for detailed information about the numbers and the names of prime ministers included in this study). Overall, a total of 350 prime ministers have served in parliamentary and semi-presidential democracies, including 200 from the 'old' Western Europe, 115 from Central-Eastern Europe, and 35 from the three South European countries after they transitioned from autocracy to democracy. The 'democratic life' of these 26 democracies ranges from a minimum of 16 years (Croatia) to a maximum of 79 years (United Kingdom). During the same time, nearly 10,000 ministers have served in cabinets directed by these prime ministers (Ennser-Jedenastik, 2020, p. 3). Thus, on average, only three ministers out of a hundred may become prime ministers. This empirical observation impressively underlines the normative argument that the prime ministerial job represents the summit of a politician's political career.

Outline of the Book

This book consists of six chapters. Following this Introduction, *Chap. 2* sets the scene by providing a novel comparative exploration of similarities and differences in the individual background characteristics of prime ministers in Europe, including their socio-demographic composition, their political experience, their partisan background, and their duration in office over the past seven decades. The descriptive analysis shows that prime ministers in Europe are not at all an internally coherent and homogeneous group of politicians, as is often assumed in the literature.

Chapter 3 presents the theoretical framework for studying changes in the career experience and the career profiles of prime ministers that will be applied to the empirical analysis in Chaps. 4 and 5. Our basic argument states that the decline of party government has supported the emergence of populist, technocratic, and presidentializing trends in European democracies. These trends have been jointly conducive to decreasing levels of prime ministerial political experience and increasing levels of technical experience, as well as to shifting prime ministers' career profiles from a 'party-agent' to a 'party-principal' type.

1 STUDYING PRIME MINISTERS' CAREERS: AN INTRODUCTION   21

Chapter 4 assesses changes in prime ministers' career experiences across Europe and between the European regions. The empirical analysis confirms that prime ministers' political experience in positions such as member of national parliament and/or cabinet and/or party leader, has declined over the past decades, albeit with regional variations. The same holds true for their duration in these political offices. The technical experiences of prime ministers, in turn, show some increase relative to their political experiences over time. Although the proportion of prime ministers with former experience in private enterprises, interest groups, state bureaucracies, and international organizations has increased moderately, these background characteristics remain less important than experiences gained in national political institutions and political parties for a successful prime ministerial career. In sum, our analysis confirms that the career experiences of European prime ministers have become moderately 'less political' and 'more technical'.

Chapter 5 examines the development of prime ministers' career profiles over time. Based on a factor analysis, we identify two primary types of career profiles: party-agents and party-principals. While the former is defined by previous experience in parliament and cabinet as a delegate of the political party, the latter is characterized by former occupation in international organizations or as head of the party. Overall, the analysis shows that prime ministers with a 'party-principal' career profile have become more common than prime ministers with a 'party-agent' career profile. In fact, the party-principal profile became the dominant career profile in the 1990s, following the decline of party government and the increase of the presidentialization of politics. The subsequent sections examine several additional relevant factors that may affect career profiles, including the form of party government, electoral volatility, prime ministers' formal agenda-setting power, party family membership, and the proportion of female prime ministers. Our empirical findings suggest that all five factors affect prime ministers' career profile, albeit in different directions.

Chapter 6 summarizes our major findings and considers their implications for the changes in democratic representation and democratic governance across Europe. It also proposes some new directions for future research on prime ministers in liberal democracies.

In sum, this book provides comprehensive empirical findings about the extent to which European prime ministers' personal and professional backgrounds have changed over time. It also contributes theoretical and empirical insights to the vigorous debate about the consequences of the decline of party government in the 'New' Europe.

Notes

1. Our book's argument is not meant to be valid for all existing political regimes nor for all advanced democracies. Rather, it holds for European liberal democracies and their patterns of party representation. In the United States, for example, populism has developed in a significantly different political environment, characterized by polarized partisanship in the context of a fairly closed two-party system.
2. In countries adopting the president-parliamentary version of semi-presidentialism, the prime minister can be dismissed by the elected president. Semi-presidential systems can, in fact, be distinguished into two sub-types: the premier-presidential sub-type, where the prime minister and the cabinet are accountable solely to the parliament, and the president-parliamentary sub-type, where the prime minister and the cabinet are accountable to both the parliament and the president (Shugart & Carey, 1992). Most semi-presidential democracies in the world have adopted the first version, whereas only a couple of democratic regimes have opted for the second version (Müller-Rommel & Vercesi, 2020, pp. 765–766).
3. Parts of this section are drawn from an earlier publication (Müller-Rommel et al., 2020).
4. According to our criteria based on the Polity V dataset, Croatia is considered democratic only from 2000 onwards.
5. The United Kingdom was still member of the European Union on 31 December 2019, which is the time limit of our observations in the dataset (see Appendix).
6. According to the Polity V dataset, France scores only 2 for 1958.

References

Alexiadou, D. (2015). Ideologues, Partisans, and Loyalists: Cabinet Ministers and Social Welfare Reform in Parliamentary Democracies. *Comparative Political Studies, 48*(8), 1051–1086.

Allen, N., Magni, G., Searing, D., & Warncke, P. (2020). What Is a Career Politician? Theories, Concepts, and Measures. *European Political Science Review, 12*(2), 199–217.

Almond, G., & Powell, B. G. (1966). *Comparative Politics. A Developmental Approach*. Little Brown.

Anckar, D. (1999). Homogeneity and Smallness: Dahl and Tufte Revisited. *Scandinavian Political Studies, 22*(1), 29–44.

Andeweg, R. B. (2000). Ministers as Double Agents? The Delegation Process between Government and Ministers. *European Journal of Political Research, 37*(3), 377–395.

Bäck, H., Dumont, P., Meier, H. E., Persson, T., & Vernby, K. (2009). Does European Integration Lead to a 'Presidentialization' of Executive Politics? Ministerial Selection in Swedish Postwar Cabinets. *European Union Politics*, *10*(2), 226–252.

Bakema, W. E. (1991). The Ministerial Career. In J. Blondel & J.-L. Thiebault (Eds.), *The Profession of Government Ministers in Western Europe* (pp. 79–98). Macmillan.

Barnes, T. D., & Taylor-Robinson, M. M. (2018). Women Cabinet Ministers in Highly Visible Posts and Empowerment of Women: Are the Two Related? In A. C. Alexander, C. Bolzendahl, & F. Jalalzai (Eds.), *Measuring Women's Political Empowerment across the Globe Strategies, Challenges and Future Research* (pp. 229–255). Palgrave Macmillan.

Baylis, T. A. (2007). Embattled Executives: Prime Ministerial Weakness in East Central Europe. *Communist and Post-Communist Studies*, *40*(1), 81–106.

Beckwith, K. (2015). Before Prime Minister: Margaret Thatcher, Angela Merkel, and Gendered Party Leadership Contests. *Politics & Gender*, *11*(4), 718–745.

Berlinski, S., Dewan, T., & Dowding, K. (2012). *Accounting for Ministers. Scandal and Survival in British Governments 1945–2007*. Cambridge University Press.

Bertsou, E., & Pastorella, G. (2017). Technocratic Attitudes: A Citizens' Perspective of Expert Decision-Making. *West European Politics*, *40*(2), 430–458.

Berz, J. (2019). Potent Executives: The Electoral Strength of Prime Ministers in Central Eastern Europe. *East European Politics*, *35*(4), 517–537.

Blondel, J. (1985). *Government Ministers in the Contemporary World*. SAGE.

Blondel, J., Müller-Rommel, F., & Malová, D. (2007). *Governing New European Democracies*. Palgrave Macmillan.

Blondel, J., & Thiébault, J.-L. (Eds.). (1991). *The Profession of Government Minister in Western Europe*. Macmillan.

Boin, A., 't Hart, P., & van Esch, F. (2012). Political Leadership in Times of Crisis: Comparing Leader Responses to Financial Turbulence. In L. Helms (Ed.), *Comparative Political Leadership* (pp. 119–141). Palgrave Macmillan.

Bucur, C., & Cheibub, J. A. (2017). Presidential Partisanship in Government Formation: Do Presidents Favor Their Parties When They Appoint the Prime Minister? *Political Research Quarterly*, *70*(4), 803–817.

Budge, I., & Keman, H. (1990). *Parties and Democracy: Coalition Formation and Government Functioning in Twenty States*. Oxford University Press.

Budge, I., Newton, K., McKinley, R. D., Kirchner, E., Urwin, D., Armingeon, K., Müller-Rommel, F., Waller, M., Shugart, M. S., Nentwich, M., Kuhnle, S., Keman, H., Klingemann, H.-D., Wessels, B., & Frank, P. (1997). *The Politics of the New Europe. Atlantic to Urals*. Longman.

Byrne, C., Randall, N., & Theakston, K. (2017). Evaluating British Prime Ministerial Performance: David Cameron's Premiership in Political Time. *The British Journal of Politics and International Relations*, *19*(1), 202–220.

Carnes, N. (2013). *White Collar Government: The Hidden Role of Class in Economic Policy Making.* University of Chicago Press.

Casal Bértoa, F., & Enyedi, Z. (2021). *Party System Closure. Party Alliances, Government Alternatives, and Democracy in Europe.* Oxford University Press.

Corbett, J., & Veenendaal, W. (2018). *Democracy in Small States. Persisting Against All Odds.* Oxford University Press.

Dahl, R. (1961). *Who Governs? Democracy and Power in an American City.* Yale University Press.

Dowding, K. (2013). The Prime Ministerialisation of the British Prime Minister. *Parliamentary Affairs, 66*(3), 617–635.

Dowding, K., & Dumont, P. (Eds.). (2009). *The Selection of Ministers in Europe. Hiring and Firing.* Routledge.

Dowding, K., & Dumont, P. (Eds.). (2015). *The Selection of Ministers around the World.* Routledge.

Dyson, S. B., & Preston, T. (2006). Individual Characteristics of Leaders and the Use of Analogy in Foreign Policy Decision-Making. *Political Psychology, 27*(2), 265–288.

Elgie, R. (2020). Methodology and the Study of the Political Executive. In R. B. Andeweg, R. Elgie, L. Helms, J. Kaarbo, & F. Müller-Rommel (Eds.), *The Oxford Handbook of Political Executives* (pp. 186–206). Oxford University Press.

Elgie, R., & Passarelli, G. (2019). Presidentialisation: One Term, Two Uses—Between Deductive Exercise and Grand Historical Narrative. *Political Studies Review, 17*(2), 115–123.

Ennser-Jedenastik, L. (2020). The 'De-Party Politicization' of Europe's Political Elites. Research proposal. Retrieved August 12, 2021, from https://homepage.univie.ac.at/laurenz.ennser/ERC_StG_2020_B1_DEPART.pdf

Ferreira da Silva, F., Garzia, D., & De Angelis, A. (2021). From Party to Leader Mobilization? The Personalization of Voter Turnout. *Party Politics, 27*(2), 220–233.

Foley, M. (2000). *The British Presidency. Tony Blair and the Politics of Public Leadership.* Manchester University Press.

Garzia, D. (2014). *Personalization of Politics and Electoral Change.* Palgrave Macmillan.

Gift, T., & Krcmaric, D. (2017). Who Democratizes? Western-Educated Leaders and Regime Transitions. *Journal of Conflict Resolution, 61*(3), 671–701.

Grotz, F., & Kukec, M. (2021). Prime Ministers and Party Governments in Central and Eastern Europe. *East European Politics, 37*(3), 401–416.

Grotz, F., Müller-Rommel, F., Berz, J., Kroeber, C., & Kukec, M. (2021). How Political Careers affect Prime-Ministerial Performance: Evidence from Central and Eastern Europe. *Comparative Political Studies, 54*(11), 1907–1938.

Grotz, F., & Weber, T. (2017). Prime Ministerial Tenure in Central and Eastern Europe: The Role of Party Leadership and Cabinet Experience. In P. Harfst, I. Kubbe, & T. Poguntke (Eds.), *Parties, Governments and Elites. The Comparative Study of Democracy* (pp. 229–248). Springer.

Hallerberg, M., & Wehner, J. (2018). When Do You Get Economists as Policy Makers? *British Journal of Political Science, 50*(3), 1193–1205.

Heffernan, R. (2005). Why the Prime Minister cannot Be a President: Comparing Institutional Imperatives in Britain and America. *Parliamentary Affairs, 58*(1), 53–70.

Helms, L. (2020). Heir Apparent Prime Ministers in Westminster Democracies: Promise and Performance. *Government and Opposition, 55*(2), 260–283.

Hennessy, P. (2012). *Distilling the Frenzy: Writing the History of One's Own Time*. Biteback.

Jahr, S., & Edinger, M. (2015). Making Sense of Multi-Level Parliamentary Careers: An Introduction. In M. Edinger & S. Jahr (Eds.), *Political Careers in Europe. Career Patterns in Multi-Level Systems* (pp. 9–26). Baden-Baden.

Jalalzai, F. (2011). A Critical Departure for Women Executives or More of the Same? The Powers of Chancellor Merkel. *German Politics, 20*(3), 428–448.

Jalalzai, F. (2013). *Shattered, Cracked, or Firmly Intact? Women and the Executive Glass Ceiling Worldwide*. Oxford University Press.

Jalalzai, F. (2014). Gender, Presidencies, and Prime Ministerships in Europe: Are Women Gaining Ground? *International Political Science Review, 35*(5), 577–594.

Jensen, J. S. (2008). *Women Political Leaders: Breaking the Highest Glass Ceiling*. Palgrave Macmillan.

Jentleson, B. W. (2018). *The Peacemakers. Leadership Lessons for Twentieth-Century Statesmanship*. W. W. Norton.

Jones, G. W. (Ed.). (1991). *West European Prime Ministers*. Frank Cass.

Karvonen, L. (2010). *The Personalization of Politics. A Study of Parliamentary Democracies*. ECPR.

Keman, H., & Müller-Rommel, F. (2012). The Life Cycle of Party Government across the New Europe. In H. Keman & F. Müller-Rommel (Eds.), *Party Government in the New Europe* (pp. 3–24). Routledge.

Key, V. O. (1956). *American State Politics: An Introduction*. Alfred Knopf Publisher.

King, A. (1981). The Rise of the Career Politician in Britain—And Its Consequences. *British Journal of Political Science, 11*(3), 249–285.

Krcmaric, D., Nelson, S. C., & Roberts, A. (2020). Studying Leaders and Elites: The Personal Biography Approach. *Annual Review of Political Science, 23*, 133–151.

Lijphart, A. (2012). *Patterns of Democracy. Government Forms and Performance in Thirty-Six Democracies. Second Edition*. Yale University Press.

MacKenzie, S. A., & Kousser, T. (2014). Legislative Careers. In S. Martin, T. Saalfeld, & K. Strøm (Eds.), *Oxford Handbook of Legislative Studies* (pp. 286–307). Oxford University Press.

Mair, P. (2013). *Ruling the Void. The Hollowing of Western Democracy.* Verso Books.

Marshall, M. G., Gurr, T. R., & Jaggers, K. (2018). *POLITY IV Project: Political Regime Characteristics and Transitions, 1800–2018. Dataset and User's Manual.* Center for Systemic Peace.

Martocchia Diodati, N., Marino, B., & Carlotti, B. (2018). Prime Ministers Unchained? Explaining Prime Minister Policy Autonomy in Coalition Governments. *European Political Science Review, 10*(4), 515–536.

Müller, W. C., & Philipp, W. (1991). Prime Ministers and other Government Heads. In J. Blondel & J.-L. Thiébault (Eds.), *The Profession of Government Minister in Western Europe* (pp. 31–43). Macmillan.

Müller-Rommel, F. (2008). Prime Ministerial Staff in Post-Communist Central and Eastern Europe. *East European Politics, 24*(2), 256–271.

Müller-Rommel, F., Kroeber, C., & Vercesi, M. (2020). Political Careers of Ministers and Prime Ministers. In R. B. Andeweg, R. Elgie, L. Helms, J. Kaarbo, & F. Müller-Rommel (Eds.), *The Oxford Handbook of Political Executives* (pp. 229–250). Oxford University Press.

Müller-Rommel, F., & Vercesi, M. (2017). Prime Ministerial Careers in the European Union: Does Gender Make a Difference? *European Politics and Society, 18*(2), 245–262.

Müller-Rommel, F., & Vercesi, M. (2020). Executive Power. In D. Berg-Schlosser, B. Badie, & L. Morlino (Eds.), *The SAGE Handbook of Political Science* (pp. 760–775). SAGE.

Musella, F. (2018). *Political Leaders beyond Party Politics.* Palgrave Macmillan.

O'Malley, E. (2007). The Power of Prime Ministers: Results of an Expert Survey. *International Political Science Review, 28*(1), 7–27.

Peters, B. G., Rhodes, R. A. W., & Wright, V. (2000). The Struggle for Control. In B. G. Peters, R. A. W. Rhodes, & V. Wright (Eds.), *Administering the Summit. Administration of the Core Executive in Developed Countries* (pp. 265–270). Palgrave Macmillan.

Poguntke, T., & Webb, P. (Eds.). (2005). *The Presidentialization of Politics. A Comparative Study of Modern Democracies.* Oxford University Press.

Poguntke, T., & Webb, P. (2015). Presidentialization and the Politics of Coalition: Lessons from Germany and Britain. *Italian Political Science Review, 45*(3), 249–275.

Protsyk, O. (2005). Prime Ministers' Identity in Semi-Presidential Regimes: Constitutional Norms and Cabinet Formation Outcomes. *European Journal for Political Research, 44*(5), 721–748.

Putnam, R. D. (1976). *The Comparative Study of Political Elites.* Prentice Hall.

Rahat, G., & Kenig, O. (2018). *From Party Politics to Personalized Politics? Party Change and Political Personalization in Democracies.* Oxford University Press.

Samuels, D. J., & Shugart, M. S. (2010). *Presidents, Parties, and Prime Ministers. How the Separation of Powers Affects Party Organization and Behavior.* Cambridge University Press.

Schleiter, P., & Morgan-Jones, E. (2009). Party Government in Europe? Parliamentary and Semi-Presidential Democracies Compared. *European Journal of Political Research, 48*(5), 665–693.

Schleiter, P., & Morgan-Jones, E. (2010). Who's in Charge? Presidents, Assemblies, and the Political Control of Semipresidential Cabinets. *Comparative Political Studies, 43*(11), 1415–1441.

Shugart, M. S., & Carey, J. M. (1992). *Presidents and Assemblies. Constitutional Design and Electoral Dynamics.* Cambridge University Press.

Simon, H. A. (1985). Human Nature in Politics: The Dialogue of Psychology with Political Science. *American Political Science Review, 79*(2), 293–304.

Strangio, P., 't Hart, P., & Walter, J. (2013). Prime Ministers and the Performance of Public Leadership. In P. Strangio, P. 't Hart, & J. Walter (Eds.), *Understanding Prime-Ministerial Performance: Comparative Perspectives* (pp. 1–28). Oxford University Press.

Strøm, K. (2000). Delegation and Accountability in Parliamentary Democracies. *European Journal of Political Research, 37*(3), 261–290.

Theakston, K., & Gill, M. (2006). Rating 20th-Century British Prime Ministers. *The British Journal of Politics and International Relations, 8*(2), 193–213.

Weber, M. (1919). Politik als Beruf. In M. Weber (Ed.), *Geistige Arbeit als Beruf. Vier Vorträge vor dem Freistudentischen Bund. Zweiter Vortrag.* Duncker & Humblot.

Weller, P. (1985). *First Among Equals. Prime Ministers in Westminster Systems.* Allen and Unwin.

Weller, P. (2014). The Variability of Prime Ministers. In R. A. W. Rhodes & P. 't Hart (Eds.), *The Oxford Handbook of Political Leadership* (pp. 489–503). Oxford University Press.

Weller, P. (2018). *The Prime Ministers' Craft: Why Some Succeed and Others Fail in Westminster Systems.* Oxford University Press.

Wiliarty, S. E. (2008). Chancellor Angela Merkel: A Sign of Hope or the Exception that Proves the Rule? *Politics & Gender, 4*(3), 485–496.

CHAPTER 2

The Background of Prime Ministers: Who They Are

This chapter examines the individual background characteristics of prime ministers in European parliamentary and semi-presidential democracies before being appointed to the office *for the first time* in their life. We first consider the patterns of prime ministers' socio-demographic background. In a second step, we describe the political experiences that prime ministers gained in various political positions prior to entering office. Third, we search for the partisan background of prime ministers by examining their membership in various party families. Finally, we relate their duration in office to their overall impact on governmental policy. The empirical evidence which follows from this inductive analysis suggests that European prime ministers are neither internally coherent nor a homogeneous group, as previous scholarship has claimed in relation to Western Europe (Müller & Philipp, 1991). On the contrary, we find remarkable differences between prime ministers in various European democracies regarding their individual background characteristics and their duration in office.

Socio-Demographic Background

The socio-demographic composition of the executive elite highlights how 'open' and 'close' politicians find pathways to executive careers. Previous research claims that politicians with certain personal background characteristics, such as higher social status, are more likely to reach executive

© The Author(s), under exclusive license to Springer Nature Switzerland AG 2022
F. Müller-Rommel et al., *Prime Ministers in Europe*, Palgrave Studies in Political Leadership,
https://doi.org/10.1007/978-3-030-90891-1_2

office than others (Putnam, 1976; Blondel, 1980). A major comparative study, aiming to understand who gets into the cabinet of West European democracies presents similar findings: ministers and prime ministers are characterized by exceptional social backgrounds when compared to the average population in their country (Blondel & Thiébault, 1991). They usually belong to a highly educated, middle class, and in terms of age, gender, occupation, and education, they represent an internally coherent and homogeneous sector of society (see also Dogan, 2003). This political elite does not reflect the social composition of the ordinary citizenry. Yet, the crucial issue in the contemporary discussion is not how well prime ministers mirror their country's socio-demographic profile. Rather, the most salient questions are whether the socio-demographic background of prime ministers makes any difference for prime ministers' political careers and whether these personal characteristics are linked to their political behavior in office.

The most obvious answer to the first question is that politicians have to pass a series of 'gates' guarded by political parties on their way to the prime ministerial office. 'Gate-keepers' may consider the socio-demographic background of a prime ministerial aspirant prior to their selection and nomination, blocking those who do not meet the party's criteria. In many cases, the selectors look for candidates with an analogous demographic profile to their own. The literature frequently observes that candidates with a similar background to gate-keepers' have easier access to the prime ministerial office, partly because they share characteristics such as age, education, or profession (Norris & Lovenduski, 1995; Cheng & Tavits, 2011).

The answer to the second question is more complicated since the relation between socio-demographic background and political behavior of prime ministers remains unknown. As Putnam has put it 'we know much more about the social background of political elites than we do about what difference it all makes for politics' (1976, p. 41). Yet, Headey claims that, for ministers of British cabinets, their social background indicates their 'substantive or specialized knowledge of particular policy areas and their ability to serve as chief executive' (1974, p. 67). Put differently, the social background of prime ministers may tell us more about their leadership style and their policy preferences than expected. Although the link between social background and political behavior is under-analyzed, we assume that prime ministers' political behavior is one function (among several others!) of their social origin (Hayo & Neumeier, 2016; Horowitz & Stam, 2014).

The Proportion of Male and Female Prime Ministers

Between 1945 and 2019, only 7 percent of all European prime ministers were women, indicating that they face substantial difficulties accessing the top political position in parliamentary and semi-presidential democracies. This underrepresentation of female prime ministers is not surprising since the literature already tells us that female members of parliament and cabinet need to have higher education and advanced professional credentials than men before reaching a leadership position (Milyo & Schosberg, 2000; Escobar-Lemmon & Taylor-Robinson, 2016). Does this argument also hold true for prime ministerial positions in Europe?

Contrary to the findings on female cabinet ministers, the empirical evidence shows that there are no major differences in occupation, education, and age between male and female prime ministers. Although men are more likely than women to start political careers and enter prime ministerial offices, all female, and nearly all male, prime ministers held a university education prior to entering office, which reflects their equal academic preparation to rule. There are, however, substantial differences among the level of political expertise between female and male prime ministers. Women have clearly stockpiled more experiences in parliament and cabinet before entering the prime ministerial office than their male counterparts. This indicates that women need more credentials than men to reach the same political posts. Previous findings already showed that fewer female prime ministers were party leaders before entering the chief executive (Müller-Rommel & Vercesi, 2017) which confirms O'Brien et al.'s (2015, p. 693) observation that men traditionally dominate party leadership posts. Thus, the remarkable underrepresentation of women in prime ministerial positions is probably not related to their professional qualifications, but rather a consequence of 'demand side' (rather than 'supply side') factors in the political recruitment process (Norris & Lovenduski, 1995). It is indeed surprising that the majority of prime ministerial positions are still in the hands of men, although we find an increasing number of women represented in European parliaments and cabinets. This might imply that the gendered nature of the pathway to prime ministerial office is still indicative of an 'unfriendly' gate-keeping role of male-dominated party politics. However, this trend is likely to change in the forthcoming years since several major parties have adopted gender quotas already in the 1990s (Claveria, 2014). In the long run, 'gender parity' will therefore provide more opportunities for women to enter prime ministerial offices, as observed in the recent appointment of female prime ministers in Estonia, Denmark, Finland, Lithuania, and Norway.

Another finding of our analysis indicates that the distribution of women prime ministers varies between single countries within the European regions (Table 2.1).

The numbers in Table 2.1 show that 17 out of 26 European democracies (65 percent) were governed by a female prime minister at least once. In nine countries, no female politician has ever been appointed as prime minister, four from the 'old' Europe (Ireland, Italy, Netherlands, Sweden) and five from the 'new' democracies (Czech Republic, Estonia, Hungary, Lithuania, Spain). Moreover, the proportional representation of female prime ministers is slightly higher in Central-Eastern Europe (8 percent of all prime ministers) than in Western and Southern Europe (6 percent in the two regions, respectively).

In absolute numbers, however, we find more female prime ministers in Western than in either Central-Eastern Europe or Southern Europe which is, of course, due to the different time periods covered in the three regions. In Western Europe, 13 women entered the prime ministerial office, among them Margaret Thatcher and Theresa May in the United Kingdom (1979–1990 and 2016–2019); in Norway, Gro Harlem Brundtland (1981, 1986–1989, 1990–1995) and Erna Solberg (2013–present); Édith Cresson in France (1991–1992); in Finland, Annelli Jäätteenmäki (2003), Mari Kiviniemi (2010–2011), and Sanna Marin (2019–present); Angela Merkel in Germany (2005–2021); in Denmark, Helle Thorning-Schmidt (2011–2015) and Mette Frederiksen (2019–present); Sophie Wilmès in Belgium (2019–2020); and Brigitte Bierlein in Austria (2019–2020). In Central-Eastern Europe, on the other hand, nine women managed to enter the chief executive office. The first were Hanna Suchocka in Poland, who was elected in 1992, and Reneta Indzhova, appointed in 1994 in Bulgaria. It took another 15 years before Jadranka Kosor was selected to serve in Croatia. Other female prime ministers were appointed in Slovakia (Iveta Radičová in 2010), in Slovenia (Alenka Bratušek in 2013), in Latvia (Laimdota Straujuma, who led two cabinets, in 2014), again in Poland (Ewa Kopacz in 2014 and Beata Szydło in 2015), and in Romania (Viorica Dăncilă in 2018). In Southern Europe, two women served as prime ministers: Maria de Lourdes Pintasilgo in Portugal between 1979 and 1980 and Vassiliki Thanou-Christophilou in Greece in 2015. Of the women on this list only Thatcher, Brundtland, and Pintasilgo were elected prior to 1990.

Table 2.1 Female and male prime ministers by country

Country	N Female (%)	N Male (%)	Total
Western Europe			
Austria	1 (7)	13 (93)	14 (100)
Belgium	1 (5)	19 (95)	20 (100)
Denmark	2 (13)	13 (87)	15 (100)
Finland	3 (11)	25 (89)	28 (100)
France	1 (4)	21 (95)	22 (100)
Germany	1 (12)	7 (88)	8 (100)
Ireland	0	12 (100)	12 (100)
Italy	0	29 (100)	29 (100)
Netherlands	0	14 (100)	14 (100)
Norway	2 (14)	12 (86)	14 (100)
Sweden	0	9 (100)	9 (100)
United Kingdom	2 (13)	13 (87)	15 (100)
Subtotal	*13 (6)*	*187 (94)*	*200 (100)*
Central-Eastern Europe			
Bulgaria	1 (8)	11 (92)	12 (100)
Croatia	1 (17)	5 (83)	6 (100)
Czech Republic	0	12 (100)	12 (100)
Estonia	0	9 (100)	9 (100)
Hungary	0	7 (100)	7 (100)
Latvia	1 (7)	13 (93)	14 (100)
Lithuania	0	10 (100)	10 (100)
Poland	3 (21)	11 (79)	14 (100)
Romania	1 (6)	16 (94)	17 (100)
Slovakia	1 (17)	5 (83)	6 (100)
Slovenia	1 (12)	7 (88)	8 (100)
Subtotal	*9 (8)*	*106 (92)*	*115 (100)*
Southern Europe			
Greece	1 (7)	14 (93)	15 (100)
Portugal	1 (7)	12 (93)	13 (100)
Spain	0	7 (100)	7 (100)
Subtotal	*2 (6)*	*33 (94)*	*35 (100)*
Total	*24 (7)*	*326 (93)*	*350 (100)*

Obviously, the distribution of female prime ministers was not even across the single countries within the three regions. There is, for instance, a perceptible tendency to appoint women more frequently in the Nordic countries (Denmark, Finland, Norway). The so-called Scandinavian effect of female representation in parliaments also holds true for prime ministerial posts in these countries (Siaroff, 2000). The proportion of female prime ministers is also fairly high in some Central-East European governments, particularly in Poland, where three women prime ministers have ruled cabinets (out of 14 prime ministers in total). In Croatia and Latvia female prime ministers served in two cabinets each, followed by Bulgaria, Romania, Slovakia, and Slovenia, each with one female head executive. In the remaining four Central-East European countries women have never reached a prime ministerial position.

Overall, the increasing number of female prime ministers in Europe after 1990 may be explained by the regime transition in Central-East Europe and the implementation of semi-presidential executive structure with its dominant elected presidents in countries such as Bulgaria, Croatia, Poland, Romania, Slovakia (since 1998), and Slovenia (Jalalzai, 2014), but also by the fragmentation of European party systems, the introduction of quotas, and the rise of new parties in nearly all European countries, which created new opportunities for women to be selected as the chief executive (Krook, 2006; Galligan et al., 2007).

The Degree of Seniority

The age when prime ministers reach office is an important individual background variable for at least two reasons: first, age often corresponds to political and administrative experience. A politician in her 50s usually has more professional experiences over one in her 40s and therefore may have an advantage in getting selected by their party officials. Second, voters may expect older prime ministers to run a cabinet government more professionally than younger candidates. Table 2.2 provides the following empirical findings on the age and the seniority of European prime ministers.

A first observation indicates that the days when 'silver hair' politicians governed Europe (e.g., Konrad Adenauer, Winston Churchill) belong to the past. The average age of prime ministers in Europe is 53. More precisely, European prime ministers entered government—on average—at the age of 51 and left the office at 55. There are, however, several differences in the age of prime ministers between and within the regions. For instance, the average age of prime ministers when entering and leaving office (seniority) is higher in Western and Southern Europe than in Central-Eastern Europe. While prime ministers in Western Europe start their job on average at the age of 52 and remain in office for six years, their counterparts in Central and Eastern Europe already leave office by the age

Table 2.2 Age and seniority of prime ministers by country

Country	Average age at first investiture	Age at investiture by category N (%)			Average age at last term in office	Average seniority[a]	N
		Under 50 years	50–64 years	65 years and over			
Western Europe							
Austria	52	6 (42)	7 (50)	1 (8)	56	54	14
Belgium	51	11 (55)	7 (35)	2 (10)	56	53	20
Denmark	49	11 (73)	3 (20)	1 (7)	55	52	15
Finland	49	14 (30)	12 (43)	2 (7)	54	52	28
France	53	5 (23)	16 (73)	1 (4)	56	55	22
Germany	59	0	6 (75)	2 (25)	67	63	8
Ireland	52	5 (42)	7 (58)	0	58	55	12
Italy	55	7 (24)	19 (65)	3 (11)	59	57	29
Netherlands	50	7 (50)	7 (50)	0	56	53	14
Norway	52	5 (36)	9 (64)	0	58	55	14
Sweden	47	6 (67)	3 (33)	0	56	51	9
United Kingdom	55	4 (27)	10 (67)	1 (6)	61	58	15
Subtotal	*52*	*81 (40)*	*106 (53)*	*13 (7)*	*58*	*55*	*200*
Central-- Eastern Europe							
Bulgaria	50	5 (42)	6 (50)	1 (8)	52	51	12
Croatia	50	2 (33)	4 (66)	0	54	52	6
Czech Republic	50	4 (33)	8 (66)	0	52	51	12
Estonia	43	6 (66)	3 (33)	0	47	45	9
Hungary	52	3 (43)	3 (43)	1 (14)	57	55	7
Latvia	45	9 (64)	5 (36)	0	49	47	14
Lithuania	50	5 (50)	4 (40)	1 (10)	54	52	10
Poland	51	6 (43)	8 (57)	0	53	52	14
Romania	49	9 (53)	7 (41)	1 (6)	50	49	17
Slovakia	46	5 (83)	1 (17)	0	51	49	6
Slovenia	45	6 (75)	2 (25)	0	49	47	8
Subtotal	*48*	*60 (52)*	*51 (44)*	*4 (3)*	*52*	*50*	*115*
Southern Europe							
Greece	61	2 (13)	8 (53)	5 (33)	64	63	15
Portugal	47	10 (77)	3 (23)	0	51	49	13

(*continued*)

Table 2.2 (continued)

Country	Average age at first investiture	Age at investiture by category N (%)			Average age at last term in office	Average seniority[a]	N
		Under 50 years	50–64 years	65 years and over			
Spain	47	5 (72)	2 (28)	0	53	50	7
Subtotal	52	17 (49)	13 (37)	5 (14)	56	54	35
Total	51	158 (45)	170 (49)	22 (6)	55	53	350

Note: Average departing age and seniority have been rounded

[a]Average seniority is calculated by the average age of prime ministers when entering and leaving office

of 52. Consequently, prime ministers in Western and Southern Europe are substantially older than their counterparts in Central-Eastern Europe: in Western Europe the average seniority age is 55 years, in Southern Europe 54 years, and in Central-Eastern Europe 50 years. It is also remarkable that the average age of prime ministers is above 51 years in all West European countries, while their colleagues in some Central-East European countries are much younger, for example, in Estonia the average age of all prime ministers when entering office for the first time was 45 years, in Latvia and Slovenia 47 years, and in Romania and Slovakia 49 years.

Table 2.2 also shows that more than half of all European prime ministers tend to come to office in their 50s and 60s. Most of the remaining prime ministers were in their 40s. More precisely, 60 percent of all prime ministers in the 'old' Europe have entered office as 'elder politicians' (between 50 and 65 years and above), while their counterparts in South and Central-East European democracies tend to be appreciably younger, reaching office below the age of 50. In three countries prime ministers were already comparatively old when entering government: all German prime ministers were above 50 years, followed by nearly all prime ministers in Greece and the more than two-thirds of their counterparts in the United Kingdom. In three other countries more than 70 percent of all prime ministers were below 50 years old when entering the executive office (in Denmark 73 percent, in Slovakia 83 percent, and in Slovenia 75 percent). However, the number of prime ministers who reached office in their 30s is relatively low (7 percent). Among them are Sebastian Kurz (31) in Austria; Charles Michel (38) in Belgium; Philip Dimitrov (36), Zhan Videnov (35), and Sergei Stanishev (39) in Bulgaria; Stanislav Gross (34) in the Czech Republic; Mart Laar (32), Juhan Parts (36), Taavi Rõivas (34), and Jüri Ratas (38) in Estonia; Esko Aho (36), Jyrki Kataine (39),and Sanna Marin (34) in Finland; Viktor Orbán (35) in Hungary; Leo Varadkar (38) in Ireland; Matteo Renzi (39) in Italy; Ivars Godmanis (38), Andris Šķēle (37), Guntars Krasts (39), Aigars Kalvītis (38), and Valdis Dombrowski (37) in Latvia; Gediminas Vagnorius (37) in Lithuania; Waldemar Pawlak (34) in Poland; Victor Ponta (39) in Romania. Overall, these distributions show that West and South European countries have been more resistant to young, presumably less politically experienced, prime ministers than post-communist democracies. It is still too early to say whether the higher proportion of younger prime ministers in Central-Eastern Europe is the product of a 'new trend' or merely the result of these countries having spent fewer years as democratic nations.

To summarize, the investiture age of prime ministers in new democracies are more similar to each other than they are to their counterparts in the old European liberal democracies. Compared to Western Europe, prime ministers in Central-Eastern Europe and in two South European countries come to office relatively early in life, but also leave office at a relatively young age, for example, in Estonia, Latvia, Portugal, Romania, Slovakia, Slovenia, and Spain. In these cases, the job of a prime minister can be viewed as a 'professional intermezzo'.

Educational and Occupational Variations

Education constitutes another core characteristic of prime ministers. In very general terms, formal education stands as an indicator for the cognitive ability of politicians. Previous research has shown that cabinet ministers with higher educational levels (i.e., with university degrees) not only have better communication skills *vis-à-vis* cabinet, parliament, and media but also exhibit more problem-solving skills, are more open to policy reform, and are less likely to leverage their public position for private gain than politicians with lower educational background (Besley et al., 2011; Fettelschoss & Nikolenyi, 2009). Moreover, educational attainment has an effect on the general views of politicians: higher education is related to 'new' value orientation and a cosmopolitan view, whereas lower education is associated with 'old' value orientations and nationalist positions (Bovens

& Wille, 2017). Finally, the educational background of cabinet members seems to affect their longevity in office. Berlinski et al. (2012) find that in the British case, cabinet members with a university degree, for example, from Oxford and Cambridge, survived longer in office than their colleagues with a lower educational background.

Although no formal educational qualifications are required for entering the position of prime minister, nearly all of them obtained a university degree.[1] This is particularly true for prime ministers in the 'new' democracies. All of them except for one (Boyko Borisov from Bulgaria) earned a university degree before starting their political career. In comparison, the average educational level among prime ministers is somewhat lower in Western Europe. Yet, even in this region the majority of prime ministers have received a bachelor's degree. Except for three Scandinavian countries, between 80 and 100 percent of all prime ministers in Western Europe held a university degree. The relatively low educational level among prime ministers in Denmark, Norway, and Sweden reflects the high proportion of manual workers among the members and office holders of the Social Democrats which have dominated party governments in these countries between 1950 and 1980 (Woldendorp et al., 2000).

The bulk of prime ministers held university degrees in four broad academic fields: natural sciences, social sciences and humanities, economics, and law. As can be seen in Table 2.3, the academic background of prime ministers varies across the three European regions. While the majority of the chief executives in Western and Southern Europe hold university degrees in law (followed by social sciences and humanities in Western Europe and by natural sciences in Southern Europe), their counterparts in Central-Eastern predominantly hold degrees in economics (followed by natural sciences).

A prime ministers' occupation often matches their education. Thus, we see many cases of lead executives holding (upper-) middle-class jobs, such as university professors and teachers, lawyers, civil servants, and journalists. These, and other occupations in the public and private service sector, provide great opportunities to learn and practice politically relevant skills, such as writing and public speaking, and to develop the networks and 'political capital' necessary to become a career politician (King, 1981; Cairney, 2007).

According to Blondel (1980, p. 130), 'lawyers are "representatives"; they […] view themselves as men who represent the ideas of clients—and constituents. Civil servants are fundamentally "managers": they are

Table 2.3 Educational background of prime ministers by country

Country	University degree %	Field of university degree N (%)					
		Natural sciences	Social sciences/ humanities	Economics	Law	Other degrees	Total
Western Europe							
Austria	86	3 (25)	2 (17)	2 (17)	4 (33)	1 (8)	12 (100)
Belgium	90	1 (6)	6 (33)	2 (11)	6 (33)	3 (17)	18 (100)
Denmark	67	0	5 (50)	3 (30)	2 (20)	0	10 (100)
Finland	93	4 (15)	11 (42)	1 (4)	10 (38)	0	26 (100)
France	95	0	5 (24)	2 (10)	8 (38)	6 (29)	21 (100)
Germany	88	1 (14)	0	1 (14)	1 (14)	4 (57)	7 (100)
Ireland	83	1 (10)	1 (10)	1 (10)	7 (70)	0	10 (100)
Italy	93	0	5 (19)	5 (19)	15 (56)	2 (7)	27 (100)
Netherlands	100	1 (8)	1 (8)	5 (38)	5 (38)	1 (8)	13 (100)
Norway	64	3 (33)	1 (11)	2 (22)	2 (22)	1 (11)	9 (100)
Sweden	56	0	1 (25)	1 (25)	1 (25)	1 (25)	4 (100)
United Kingdom	80	1 (9)	4 (36)	0	2 (18)	4 (36)	11 (100)
Subtotal	*83*	*15 (8)*	*42 (25)*	*25 (15)*	*63 (38)*	*23 (14)*	*168 (100)*
Central-- Eastern Europe							
Bulgaria	92	0	2 (18)	6 (55)	2 (18)	1 (9)	11 (100)
Croatia	100	0	1 (17)	1 (17)	4 (67)	0	6 (100)
Czech Republic	100	2 (17)	1 (8)	7 (58)	2 (17)	0	12 (100)

(*continued*)

Table 2.3 (continued)

Country	University degree %	Field of university degree N (%)					
		Natural sciences	Social sciences/ humanities	Economics	Law	Other degrees	Total
Estonia	100	4 (44)	1 (11)	3 (33)	1 (11)	0	9 (100)
Hungary	100	0	1 (14)	3 (43)	2 (29)	1 (14)	7 (100)
Latvia	100	8 (57)	2 (14)	3 (21)	0	1 (7)	14 (100)
Lithuania	100	7 (70)	0 (0)	3 (30)	0	0	10 (100)
Poland	100	4 (29)	3 (21)	3 (21)	4 (29)	0	14 (100)
Romania	100	5 (29)	2 (12)	3 (18)	4 (24)	3 (18)	17 (100)
Slovakia	100	1 (17)	1 (17)	1 (17)	3 (50)	0	6 (100)
Slovenia	100	0	2 (29)	4 (57)	1 (14)	0	7 (100)
Subtotal	*99*	*31 (27)*	*16 (14)*	*37 (33)*	*23 (20)*	*6 (5)*	*113 (100)*
Southern Europe							
Greece	100	2 (14)	1 (7)	2 (14)	4 (29)	5 (36)	14 (100)
Portugal	100	4 (31)	0	2 (15)	5 (38)	2 (15)	13 (100)
Spain	100	1 (14)	0	1 (14)	5 (71)	0	7 (100)
Subtotal	*100*	*7 (21)*	*1 (3)*	*5 (15)*	*14 (41)*	*7 (21)*	*34 (100)*
Total	*91*	*53 (17)*	*59 (19)*	*67 (21)*	*100 (32)*	*36 (11)*	*315 (100)*

Note: Information on the university education of Prime Minister Tzannetakis (Greece) was not available. This reduces the number of cases for Southern Europe from 35 to 34. Prime Ministers Churchill (United Kingdom) and Janša (Slovenia) undertook military studies, which are not included in the degree categories

concerned with policy-implementation and often with policy-making as well.' Moreover, lawyers, teachers, and journalists are usually great 'communicators' who learn to argue for and against certain positions, which enables them to formulate and defend specific policies in the cabinet decision-making process. On the other hand, prime ministers who held an occupation in private business or public companies may be less rhetorically fluent, while having a more refined set of managerial skills (Dowding & Lewis, 2015, p. 52). Table 2.4 shows that nearly half of all prime ministers in Europe held occupations in the public service sector before entering office. Most of them have been teachers and university professors (23 percent) and civil servants (15 percent), while prime ministers with a professional background, for instance, in business, economics, and finance are clearly less represented (11 percent).

As with the other socio-demographic background characteristics, we observe major geographical variation across the single European countries and its regions. First, the proportion of career politicians is higher in Southern and Western Europe (20 and 17 percent, respectively) than in Central-Eastern Europe, where only three (out of 115) prime ministers (Waldemar Pawlak in Poland, Borut Pahor in Slovenia, and Bohuslav Sobotka in the Czech Republic) have been full-time politicians before entering office. Second, compared to the other two regions, Western Europe has a much more diverse cast of prime ministers since 24 percent of them do not belong to any of the major occupational groups. Third, the group of lawyers among the prime ministers is much higher in Southern Europe, particularly in Greece, than in the other two regions. Fourth, teachers and university professors succeeded particularly well in Central--Eastern Europe, where they correspond to more than one-third of all prime ministers (37 percent). They were most likely to enter office immediately after the political transition. At that time, the newly founded political parties in this region were looking for new personal from outside the former (discredited) communist political sphere (Szelényi & Szelényi, 1995). This also explains the fairly high number of teachers and university professors in Southern Europe (20 percent), who often belonged to the political opposition under the former authoritarian regime. Fifth, civil servants are most prominently represented among prime ministers in Western and Central-Eastern Europe, respectively, 16 percent and 14 percent, while they play only a relatively small role in Southern Europe (9 percent). The highest number of civil servants is among the prime ministers in France, while former teachers and university professors frequently held the chief executive post in Italy, Latvia, Poland, and Romania. Sixth, in some countries the business and financial background of prime ministers is appreciably high. Countries with the largest proportion of prime ministers

Table 2.4 Occupational background of prime ministers by country N (%)

Country	First occupation									
	Business/ finance	Lawyer	Technician	Journalist	Teacher/ professor	Civil servant	Full-time politician	Others	Total
Western Europe									
Austria	3 (21)	1 (7)	0	1 (7)	0	1 (7)	4 (29)	4 (29)	14 (100)
Belgium	1 (5)	4 (20)	0	1 (5)	4 (20)	4 (20)	2 (10)	4 (20)	20 (100)
Denmark	1 (7)	2 (13)	0	0	0	3 (20)	2 (13)	7 (47)	15 (100)
Finland	0	4 (14)	1 (4)	3 (11)	3 (11)	3 (11)	4 (14)	10 (36)	28 (100)
France	1 (5)	2 (9)	0	0	4 (18)	11 (50)	1 (5)	3 (14)	22 (100)
Germany	1 (13)	3 (38)	0	1 (13)	1 (13)	1 (13)	1 (13)	0	8 (100)
Ireland	2 (17)	2 (17)	0	0	0	1 (8)	6 (50)	1 (8)	12 (100)
Italy	3 (10)	2 (7)	0	3 (10)	13 (45)	1 (3)	4 (14)	3 (10)	29 (100)
Netherlands	2 (14)	1 (7)	0	1 (7)	3 (21)	4 (29)	0	3 (21)	14 (100)
Norway	1 (7)	1 (7)	1 (7)	0	1 (7)	1 (7)	5 (36)	4 (29)	14 (100)
Sweden	0	0	0	0	0	0	2 (22)	7 (78)	9 (100)
United Kingdom	3 (20)	1 (7)	1 (7)	1 (7)	3 (20)	2 (13)	2 (13)	2 (13)	15 (100)
Subtotal	*18 (9)*	*23 (12)*	*3 (2)*	*11 (6)*	*32 (16)*	*32 (16)*	*33 (17)*	*48 (24)*	*200 (100)*
Central-Eastern Europe									
Bulgaria	1 (8)	1 (8)	0	1 (8)	5 (42)	2 (17)	0	2 (17)	12 (100)
Croatia	1 (17)	0	0	2 (33)	1 (17)	2 (33)	0	0	6 (100)
Czech Republic	4 (33)	0	2 (17)	0	2 (17)	1 (8)	1 (8)	2 (17)	12 (100)
Estonia	1 (11)	0	2 (22)	0	2 (22)	2 (22)	0	2 (22)	9 (100)
Hungary	2 (29)	0	0	0	2 (29)	3 (43)	0	0	7 (100)
Latvia	2 (14)	0	2 (14)	0	7 (50)	2 (14)	0	1 (7)	14 (100)
Lithuania	2 (20)	0	2 (20)	0	2 (20)	2 (20)	0	2 (20)	10 (100)

Poland	1 (7)	0	0	0	8 (57)	1 (7)	1 (7)	3 (21)	14 (100)
Romania	1 (6)	4 (24)	3 (18)	0	7 (41)	2 (12)	0	0	17 (100)
Slovakia	1 (17)	2 (33)	0	0	3 (50)	0	0	0	6 (100)
Slovenia	1 (13)	0	1 (13)	2 (25)	3 (38)	0	1 (13)	0	8 (100)
Subtotal	*17 (15)*	*7 (6)*	*12 (10)*	*5 (4)*	*42 (37)*	*17 (15)*	*3 (3)*	*12 (10)*	*115 (100)*
Southern Europe								
Greece	1 (7)	5 (33)	1 (7)	0	3 (20)	0	4 (27)	1 (7)	15 (100)
Portugal	1 (8)	3 (23)	2 (15)	1 (8)	3 (23)	0	2 (15)	1 (8)	13 (100)
Spain	1 (14)	1 (14)	0	0	1 (14)	3 (43)	1 (14)	0	7 (100)
Subtotal	*3 (9)*	*9 (26)*	*3 (9)*	*1 (3)*	*7 (20)*	*3 (9)*	*7 (20)*	*2 (6)*	*35 (100)*
Total	*38 (11)*	*39 (11)*	*18 (5)*	*17 (5)*	*81 (23)*	*52 (15)*	*43 (12)*	*62 (18)*	*350 (100)*

who were trained in business or the private sector are particularly represented in two Baltic countries (Estonia and Lithuania) as well as in the Czech Republic and in Portugal. Moreover, in some Western Europe countries, such as in Austria, Ireland, Italy, and the United Kingdom, we also find several prime ministers with a professional background in business and finance who climbed up the ladder to the chief executive.

Overall, despite several similarities, particularly in the educational background, two socio-demographic characteristics of prime ministers, age and gender, differ remarkably across the three European regions.

POLITICAL EXPERIENCES

While it is difficult to relate the social background characteristics of prime ministers directly to their political skills, the political experiences that prime ministers have gained on their pathway to the top is arguably the most important predictor for their behavior in office. Membership in a politically relevant institution or a political party instills not only specific political values and norms but also a degree of individual party loyalty. Thus, the more political posts a prime minister held before entering office, the more we can define party control over government as a function of the prime ministers' political socialization. Moreover, previous research on cabinet ministers shows that ministers who held preceding posts and gained valuable political experience performed better than those with less experience (Fischer et al., 2012; Bright et al., 2015). In a similar vein, we argue that holding various political offices enable potential prime ministers to acquire specific knowledge and skills that will help them to perform better as heads of governments. Most politicians tend to hold at least one of the following three offices prior to ascending to the post of prime minister: member of the national parliament, cabinet member, or head of a political party. Additionally, leading the opposition party in parliament or holding a prestigious cabinet portfolio may supply political experiences which prepare a politician on their way to become prime minister. The accumulated political experience of politicians holding these positions provides them with a reservoir of skills essential for governing.

Table 2.5 presents the proportion of prime ministers who held one or more of these three important political posts prior to entering the chief executive office. Nearly 80 percent of all European prime ministers were members of the parliament, two-thirds of them held a post as cabinet member, and about half of them served as party heads before reaching the prime ministerial position.

Table 2.5 Prime ministers by political positions in the European regions prior to entering office, N (%)

Region	Political position			Number of PMs
	Member of parliament	Member of cabinet	Party head	
Western Europe	172 (86)	153 (77)	103 (52)	200
Central-Eastern Europe	78 (68)	61 (53)	52 (45)	115
Southern Europe	28 (80)	20 (57)	23 (66)	35
Total	*278 (79)*	*234 (67)*	*178 (51)*	*350*

Source: Accumulated calculations based on country data in Table 2.6

Note: Percentages in parentheses are based on the number of prime ministers. Prime ministers may have held multiple political positions

There are, however, several similarities and differences between the political experiences of prime ministers in the three European regions. While the majority of all prime ministers in these regions were members of parliament, their political experience as cabinet member and as head of a political party varies considerably. First, the proportion of prime ministers with cabinet experience is 20 percent higher in Western Europe than in the other two regions. Second, the percentage of prime ministers with political experiences as party head is the highest in Southern Europe. Third, the number of Central-East European prime ministers with political experiences in each of the three posts is relatively low (see Table 2.6). As we will see below, several of the prime ministers of this region were recruited as 'political outsiders' with no, or hardly any, party-based political experience, especially during the time of democratic transition.

These patterns of position holding are not as clear cut when looking at the country level. In 14 countries, a large majority of prime ministers held a parliamentary seat prior to entering office, while the parliamentary experiences of their counterparts in 12 countries was much lower. For instance, all prime ministers in Germany, Ireland, Sweden, Norway, the United Kingdom, and Spain were members of parliament before reaching the executive office. Similarly, in Belgium, Denmark, Netherlands, Norway, Croatia, Estonia, Poland, Slovakia, and Portugal, 80–90 percent of all prime ministers held parliamentary experiences. Moreover, with the exception of France and Italy, 50 percent or more of the prime ministers in each West European country served as party head prior to entering the chief

Table 2.6 Prime ministers by held political positions in the European countries prior to entering office, N (%)

Country	Political position			Number of PMs
	Member of parliament	Member of cabinet	Party head	
Western Europe				
Austria	11 (78)	9 (64)	9 (64)	14
Belgium	18 (90)	18 (90)	10 (50)	20
Denmark	14 (93)	11 (73)	9 (60)	15
Finland	20 (71)	22 (78)	14 (52)	28
France	17 (77)	18 (82)	5 (23)	22
Germany	8 (100)	4 (50)	4 (50)	8
Ireland	12 (100)	11 (92)	7 (58)	12
Italy	22 (76)	21 (72)	10 (34)	29
Netherlands	13 (93)	12 (86)	9 (64)	14
Norway	13 (93)	9 (64)	9 (64)	14
Sweden	9 (100)	5 (56)	6 (67)	9
United Kingdom	15 (100)	13 (87)	11 (73)	15
Subtotal	*172 (86)*	*153 (77)*	*103 (52)*	*200*
Central-Eastern Europe				
Bulgaria	8 (67)	2 (17)	6 (50)	12
Croatia	5 (83)	2 (33)	5 (83)	6
Czech Republic	9 (75)	8 (67)	8 (67)	12
Estonia	8 (89)	5 (56)	4 (44)	9
Hungary	3 (43)	5 (71)	3 (43)	7
Latvia	9 (64)	10 (71)	3 (21)	14
Lithuania	6 (60)	5 (50)	3 (30)	10
Poland	12 (86)	6 (43)	4 (28)	14
Romania	9 (53)	11 (65)	6 (35)	17
Slovakia	5 (83)	5 (83)	3 (50)	6
Slovenia	4 (50)	2 (25)	7 (87)	8
Subtotal	*78 (68)*	*61 (53)*	*52 (45)*	*115*
Southern Europe				
Greece	10 (67)	8 (53)	8 (53)	15
Portugal	11 (85)	9 (69)	10 (77)	13
Spain	7 (100)	3 (43)	5 (71)	7
Subtotal	*28 (80)*	*20 (57)*	*23 (66)*	*35*
Totals	*278 (79)*	*234 (67)*	*178 (51)*	*350*

Note: Average political experiences have been rounded. Percentages in parentheses are based on the number of prime ministers. Prime ministers may have held multiple political positions executive office. In Central-Eastern Europe, this holds true for five countries (Bulgaria, Croatia, Czech Republic, Slovakia, and Slovenia). The proportion of prime ministers with cabinet experience is particularly high in Belgium, France, Ireland, Netherlands, the United Kingdom, and Slovakia (above 80 percent) and relatively low in Croatia and Slovenia (below 30 percent). In all other countries, the cabinet experience of prime ministers ranges between these two poles.

Turning to an analysis of specific cases, we observe that prime ministers in the United Kingdom have the highest political experiences among the European chief executives. All of them held a seat in national parliament, 87 percent were cabinet members and 73 percent chaired their party prior to entering office. Similarly, all prime ministers in Sweden were members of parliament and more than two-thirds also held the title of party leader before reaching office. However, Sweden also has the second lowest percentage of cabinet members to become prime minister, implying that in this system, executive experience is less valuable than legislative participation. Moreover, we also observe the case of Germany where all heads of government were parliamentarians before being appointed, but only half were either cabinet members or party heads. On the other hand, the percentage of Austrian chancellors who served in either parliament or cabinet are relatively low, while their experience as party head is among the highest values in Western Europe. Regarding the other countries, Italy has, on average, the least experienced prime ministers. It is no coincidence that this finding refers to a country where, after 1992, the number of political 'outsiders' and technocrats among prime ministers has increased substantially.

Moving to Central-Eastern Europe, the prime ministers of Hungary and Latvia share the highest percentage of former cabinet membership (71 percent). However, interestingly enough, Hungary has the lowest percentage of former parliamentarians (43 percent), and Latvia has the lowest percentage of former party leaders (21 percent). In contrast, prime ministers of Bulgaria and Slovenia have the lowest percentage of former cabinet members (17 and 25 percent, respectively), but Slovenia offsets this with the highest percentage of party leaders among prime ministers (87 percent).

In Southern Europe, a similar pattern exists in Spain and Portugal, where prime ministerial experience in former cabinets is lower than the one in national parliament and as party heads. This pattern is most common in situations when a prime minister formerly belonged to an opposition party in parliament without having had a chance to gain a ministerial post.

It is precisely for this reason that we additionally consider the role of opposition leader held by a prime minister prior to entering office as a major source for their political experiences. Being a leader of a parliamentary opposition party may endow a politician with significant knowledge about intra-parliamentary and party procedures. These leaders may, for instance, develop specific bargaining abilities for negotiating with parties in government in order to get policy pay-offs. Angela Merkel is a prominent example of a former parliamentary opposition leader who later became prime minister. Merkel was elected as the leader of the Christian Democratic Party (CDU) in 2000 and, after supporting the losing candidate to the chancellery, Edmund Stoiber (Christian Social Union-CSU), at the 2002 German general election, she replaced Friedrich Merz as leader of the CDU/CSU parliamentary party (*Fraktion*) in the lower chamber during Schröder's 'red-green' coalition government.

As Table 2.7 shows, the proportion of prime ministers who held political experiences as leader of an opposition party in parliament is particularly high in Southern Europe (34 percent). This is not surprising, since these countries are characterized by regular alternations between governing and opposition parties. These majoritarian dynamics make the systems more similar to Westminster democracies, in that large parties are more likely to direct single-party governments, led by prime ministers who have been, and remain, party leaders while in office. By contrast, in Western and

Table 2.7 Prime ministers' former cabinet portfolios and opposition parliamentary party leader, N (%)

	Western Europe	Central-Eastern Europe	Southern Europe	Total
Prestigious cabinet portfolio				
Finance	52 (26)	13 (11)	3 (9)	68 (19)
Economy	17 (9)	7 (6)	5 (14)	29 (8)
Foreign affairs	29 (15)	5 (4)	6 (17)	40 (11)
Defense	11 (6)	2 (2)	0	13 (4)
Opposition party leader in parliament	32 (16)	18 (16)	12 (34)	62 (18)

Note: Numbers are not mutually exclusive. A prime minister could have potentially controlled more than one portfolio during her career at different points in time, for example, in both the finance and defense ministry

Central-Eastern Europe, this tendency is less common: only 16 percent of all prime ministers in either region have been former opposition party leaders in parliament.

Finally, we also examine the ministerial portfolio that a prime minister held prior to their investiture. Some ministries receive greater public attention, manage more resources (personnel and monetary), and exercise greater political influence on government policies than others. For instance, while the minister of finance controls the monetary resources of the whole government and exerts major control over cabinet members by allocating funds to the other ministries, the ministers of family, youth, and science (to name but a few) are often only in charge of a few financial resources. They also have limited influence on the overall government policy.

Although all ministers who oversee cabinet portfolios gain political experiences while in office, those who direct large and more prestigious ministers have a 'wider' spectrum of political responsibilities and therefore receive more political experiences than their counterparts in small and less influential ministries. One important difference between these two types of ministers is, for instance, the experience they gathered in dealing with mass media. In most cases, ministers who run highly prestigious portfolios have more political experience in managing the public spotlight than their counterparts in low-profile ministries.

Although there is no consensus on the definition of 'high', 'medium', and 'low' prestige ministries, the literature often describes them in these terms, and identifies four as being high prestigious: finance, economy, foreign affairs, and defense (Browne & Feste, 1975; Dogan, 1989; Laver & Schofield, 1990; Escobar-Lemmon & Taylor-Robinson, 2016). These ministries are very visible and exert significant control over government policy. 'Medium prestige ministries' control significant financial resources, but have lower visibility and policy impact. These include, for instance, the ministries of interior, agriculture, education, labor, justice, health transport, and economic development. 'Low prestige ministries' have hardly any public visibility and are characterized by a lack of resources for patronage, for example, the ministry of family and youth.

The distribution shows that 42 percent of all prime ministers have formerly been chiefs of at least one highly prestigious ministry. Among them, 27 percent held positions as ministers of finance or economics, followed by ministers of foreign affairs (11 percent). Only a few prime ministers show political experience as former chiefs of the defense ministry. There is also a regional variation among the previous cabinet portfolios of prime ministers. While more than half of all prime ministers in Western Europe (56 percent) held a post in one of the four prestigious portfolios, the proportion of prime ministers with these experiences is lower in Southern Europe (40 percent) and Central-Eastern Europe (only 23 percent) (see Table 2.7).

In sum, we find remarkable variations among the political experiences of prime ministers in the three European regions. Compared to their counterparts in Central-Eastern Europe, most prime ministers in Western Europe have been members of parliament and cabinet. Moreover, half of them held prestigious ministries prior to entering office. The political experience of prime ministers in Southern Europe ranges somewhere between their colleagues in the other two regions.

Partisan Background

While the majority of prime ministers are active members of political parties, a small but increasing number of lead executives, who are usually drawn from the 'non-political' sector, have never been affiliated with any political party. It is therefore reasonable to assume that partisan and non-partisan prime ministers follow different career paths on their way to the chief executive.

Partisan prime ministers have been politically socialized into the party organization and their parliamentary group before being recruited to the prime ministerial office by their party (Blondel, 1980; Helms, 2020). This provides them with first-hand knowledge of the formal and informal policy-making procedures as well as the means to efficiently gather support from relevant actors inside the political party. Once having reached the prime ministers' office, partisan prime ministers predominantly serve as 'agents' of their party by guaranteeing the parties' control over policy decisions in government. Thereby, they enhance the chances of stabilizing their own political career (see for more details Chap. 6).

'Non-partisan' prime ministers, in turn, have followed a professional career pathway outside the national party system. They were never formal members of a political party nor did they hold a public office under the banner of a political party before entering government. Instead, they usually became prime ministers from outside the political world because of their recognized, non-partisan political expertise (Cotta, 2018, p. 272). The 'proto-type' of a 'non-partisan' prime minister reaches executive office because of his or her experience in managing private and public enterprises or their membership in large national or international organizations. They are therefore counted as politicians who lack political experiences in party politics but who have substantial expertise and a willingness to enact new (sometimes unpopular) policy reforms beyond the traditional party programs. Since these prime ministers are less rooted in the internal dynamics of party politics, they receive less support in times of cabinet crisis by the political parties in government. We therefore presume that the duration of non-partisan prime ministers in office is likely to be shorter than their partisan counterparts.

As Table 2.8 shows, the number of partisan prime ministers is indeed appreciably higher than non-partisan chief executives. Over the past decades, only 12 percent of all prime ministers in Europe held no party affiliation.[2]

There are, however, some remarkable differences between the partisan background among prime ministers in the 'old' and the 'new' democracies. In Western Europe, for instance, 94 percent of all prime ministers held a party membership while only 12 prime ministers (6 percent) belonged to the group of non-partisan chief executives. These include one prime minister in Austria (Brigitte Bierlein), four in Finland (Rainer von Fieandt, Reino Kuuskoski, Reino Ragnar Lehto, and Keijo Liinamaa), two in France (Georges Pompidou and Raymond Barre), and five in Italy (Carlo Azeglio Ciampi, Lamberto Dini, Romano Prodi, Mario Monti, and Giuseppe Conte).

The picture looks slightly different in the 'new' democracies where the party system remained weakly institutionalized during the years directly following the transition toward democracy. In Central-Eastern Europe, for example, 81 percent of all prime ministers were affiliated to one of the established political parties. In Southern Europe, this proportion was even lower (77 percent). Put differently, about one fifth of all prime ministers in Central-Eastern and Southern Europe (19 and 23 percent respectively) had no party affiliation when entering office.

According to previous research, the ideological background of a partisan prime minister impacts their career trajectory. Prime ministers with a 'left-wing' party background, for instance, reach party or public offices later in life than politicians from 'center-right-wing' parties. They are also expected to hold different cabinet portfolios and thereby gain distinct political expertise on their journey to the top. 'Prime ministers from the left are more likely to have been ministers of labor and social affairs, while prime ministers on the Right and Centre are more likely to have been at

Table 2.8 Partisan background of prime ministers by country (when entering office for the first time), N (%)

Country	Party family							Total
	Social Democrat/ Socialist	Liberal/ Green	Conservative	Christian Democrat	Agrarian	Right-wing/ Nationalist	Non-partisan	
Western Europe								
Austria	7 (50)	0	0	6 (43)	0	0	1 (7)	14 *(100)*
Belgium	4 (20)	3 (15)	0	13 (65)	0	0	0	20 *(100)*
Denmark	8 (53)	6 (40)	1 (7)	0	0	0	0	15 *(100)*
Finland	8 (29)	7 (25)	3 (11)	0	6 (21)	0	4 (14)	28 *(100)*
France	9 (41)	0	11 (50)	0	0	0	2 (9)	22 *(100)*
Germany	3 (38)	0	0	5 (63)	0	0	0	8 *(100)*
Ireland	0	0	7 (58)	5 (42)	0	0	0	12 *(100)*
Italy	6 (21)	1 (3)	1 (3)	16 (55)	0	0	5 (17)	29 *(100)*
Netherlands	3 (21)	1 (7)	0	10 (71)	0	0	0	14 *(100)*
Norway	7 (50)	0	4 (29)	2 (14)	1 (7)	0	0	14 *(100)*
Sweden	5 (56)	1 (11)	2 (22)	0	1 (11)	0	0	9 *(100)*
United Kingdom	5 (33)	0	10 (67)	0	0	0	0	15 *(100)*
Subtotal	*65 (33)*	*19 (10)*	*39 (20)*	*57 (29)*	*8 (4)*	*0*	*12 (6)*	*200 (100)*
Central-Eastern Europe								
Bulgaria	2 (17)	0	5 (42)	0	0	0	5 (42)	12 *(100)*
Croatia	2 (33)	0	0	1 (17)	0	2 (33)	1 (17)	6 *(100)*
Czech Republic	5 (42)	1 (8)	3 (25)	0	0	0	3 (25)	12 *(100)*
Estonia	1 (11)	4 (44)	2 (22)	0	0	0	2 (22)	9 *(100)*
Hungary	2 (29)	0	3 (43)	0	0	0	2 (29)	7 *(100)*
Latvia	0	7 (50)	4 (29)	0	1 (7)	0	2 (14)	14 *(100)*
Lithuania	6 (60)	0	2 (20)	0	1 (10)	0	1 (10)	10 *(100)*
Poland	3 (21)	3 (21)	1 (7)	2 (14)	1 (7)	3 (21)	1 (7)	14 *(100)*

Romania	6 (35)	2 (12)	1 (6)	3 (18)	0	0	5 (29)	17 (100)
Slovakia	2 (33)	1 (17)	1 (17)	1 (17)	0	1 (17)	0	6 (100)
Slovenia	2 (25)	4 (50)	1 (13)	0	1 (13)	0	0	8 (100)
Subtotal	31 (27)	22 (19)	23 (120)	7 (6)	4 (3)	6 (5)	22 (19)	115 (100)
Southern Europe								
Greece	4 (27)	0	6 (40)	0	0	0	5 (33)	15 (100)
Portugal	4 (31)	0	6 (46)	0	0	0	3 (23)	13 (100)
Spain	3 (43)	0	2 (29)	1 (14)	0	1 (14)	0	7 (100)
Subtotal	11 (31)	0	14 (40)	1 (3)	0	1 (3)	8 (23)	35 (100)
Total	107 (30)	41 (12)	76 (22)	65 (19)	12 (3)	7 (2)	42 (12)	350 (100)

the treasury or at the ministry for defense, justice, interior, and agriculture' (Müller & Philipp, 1991, p. 148).

The ideological background of prime ministers is empirically defined by their affiliation to one of the major party families. In Europe, partisan prime ministers were members of six party families, including the Socialists, Social Democrats, Christian Democrats, Conservatives, Agrarian, Liberals, Greens, Nationalists, and right-wing parties. These parties were grouped according to their memberships in international organizations such as international party groups and factions in the European parliament (Volkens & Klingemann, 2002, p. 157).

As Table 2.8 shows, the ideological background of prime ministers varies across the three European regions. Four observations merit note: first, in the 'old' Western democracies, prime ministers tend to have, on average, a closer affiliation to the center-right than to the center-left party families. Overall, 53 percent were members of the Conservative, the Christian Democrats, or the Agrarian party families, most obviously in Belgium, Italy, and the Netherlands. Thirty-two percent of prime ministers in Western Europe belonged to the Social Democrat/Socialist families of the left, and this occurred most frequently in the Scandinavian countries. Only 9 percent of prime ministers were members of the Liberal party family.

Second, in Southern Europe, the relationship between prime ministers belonging to center-right and the left-wing or Liberal party families is similar to the one in Western Europe. While 43 percent of all prime ministers were affiliated with the Christian Democrats and the Conservatives, 31 percent were members of the Social Democrats/Socialist party family. Contrary to the other two regions, none of the prime ministers in Southern Europe belonged to either the Liberal or the Agrarian party families.

Third, in Central-Eastern Europe, the ideological background of prime ministers differs markedly from their counterparts in Western and Southern Europe. Given that all prime ministers in Central-Eastern Europe were born before the regime transition and therefore—at least partially—associated with the former communist regime, they have a surprisingly strong affiliation with left party families. Nearly one-third of the prime ministers in these countries were members of the Social Democrat or the Socialist parties. One prime minister in Latvia belonged to the Green party (Indulis Emsis). Moreover, in Central-Eastern Europe, we find the highest affiliation of prime ministers with right wing-populist and nationalist parties. Among them Ivo Sanader and Jadranka Kosor in Croatia; Kazimierz

Marcinkiewicz, Jarosław Kaczyński, and Mateusz Morawiecki in Poland; Vladimír Mečiar in Slovakia; and Victor Orbán in Hungary.

Finally, although the partisan background of prime ministers differs across Europe, more than 80 percent of all prime ministers in Europe were affiliated in one of the center-left and center-right party families. This finding, together with the low proportion of non-partisan prime ministers, indicates that the principles of the party government model have worked well in all three regions over the past decades.

THE LONGEVITY IN OFFICE

How long prime ministers stay in office and how often they leave their post during a legislative term or after a national election is nearly as important as how they arrive in the office. Admittedly, for most politicians, holding the prime ministerial office comprises only a short period in the total duration of their political lives. Yet, the length of time that prime ministers serve in office can provide some indication of their potential impact on cabinet decision-making and on the overall governmental policy. Prime ministers with a longer tenure in office may, for instance, have greater opportunities to increase their political expertise and managerial skills as well as enhance their political networks than others colleagues who served for shorter periods. Having been in office for more than ten years, prime ministers Tage Erlander in Sweden, Margaret Thatcher in the United Kingdom, and Angela Merkel in Germany gained substantive expertise in a wide range of policy fields and developed closer links to other ministers and civil servants which helped them to pursue their individual policy preferences. This is not to say that prime ministers with longer tenure are more important than the ones who have been in office for only one year. However, if it is true that incoming prime ministers need at least one year to fully grasp the 'machinery of government' and three years (if not more) to implement their policy preferences effectively (Blondel, 1985, p. 82; Rose, 1971, p. 400; Müller & Philipp, 1991, p. 138), then we may justifiably claim that prime ministers with five or more years in office have a greater political impact on national policy-making than their counterparts with a low duration in office.

Since comparative studies on the longevity of prime ministers are relatively scarce, it is, first of all, essential to provide an overview of European prime ministers' duration in office. The longevity of prime ministers is measured by the total number of days each prime minister spent in office, from the date of appointment until December 31, 2019 (end of data collection, see Appendix), irrespective of whether the position has been continuous or interruptive. The number of days each prime minister has been in office is transformed into an index of 'average duration' (by years) on country and regional level (Blondel, 1985, p. 79ff). Table 2.9 pools all the descriptive statistics and confirms that European prime ministers were in government on average for only 3.6 years.

In very general terms, two patterns of prime ministers' duration emerge. One in which prime ministers tend to stay in office longer than the overall 'mean duration' and the other in which they remain for a shorter period of time. Within the first group we find prime ministers in seven countries in Western Europe (Austria, Denmark, Germany, Ireland, Netherlands Norway, Sweden, and United Kingdom) and four in the 'new' democracies (Hungary, Slovakia, Slovenia, and Spain). The longevity of prime ministers in the remaining 14 countries (among them, 11 in 'new' democracies) scores below the mean average duration of prime ministers in Europe. In Belgium, the duration of prime ministers' mirrors exactly the overall measure.

These aggregated findings become clearer when comparing the duration of prime ministers across the single regions and the various countries. As Table 2.9 shows, the prime ministers' duration in office was above average in Western and Southern Europe (5.0 and 4.0 years), yet the range across countries within each region was remarkable. In Germany and Sweden, for instance, the prime ministers stayed in office—on average—over eight years, while their counterparts in Belgium, Finland, France, Greece, Italy, and Portugal held office for only two to three years, on average. Prime ministers in countries with particularly stable party systems such as Austria, Denmark, Ireland, the Netherlands, Norway, Spain, and the United Kingdom stayed in office around five years on average. The average duration of prime ministers in Central-Eastern Europe was markedly lower (2.9 years) than their counterparts in the other two regions. However, the prime ministerial tenure also varied considerably in this region. In Hungary and Slovakia, prime ministers averaged more than four years in office, while the prime ministers' duration in Romania, the Czech Republic, and Poland averaged two or fewer years.

An analysis of short, medium, and long-term prime ministers in the different European countries confirms these findings. Short-term prime ministers are defined as those who held office for less than 12 months, medium-term prime ministers ruled cabinet governments between one

Table 2.9 Prime ministers' duration and interruptions in office

Country (N of prime ministers)	Duration in prime ministerial office (distribution by duration, in percent)							Interruptions	
	Average duration in years	Short term Below 1 year in %	Short term 1–4 years in %	Long term 5–7 years in %	Long term 8–10 years in %	Long term Over 10 years in %	Total long term in %	Overall number of interruptions	Average percent of interruptions
Western Europe									
Austria (14)	5.3	7	43	29	7	14	50	0	0
Belgium (20)	3.6	30	40	15	10	5	30	7	35
Denmark (15)	5.1	7	46	27	13	7	47	4	27
Finland (28)	2.7	38	48	7	7	0	14	11	39
France (22)	2.8	14	77	9	0	0	9	1	5
Germany (8)	8.8	0	37	13	13	37	63	0	0
Ireland (12)	5.5	0	50	34	8	8	50	5	42
Italy (29)	2.5	21	66	10	3	0	13	10	48
Netherlands (14)	5.3	7	58	7	14	14	35	1	07
Norway (14)	5.3	7	43	29	7	14	50	7	50
Sweden (9)	8.1	0	22	33	11	33	77	3	33
United Kingdom (15)	5.3	7	39	33	7	14	54	2	13
Subtotal (200)	*5.0*	*12*	*47*	*21*	*8*	*12*	*41*	*51*	*24*
Central-- Eastern Europe									
Bulgaria (12)	2.3	34	58	0	8	0	8	2	17
Croatia (6)	3.5	17	50	33	0	0	33	0	0
Czech Republic (12)	2.0	34	58	8	0	0	8	0	0
Estonia (9)	3.1	11	78	0	11	0	11	2	22
Hungary (7)	4.2	14	71	0	0	14	14	1	14
Latvia (14)	2.2	21	79	0	0	0	0	2	14
Lithuania (10)	2.8	20	60	20	0	0	20	3	30
Poland (14)	2.0	21	71	7	0	0	7	0	0
Romania (17)	1.7	41	59	0	0	0	0	0	0
Slovakia (6)	4.8	17	33	33	0	17	50	2	33
Slovenia (8)	3.7	13	61	13	0	13	26	2	25
Subtotal (115)	*2.9*	*22*	*62*	*10*	*2*	*4*	*16*	*14*	*14*
Southern Europe									
Greece (15)	2.6	47	33	7	13	0	20	2	13
Portugal (13)	3.3	31	46	15	8	0	23	1	8
Spain (7)	6.2	0	43	43	0	14	57	0	0

(*continued*)

Table 2.9 (continued)

Country (N of prime ministers)	Duration in prime ministerial office (distribution by duration, in percent)						Interruptions		
	Average duration in years	Short term Below 1 year in %	Short term 1–4 years in %	Long term 5–7 years in %	Long term 8–10 years in %	Long term Over 10 years in %	Total long term in %	Overall number of interruptions	Average percent of interruptions
Subtotal (35)	4.0	26	41	22	7	4	33	3	7
Total (350)	3.6	20	50	16	7	7	30	68	21

and four years, and long-term executives served at least five years. Among the countries with a short-term prime ministerial duration, four are located in Western Europe (Belgium, Finland, France, and Italy), three in Central-Eastern Europe (Bulgaria, Czech Republic, and Romania), and two in Southern Europe (Greece and Portugal). In Greece, for instance, nearly one-half (47 percent) of all prime ministers stayed in office for less than 12 months.

Half of all prime ministers in Europe held power for a medium-term duration (i.e., one to four years). Among them, 62 percent of all prime ministers in Central-Eastern Europe, 47 percent in Western Europe, and 41 percent in Southern Europe. The most obvious cases for Western Europe are France (77 percent), Italy (66 percent), Netherlands (58 percent); and for Central and Eastern Europe Latvia (79 percent), Estonia (78 percent), as well as Poland and Hungary (71 percent).

The proportion of long-term prime ministers who have been in office for more than five years is twice as high in Western and Southern Europe (40 and 33 percent) than in Central-Eastern Europe (16 percent). In the latter region there are two countries (Latvia and Romania) in which no prime minister stayed in office for over five years. In three countries, the proportion of prime ministers who have been in office for more than ten years was comparatively high (Hungary, Slovakia; Slovenia). In Western Europe the representation of long-term prime ministers is most visible in Sweden (77 percent) and Germany (63 percent), followed by the United Kingdom (54 percent), Austria, Ireland, and Norway (50 percent).

Duration in office, whether short, medium, or long, can be continuous or interrupted. All democratic regimes facilitate elite circulation and thus enable former prime ministers to come back to office. As noted above, a long continuous prime ministerial tenure reflects a politically influential career. Moreover, prime ministers with a continuous tenure in office for five or more years are regarded as being efficient and effective in managing politics at the center of government (Müller-Rommel, 1993, 2008). On the other hand, prime ministers with interrupted political careers are often considered as being less influential on governmental policy.

As Table 2.9 shows, the majority of all European prime ministers held this post only once in their life, while a minority of them (21 percent) interrupted office once or several times in succession.[3] Thereby, interruptions in the prime ministerial office are much higher in Western (24 percent) than in Central-Eastern (14 percent)—and Southern Europe (7 percent). Overall, among the 26 European democracies, there are eight countries with a high proportion of interruptions (Belgium, Finland, Ireland, Italy, Lithuania, Norway, Slovakia, and Sweden); 11 with a low proportion (Bulgaria, Denmark, Estonia, France, Greece, Hungary, Latvia, Netherlands, Portugal, Slovenia, and United Kingdom) and seven countries with no comebacks of prime ministers (Austria, Croatia, Czech Republic, Germany, Poland, Romania, and Spain).

In sum, it usually takes a long time for prime ministers to get into office and it often begins and ends by accident. However, if a prime ministers' time in office can be viewed as their career 'peak' then it becomes evident that for most of them, the 'prime time' does not last very long. This implies that many younger prime ministers—even while in office—need to consider their prospects for professional employment during their 'post-prime ministerial' career. This seems to be different among prime ministers who have entered office relatively late in life and stayed in (or returned to) office for a longer period. These prime ministers finally retire at a relative mature age (Theakston & de Vries, 2012; Musella, 2015).

Conclusion

This chapter provides the first comprehensive empirical exploration of similarities and differences in the background characteristics of prime ministers across Europe. Overall, we found several differences between prime ministers' individual background across the 26 countries and the three regions. First, although most prime ministers are older, male politicians who belong to a highly educated middle class, the differences among them remain remarkable in comparative perspective. The proportion of woman prime ministers is, for instance, proportionally higher in the 'new' than in the 'old' democracies. Moreover, within Western Europe, we find more female prime ministers in the Nordic countries than elsewhere. Similar variation exists in the degree of prime ministerial seniority. While many prime ministers in Central-Eastern Europe enter (and leave) office in their forties, their counterparts in Western Europe are not only older on average, but they also stay in office for a longer period of time. Furthermore, the occupational background of European prime ministers differs appreciably, though to a lesser extent, than most of the other background variables. In Central-Eastern Europe, their professional background in the field of education (i.e., teachers or professors) is much higher than in other parts of Europe.

Second, the political and partisan background of prime ministers looks slightly different in the 'old' and in the 'new' democracies. While nearly all prime ministers in Western Europe belong to one of the established parties, the proportion is much lower in Central-Eastern and Southern Europe. Many prime ministers in these countries are 'political outsiders' who were recruited from the 'non-political, business sector' and who were not a formal member of a political party. More than half of the partisan prime ministers in Western and Southern Europe are affiliated with one of the center-right parties, while the opposite is true for in Central-Eastern Europe—in these countries, the majority of prime ministers belonged to one of the left or Liberal parties.

Third, the differences in the longevity of prime ministers across the three European regions are striking. The average duration of prime ministers in office is, for example, considerably higher in the 'old' than in the 'new' democracies. Moreover, and not unexpectedly, the number of prime ministers who have ruled continuously across several cabinets is twice as high in Western Europe than in Central-Eastern Europe.

In sum, our analysis shows that prime ministers in Europe are not an internally homogeneous group of politicians, either socially or politically, as claimed in previous research on cabinet members in Western Europe (Blondel & Thiébault, 1991). This finding is one to which we shall return to in Chaps. 4 and 5 in more detail.

Notes

1. The doctoral level of education is not taken into account.
2. If a prime minister had no partisan affiliation at the time of investiture, but was party member in previous year, we have counted this prime minister as

'non-partisan'. An example is the Romanian Prime Minister Mihai Răzvan Ungureanu, who entered office in 2012 as independent, after being affiliated to the National Liberal Party until 2007.
3. See Appendix for the criteria for the count of the terms in office.

References

Berlinski, S., Dewan, T., & Dowding, K. (2012). *Accounting for Ministers. Scandal and Survival in British Governments 1945–2007*. Cambridge University Press.

Besley, T., Montalvo, J. G., & Reynal-Querol, M. (2011). Do Educated Leaders Matters? *The Economic Journal, 121*(554), 205–227.

Blondel, J. (1980). *World Leaders. Heads of Government in the Postwar Period*. SAGE.

Blondel, J. (1985). *Government Ministers in the Contemporary World*. SAGE.

Blondel, J., & Thiébault, J.-L. (Eds.). (1991). *The Profession of Government Minister in Western Europe*. Macmillan.

Bovens, M., & Wille, A. (2017). *Diploma Democracy. The Rise of Political Meritocracy*. Oxford University Press.

Bright, J., Döring, H., & Little, C. (2015). Ministerial Importance and Survival in Government: Tough at the Top? *West European Politics, 38*(3), 441–464.

Browne, E. C., & Feste, K. A. (1975). Qualitative Dimensions of Coalition Payoffs: Evidence From European Party Governments, 1945–1970. *American Behavioral Scientist, 18*(4), 530–556.

Cairney, P. (2007). The Professionalisation of MPs: Refining the 'Politics-Facilitating' Explanation'. *Parliamentary Affairs, 60*(2), 212–233.

Cheng, C., & Tavits, M. (2011). Informal Influences in Selecting Female Political Candidates. *Political Research Quarterly, 64*(2), 460–471.

Claveria, S. (2014). Still a Male Business? Explaining Women's Presence in Executive Office. *West European Politics, 37*(5), 1157–1176.

Cotta, M. (2018). Technocratic Government Versus Party Government? Non-Partisan Ministers and the Changing Parameters of Political Leadership in European Democracies. In A. Costa Pinto, M. Cotta, & P. Tavares de Almeida (Eds.), *Technocratic Ministers and Political Leadership in European Democracies* (pp. 267–288). Palgrave Macmillan.

Dogan, M. (Ed.). (1989). *Pathways to Power. Selecting Rulers in Pluralist Democracies*. Westview Press.

Dogan, M. (Ed.). (2003). *Elite Configurations at the Apex of Power*. Brill.

Dowding, K., & Lewis, C. (2015). Australia: Ministerial Characteristics in the Australian Federal Government. In K. Dowding & P. Dumont (Eds.), *The Selection of Ministers around the World* (pp. 44–60). Routledge.

Escobar-Lemmon, M. C., & Taylor-Robinson, M. M. (2016). *Women in Presidential Cabinets: Power Players or Abundant Tokens?* Oxford University Press.
Fettelschoss, K., & Nikolenyi, C. (2009). Learning to Rule: Ministerial Careers in Post-Communist Democracies. In K. Dowding & P. Dumont (Eds.), *The Selection of Ministers in Europe. Hiring and Firing* (pp. 204–227). Routledge.
Fischer, J., Dowding, K., & Dumont, P. (2012). The Duration and Durability of Cabinet Ministers. *International Political Science Review, 33*(5), 505–519.
Galligan, Y., Clavero, S., & Calloni, M. (2007). *Gender Politics and Democracy in Post-Socialist Europe*. Barbara Budrich.
Hayo, B., & Neumeier, F. (2016). Political Leaders' Socioeconomic Background and Public Budget Deficits: Evidence from OECD Countries. *Economics & Politics, 28*(1), 55–78.
Headey, B. W. (1974). The Role Skills of Cabinet Ministers: A Cross-National Review. *Political Studies, 22*(1), 66–85.
Helms, L. (2020). Heir Apparent Prime Ministers in Westminster Democracies: Promise and Performance. *Government and Opposition, 55*(2), 260–283.
Horowitz, M. C., & Stam, A. C. (2014). How Prior Military Experience Influences the Future Militarized Behavior of Leaders. *International Organization, 68*(3), 527–559.
Jalalzai, F. (2014). Gender, Presidencies, and Prime Ministerships in Europe: Are Women Gaining Ground? *International Political Science Review, 35*(5), 577–594.
King, A. (1981). The Rise of the Career Politician in Britain—And Its Consequences. *British Journal of Political Science, 11*(3), 249–285.
Krook, M. L. (2006). Reforming Representation: The Diffusion of Candidate Gender Quotas Worldwide. *Politics & Gender, 2*(3), 303–327.
Laver, M., & Schofield, N. (1990). *Multiparty Government: The Politics of Coalition in Europe*. Oxford University Press.
Milyo, J., & Schosberg, S. (2000). Gender Bias and Selection Bias in House Elections. *Public Choice, 105*(1–2), 41–59.
Müller, W. C., & Philipp, W. (1991). Prime Ministers and other Government Heads. In J. Blondel & J.-L. Thiébault (Eds.), *The Profession of Government Minister in Western Europe* (pp. 31–43). Macmillan.
Müller-Rommel, F. (1993). Ministers and the Role of the Prime Ministerial Staff. In J. Blondel & F. Müller-Rommel (Eds.), *Governing Together. The Extent and Limits of Joint Decision-Making in Western European Cabinets* (pp. 131–152). St. Martin's Press.
Müller-Rommel, F. (2008). Prime Ministerial Staff in Post-Communist Central and Eastern Europe. *East European Politics, 24*(2), 256–271.
Müller-Rommel, F., & Vercesi, M. (2017). Prime Ministerial Careers in the European Union: Does Gender Make a Difference? *European Politics and Society, 18*(2), 245–262.

Musella, F. (2015). Presidents in Business. Career and Destiny of Democratic Leaders. *European Political Science Review, 7*(2), 293–313.

Norris, P., & Lovenduski, J. (1995). *Political Recruitment: Gender, Race and Class in the British Parliament.* Cambridge University Press.

O'Brien, D. Z., Mendez, M., Carr Peterson, J., & Shin, J. (2015). Letting Down the Ladder or Shutting the Door: Female Prime Ministers, Party Leaders, and Cabinet Ministers. *Politics & Gender, 11*(4), 689–717.

Putnam, R. D. (1976). *The Comparative Study of Political Elites.* Prentice Hall.

Rose, R. (1971). The Making of Cabinet Ministers. *British Journal of Political Science, 1*(4), 393–414.

Siaroff, A. (2000). Women's Representation in Legislatures and Cabinets in Industrial Democracies. *International Political Science Review, 21*(2), 197–215.

Szelényi, I., & Szelényi, S. (1995). Circulation or Reproduction of Elites during the Postcommunist Transformation of Eastern Europe: Introduction. *Theory and Society, 24*(5), 615–638.

Theakston, K., & de Vries, J. (Eds.). (2012). *Former Leaders in Modern Democracies Political Sunsets.* Palgrave Macmillan.

Volkens, A., & Klingemann, H.-D. (2002). Parties, Ideologies, and Issues: Stability and Change in Fifteen European Party Systems 1945–1998. In R. Luther & F. Müller-Rommel (Eds.), *Political Parties in the New Europe. Political and Analytical Challenges* (pp. 143–168). Oxford University Press.

Woldendorp, J., Keman, H., & Budge, I. (Eds.). (2000). *Party Government in 48 Democracies (1945–1998).* Kluwer Academic Publisher.

CHAPTER 3

Change of Prime Ministers' Careers: Theoretical Considerations

This chapter presents the overarching theoretical argument of the book, which will be applied to the following two chapters. It integrates two strands of literature in empirical research on party systems and political executives in liberal democracies: changes of party government and the study of executive political careers. The research into these two individual topics is already quite deep, but this chapter's task is to link these basic concepts. We argue that the decline of party government goes along with an increase of populism, technocracy, and presidentialization, which has substantially modified the career experience and profiles of European prime ministers over time. More concretely, we claim that, under populism and technocracy, prime ministers accumulate less political experience within traditional political institutions, such as national parliaments, governments, and political parties, during their political life and more technical experience outside politics. Furthermore, we expect that presidentialization has led to prime ministers' profiles changing from a 'party-agent' to a 'party-principal' ideal-type.

THE ARGUMENT IN BRIEF

As noted in Chap. 1, research on prime ministers' political careers has received limited analytical treatment in the study of political executives. One reason for this may originate with the perception of the traditional (never changing) tasks of prime ministers in party government. In parliamentary democracies, prime ministers are the central figures in cabinet politics. They usually have the formal power to hire and fire ministers as well as to direct domestic policy-making. Moreover, in several countries, prime ministers are normally heads of a major political party and express the voice of their party in government. Notwithstanding notable variation in their age, gender, and occupational background (see Chap. 2), most prime ministers have pursued a career within the parliament, the cabinet, or their party. Therefore, they have been both 'political professionals' with profound knowledge about formal and informal decision-making within these three political arenas and 'representatives' of their party when it has come to articulating and implementing government policies. In the past decades, prime ministers with this career background guaranteed the functioning of stable party governments and they were considered subordinated to the party.

This situation has changed, however, with the decline of the party model of government, the internationalization of governance structures, and the mediatization of political leaders and domestic politics (Johansson & Tallberg, 2010; Mair, 2013; Campus, 2020). These long-term trends are partially interrelated and have some crucial implications for the way party 'representation' and the use of 'expert' knowledge are changing within contemporary governments. We argue that the decline of party government as both responsive and responsible government (Mair, 2009) has—among other things—affected prime ministers' career experiences and profiles. The significant change of the structural conditions of party competition and voters' representation has inspired new types of prime ministerial candidates to compete with the old guard. Political actors have, for instance, strategically changed their behavior in response to voters' political expectations. Put differently, in order to be represented in political offices, political parties search for prime ministers who best fit with new voters' demands. Consequently, ambitious politicians pursue new career paths in order to cultivate the expertise and skills which are demanded by the public and the parties. Behind these linkages we find causal mechanisms which consist of new campaigning strategies, new selection criteria for political personnel, and prime ministerial candidates who accordingly change their behaviors when compared to their predecessors (Siavelis & Morgenstern, 2008).[1]

Moreover, we find two additional new developments: on the one hand, the decline of party government has opened the door for more inexperienced and technically oriented prime ministers to enter cabinet government. On the other hand, according to the presidentialization of politics thesis, the personal power of prime ministers is increasing *vis-à-vis* their party organizations. Both developments have major implications on the political career of prime ministers. First, we expect that the rise of populism and populist leaders recruited within challenger parties[2] leads to a reduction in prime ministers' political experience. Second, factors such as the weakening of political ideologies and party-based politics, as well as increased international pressure on national policy-making, have fostered technocratic traits among political executives (Pastorella, 2016). These traits, in turn, have matched popular demand for 'knowledgeable elite making decisions' across European countries (Bertsou & Caramani, 2020, p. 16). In this regard, contemporary democratic governance may very well require more technical experience, rather than pure, political skills, from prime ministerial aspirants. Third, the weakening of party organizations and the increasing autonomy of single prime ministers from the parties have produced a shift of prime ministers' career profile from that of a party-agent to a new profile of party-principal.

Figure 3.1 shows the general assumptions and expectations of our theoretical argument. We argue that the changes within party government have three major consequences for political representation: increasing demands for either populist or technocratic leadership and the

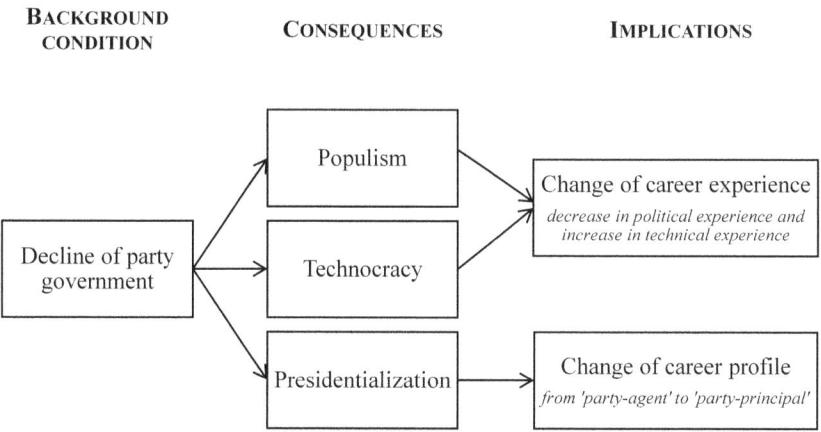

Fig. 3.1 From party government to prime ministers' career changes

presidentialization of politics. Moreover, these three phenomena are expected to have two major implications on the careers of prime ministers: first, a decrease in political experience offset by an increase in technical expertise gained prior to entering office, and, second, a shift from the party-agent profile, defined by party reliability and apprenticeship within political institutions, to the party-principal profile, defined by strong personal leadership skills and public visibility.

In the following sections, we first describe the major characteristics of declining party government. Second, we discuss the political consequences of party government decline, that is, the rise of populist and technocratic demands as well as the presidentialization of politics. Finally, we provide some theoretical implications of these three trends on the changes in prime ministers' careers in European democracies.

The Decline of Party Government

The study of party government is among the core themes within comparative politics. Particularly in Europe the comparative analysis of party government has long been on the research agenda and has been conducive to theoretical and empirical advances (Budge, 1984; Keman & Müller-Rommel, 2012). Scholarly research has shown that for modern democracies, party government is both an empirical concept and a legitimizing myth (Katz, 1987). On the one hand, it describes the way in which citizens can affect policy and hold governments accountable: that is, by voting for parties, which are expected to coordinate voters' demands, recruit political personnel, and represent (sectors of) the society. On the other hand, party government is an ideal-typical model of government, against which the legitimacy of party decisions should be assessed. Peter Mair (2008, p. 225) has provided the most comprehensive summary of party government's conditions in representative democracies:

> [p]arty government *in democratic polities* will prevail when a party or parties wins control of the executive as a result of competitive elections, when the political leaders in the polity are recruited by and through parties, when the (main) parties or alternatives in competition offer voters clear policy alternatives, when public policy is determined by the party or parties holding executive office, and when that executive is held accountable through parties. (emphasis in the original)

In real-world politics, however, these conditions of party government—whose joint presence guarantees that party government exists in its full-fledged form—seldom occur simultaneously or in their ideal-typical form. This means that party government should be understood in terms of degrees, rather than as a dichotomous concept. The notion of 'partyness of government'—that is, 'the proportion of formal governmental power exercised in accordance with the party government model' (Katz, 1986, p. 45)—captures this aspect: when the partyness of government is higher, party government is more developed.

Over the past decades, the literature has focused on different conditions of party government, depending on the function of political parties that scholars wanted to emphasize. Schattschneider (1945, p. 1151), for instance, describes the major party in a two-party system as the 'mobiliser of majorities' and 'the only political organization ... that can measure up to the requirements of modern public policy ... [based on] a mandate from the people to govern the country'. Analyses from the late 1960s and early 1970s approached this topic from a more comparative perspective. In particular, Richard Rose's article 'The Variability of Party Government' depicted the party's capacity 'to translate the possession of the highest formal offices of a regime into operational control of government' (Rose, 1969, p. 413 ff) as the crucial condition of party government. Moreover, this seminal article emphasized—similar to the later book by Rose on *The Problem of Party Government* (1974, pp. 380–383)—that the partisans in government must participate in the policy-making and be in control of the bureaucracy. Essentially, Schattschneider and Rose connected party government to either elections as mechanisms of ensuring political mandate and accountability or the partisan nature of policy-making.

In the 1980s, Castles and Wildenmann (1986) initiated a collective project on the varieties of party government in Western democracies which set the standard for further comparative studies (e.g., Blondel & Cotta, 2000). As a member of the Castles and Wildenmann project team, Richard Katz suggests that '[p]arty government is an abstraction of European parliamentary democracy in the era of mass suffrage' (1986, p. 42), which relies on three assumptions: parties are the most effective linkage mechanisms between society and state; they are entrusted with the responsibility to govern; for these reasons, governmental policies are legitimate (Katz, 1987, pp. 3–6). Moreover, he states that 'the highest officials (e.g., cabinet ministers and especially the prime minister) must be selected within their parties and be responsible to the people through their parties. Finally, positions in government must flow from support within the party rather than party positions flowing from electoral success' (Katz, 1986, p. 43). For many decades, this type of party government defined the quality of European representative democracies.

The overall success of this party government model is dependent upon the ways in which countries are practically governed, whereby the national constitutions define the formal framework for governing. Most European constitutions provide a system of responsive and responsible government which is commonly regarded as desirable and important for liberal democracies. A responsive party government is one in which members of the government reflect to a significant degree the political desires and expectations of the citizens in their political decision-making. Thus, responsiveness implies the congruence between voters' demands and policy outputs. In responsible governments political leaders, including prime ministers and cabinet members, take political decisions primarily in the collective interest of the state and the political stability of the country, even if they do not meet the immediate approval of the public. In this sense, responsible government also requires leadership. However, responsibility implies that political parties and their leaders act according to procedural norms and practices in order to avoid random or illegal decision-making. Thus, responsible party government is similar to the notions of 'good' or 'efficient' government. Overall, the whole edifice's stability of party government is in danger if one of the two pillars (responsiveness or responsibility) is absent or weak.

In the first three decades after the Second World War, the acceptance of party government as the best form of representation strongly relied on parties' ability to be responsive toward voters' demands while also being responsible in government. During this period, the trade-off between responsive and responsible party government was highly developed, and political parties could still represent voters' preferences and be flexible enough to govern responsibly (i.e., for the broader public interest). This held true for both single-party and coalition government systems in the 1960s and 1970s. Qualitative country studies on seven West European democracies (plus the United States) provided sound evidence of well-functioning conditions of the party government model, both from an empirical and a normative viewpoint. Except for Switzerland, Katz (1987) found that France's Fifth Republic, Italy, Germany, the United Kingdom, Denmark, and Sweden[3] could all be placed in the group of '"real" party governments'. These six countries, as well as others, such as Austria,

Belgium, Finland, and the Netherlands, have long been characterized as having clear party control over the selection of government members, including prime ministers (Blondel & Cotta, 1996, pp. 249–250).

Yet, since the 1980s, the gap between responsiveness and responsibility increased, and traditional parties in most of these countries lost their presence in the society, or—in other words—started to govern without representing (Katz & Mair, 2009, p. 760; Karremans, 2021, p. 1536 ff). According to Katz (1987, pp. 23–25), this process was supported by four 'ironies of party government'. First, competitive pressures made parties more prone to overpromising. The negative effect of this behavior has been an increasing gap between expectations and party performance, which forced governing parties to lower the bar with respect to previous expansive welfare programs, particularly after the economic downturns of the 1970s and 1980s. Second, parties socialized citizens into democracy to such an extent that citizens themselves began taking a more active role in the political process and looking for more participatory movements and alternative parties, such as the Greens, which developed in several European countries in the early 1980s. Third, the rise of electronic media made the flow of news continuous and more fragmented: the result was an overproduction of news that put citizens in a more difficult situation when it came to gathering clear information to keep parties accountable, with negative consequences for the legitimacy of party government. Finally, the more parties became familiar with governmental practices, the more the 'governmentness' of governing parties obfuscated the 'partyness of government', whereby the former 'refers to the degree to which parties […] are in charge, not just of the formal government apparatus, but of social power overall' and the latter to their ability to guide the executive decision-making effectively in tune with citizens' preferences (Katz, 1987, p. 8). As a consequence, established political parties have faced increasing difficulties to balance their responsive and responsible functions: parties that are responsive struggle to be responsible and those which seek to be responsible displease voters more frequently.

Hans Keman (2017) provides convincing evidence to support this observation for governing parties. He argues that in contemporary democracies, the usual relationship between voters and parties is reversed when compared to the assumptions of party government: parties act more independently from popular mandates when in government, while citizens are relatively 'ignored' by these parties. Factors such as the increased multidimensionality of political competition and the higher fragmentation of party systems, which requires more compromises in government, account for two interrelated outcomes: parties in opposition remain responsive, whereas 'parties in government tend to be coalescent and prone to responsible behavior' (Keman, 2017, p. 42). As Frognier (2000) already argued, the trade-off between responsiveness and responsibility is inherent to the myth of party government. The 'imperative' mandate from voters to parties (responsive government) and the 'trusteeship' mandate between voters and party officers (responsible government) 'gives those who are elected the right to carry out … in the executive … the policies which have been formulated in the programme …, but also leave[s] the government some room of manoeuvre' (Frognier, 2000, p. 29). In this regard, the empirical literature has found that 'parties do seek to implement policies that are consistent with their ideology or election promises, but this is not to say that parties in government only pursue policies for which they have a popular mandate' (Andeweg, 2020, p. 465).[4] While the ideal-type of party government implies a balance between 'imperative' mandate and 'trusteeship', real governments can lean away from the former or from the latter. Not surprisingly, responsiveness, or the fulfillment of party pledges, in multi-party, coalition governments, is for example lower than in single-party (majority) cabinets because, in coalitions, parties need to find agreeable compromises with their governing partners (Thomson et al., 2017). This suggests that institutional constraints can negatively impact government responsiveness and skew party government to the side of responsibility (Keman, 2017).

Over the last three decades, the basic principle of the 'old' party government (i.e., the balance between responsive and responsible decision-making) has evidently changed in at least two ways: a change in partisan policy-making due to changes in the ideological distance between the established parties (supply side of party government) and an increasing dissatisfaction of citizens with the political behavior of established parties (demand side of party government) (Mair, 2008, p. 218).

On the supply side, the conflict between traditional political parties has diminished because the ideological polarization of European party systems (particularly the ideological distance between left- and right-wing parties) has substantially decreased over the years. Parties that used to be anti-system and non-coalitionable during the Cold War have either disappeared or moderated their political stances. For example, the former Italian Communist Party (PCI) converted itself into a Social Democratic Party, the Democratic Party of the Left (PDS), and entered government for the first time as the main coalition partner in 1996. Likewise, the extreme right-wing Italian Social Movement (MSI), searching for a more moderate, conservative profile, entered a center-right coalition government led by Silvio Berlusconi and renamed itself the National Alliance (AN) in 1995. Similarly, after a transitional decade, the Spanish People's Alliance (AP) renamed itself the People's Party (PP) in order to distance itself from its Francoist heritage; in 1996, the People's Party formed a single-party government under the leadership of the former Prime Minister José María Aznar. Moreover, some anti-system (but not anti-democratic)[5] parties, such as the German Greens (in government from 1998 to 2005 and back in 2021) and the Greek *SYRIZA* (in government from 2015 to 2019), have gradually integrated themselves without changing the roots of their original identity (Zulianello, 2018). Between the twentieth and the twenty-first century, parties with remarkable anti-system stances, such as the Austrian Freedom Party (FPÖ) in Austria or the Italian Northern League (LN) and Five Star Movement (M5S), even entered into coalition governments.

Moreover, the so-called mainstream parties have moved to the center of the ideological spectrum by promoting catch-all electoral strategies and blurring their programmatic differences. The 'Third Way' advocated by the British Labour Party under the leadership of Prime Minister Tony Blair (in office from 1997 to 2007) is a straightforward example of a left-wing party moving toward the center. The conservative German Christian Democratic Union (CDU) also took on more centrist positions, thus shifting away from the ideological right, during the chancellorship of Angela Merkel.

While moving ideologically closer to each other, political parties have also increasingly endowed expert bodies, or non-majoritarian institutions, with increasing policy-making power: regulatory authorities, independent central banks, and supranational courts of justice now take myriad decisions that have substantial impact on societies without direct political legitimation (Thatcher & Stone Sweet, 2002). Overall, programmatic convergence and de-politicization have decreased the level of policy-making's partisanship (Mair, 2008, pp. 215–217).

On the demand side, we find an erosion of the party government model since citizens are increasingly dissatisfied with the behavior of the mainstream political parties and the political leaders to come to grips with new policy approaches that respond more adequately to their demands. Established parties are indeed unable (or unwilling) to respond to the new demands of voters in an age of increasing globalization and mediatization (Kriesi et al., 2013) because of the time-consuming and demanding decision-making processes in government as well as the external constraints posed by organizations such as the European Union. The negative experiences made by many citizens with large established parties in government and opposition have an impact on the decrease of party identification, the decline in party membership among citizens, an increasing electoral volatility, and lower electoral turnout rates. These four phenomena signal the inability of parties to mobilize and keep bonds with the society (Dalton et al., 2011, p. 10).

Citizens' identification with political parties is one of the most important features for a party-based democracy. Partisan ties bind voters to their preferred political party. If political parties react adequately to the political demands of the citizens, partisanship is high. Cross-national and longitudinal surveys show, however, that party identification decreased dramatically across West European countries between the 1960s and 1990s (Dalton, 2000, p. 25). Recent analyses confirm these findings, although the pace of decline has slowed, at least in countries such as Germany and the United Kingdom (Dalton, 2016, p. 11). In Central-Eastern Europe, partisan identification has also been consistently low across all time periods, with only minor adjustments (Webb & White, 2007).

The decrease in party membership is even more striking. An analysis of 19 European countries[6] shows that, between 1980 and 2009, the percentage of party members in the entire electorate, as well as the absolute number of party members, decreased in both Western and Central-Eastern Europe. An inverse trend exists in three Mediterranean countries: in Spain, as well as in Greece and Portugal, although in the latter two countries only in the absolute number of party members (Van Biezen et al., 2012, p. 34). Interestingly enough, we have some evidence of within-country variation: older parties lose more members while newer parties perform better in this respect (Kölln, 2016).

Electoral volatility, in turn, has been on the rise for a long time. In this regard, major changes in Western Europe have occurred since the 1990s and persisted after 2010, with significant alarm bells ringing already in the two previous decades in countries such as the Netherlands and Norway (Chiaramonte & Emanuele, 2017, p. 380). In contrast, Central-Eastern Europe has experienced a slight decrease in electoral volatility, although this is likely due to the fact that the region had very high levels of volatility during the years of democratic transition (Sikk, 2005; Keman & Müller-Rommel, 2012, p. 4).

The lack of trust in party government is further indicated by the decline of electoral participation. In the Western-established democracies voter turnout dropped by 5 percent, on average, between 1970 and 2000 (Franklin, 2004, p. 10). Similar trends exist in Southern Europe (except for Spain) and in Central-Eastern Europe (except for Hungary) (Keman & Müller-Rommel, 2012, p. 8; Kostelka, 2017). Even the success of populist challenger parties has not increased voter turnout among European democracies, with the exception of some Central-East European cases (Leininger & Meijers, 2021).

The discussion about supply and demand of party government casts light on its overall decline in European democracies. Longitudinal trends tell us that most of the key conditions of party government do not exist, or have become greatly attenuated. This point has been raised by Mair (2008, pp. 226–230) who confirms that party government is waning. Following his argument, we can state that, first, mainstream political parties cannot offer clear policy alternatives anymore because of lower ideological polarization within European party systems and less distinguishable party programs between left- and right-wing parties. Second, because of the de-politicization of policy-making, there is less room for alternative policy choices and mainstream parties do not determine governmental policy to the extent they were used in the past. Third, because of the loss of coherence of the left-right dimension as the main ideological divide and the fragmented interest representation in government, it becomes more difficult for citizens to hold the executive accountable through mainstream parties. Finally, and most important for our analysis, government personnel and leaders 'continue to be recruited by party, [… but] they are less likely to be recruited *through* parties' (Mair, 2008, p. 227).

In sum, party government, as it developed in the second post-World War period in Europe is 'malfunctioning' and its legitimacy as a doctrine of government is in decline: political parties have converged on policy positions and (mainstream) parties have suffered a loss of popular legitimacy (Webb, 2000). These processes have opened the door to challenging views of representation, which we expect to provide changes in the level of prime ministers' career experiences and in their career profiles (see Chaps. 4 and 5). These changes have been particularly fostered by the diffusion of populism, technocracy, and the presidentialization of politics in European democracies.

Consequences of Declining Party Government

Why is the waning of party government conducive to populism, technocracy, and presidentialization? The answer could read as follows: 'the constraints on government have become much greater, the ability to respond to voters has been much curtailed, and the parties' capacity to use their political and organizational resources to bridge or even manage the resulting gap has become severely limited' (Mair, 2009, p. 16). As mentioned above, when parties in government try to behave responsibly, their room of maneuver narrows down and the representation of citizens' demands gets harder; in particular, problems of responsiveness emerge when governing parties are constrained by expert institutions or by contested supranational actors such as the European Union. Given that the party government model requires parties to propose *and* produce policies that match citizens' demands, the (increasing) disconnection between voter demands and party supply undermines parties' representative legitimacy.

The lack of traditional political representation, in turn, favors the rise of populism, technocracy, and presidentialization while also undercutting traditional modes of party government. Populism and technocracy offer different solutions to the diminished legitimacy of party government. The former focuses on the promise of party responsiveness, whereas the latter stresses the responsible political behavior of individual rulers, who are evaluated on the basis of their performance in office and irrespective of initial citizens' policy demands. While populism claims 'that political action must be guided by the unconstrained will of the people', technocracy stresses 'the prominence of expertise in the identification and implementation of objective solutions to societal problems' (Caramani, 2017, p. 55). Presidentialization, in turn, challenges the traditional party government model by asking for a more 'personalized' type of government run by prime ministers who are freed from party constraints and therefore able to promise a 'personal' (i.e., direct) linkage to voters.

Populism and Technocracy

In Europe, the populist movements and parties developed in the 1970s.[7] Since then, the number of populist parties has increased constantly, although at various speeds and intensities across the European regions. These non-mainstream parties challenge established parties and party government by publicly articulating the discontent of voters with the latter.

They argue that mainstream political parties are incapable of representing citizens' preference and dealing with contemporary challenges, such as economic crises and mass migration. Therefore, they claim to be the responsive political actors, filling the void left by the mainstream parties. In this sense, populism has been 'a means of linking an increasingly undifferentiated and depoliticized electorate with a largely neutral and non-partisan system of governance' (Mair, 2002, p. 84). Examples of successful populist parties are numerous, both on the left and on the right of the political spectrum. A famous long-standing case is the right-wing French *Front National* (now *Rassemblement National*). Another case is the Danish Progress Party founded by Mogens Glistrup in the 1970s. This party has generated the right-wing Danish People's Party in 1995, which obtained fairly high electoral support in the 2000s. The Austrian FPÖ, the German *Alternative für Deutschland* (AfD), and the Italian Northern League are also cases in point. Moreover, we can find *Podemos* in Spain and *SYRIZA* in Greece on the left as well as the Italian anti-corruption Five Star Movement on more centrist position. The situation is similar in Central-Eastern Europe. Populist parties were formed after the transitional period and some have been successful by providing prime ministers, such as the centrist Juhan Parts from *Res Publica* and Valdis Dombrovskis from New Era in Estonia, as well as right-wing populists, for example, Beata Szydło and Mateusz Morawiecki from Law and Justice (PiS), who entered office in Poland, and Viktor Orbán from *Fidesz* (Hungarian Civic Alliance) in Hungary. In the 2000s, the increased support for populist parties in Europe has been so monotonic and ubiquitous that some have wondered if one can speak of 'populist contagion' (Rooduijn et al., 2014).

There is preliminary evidence that populist parties are indeed responsive and, most importantly, that they fill representative gaps on the supply side of party government (Werner & Giebler, 2019). First, populists can offer substantive representation for underrepresented groups or policy positions that are not usually covered by mainstream parties. Second, they can be instruments for symbolic representation, as symbols of anti-establishment and anti-politics sentiments. Third, populist leaders can claim to provide descriptive representation, in that populist politicians 'mirror' the socio-demographic background of the general population, for example, in terms of age, sex, education, or occupation. A comparative study of the German AfD and the Austrian FPÖ has, for instance, shown that the socio-demographic background of the members of radical right-wing populist parties fits with such claims of descriptive representation for specific groups (among others: families, pensioners, police, and the military) (Heinisch & Werner, 2019, pp. 487–488). Radical right-wing populists also prove to be faster in discussing issues that are salient for citizens than their left-wing counterparts (Plescia et al., 2019).

Overall, by reconnecting citizens' demands with party supply, populism challenges representative politics by presenting itself as the 'cure' for the democratic deficit created by traditional parties. As claimed by Berman and Snegovaya (2019, pp. 15–16), '[i]f traditional parties stop fulfilling [their ...] representative function, voters who believe their interests, demands, and preferences are being consistently ignored may become susceptible to appeals made by parties that question the legitimacy of liberal democracy itself'. Thus, populism brings anti-party leaders to the forefront of the political scene.

Compared to the traditional party government model, as defined by Katz (1986, 1987), populism is 'partyless'. While political parties remain important representative vehicles, populism calls for the disintermediation between citizens and leaders, including prime ministers. In contrast with the growing complexity of contemporary societies, populism conceives of only one popular will, which is opposed to corrupt, mainstream elites (Mudde, 2004, p. 543). Moreover, as Blondel and Thiébault (2010, p. 255) state, European populism is characterized by leaders of new parties rather than those of old parties. However, not all populist leaders necessarily belong to the type of political 'outsiders' who have hardly any political experience. Populism also paves the way for party politicians to receive popular support in spite of (or because of) their unpopularity within their own party organization. The former Italian Prime Minister Matteo Renzi is an example (Bordignon, 2014). Even party figures with previous political experience can be social or psychological outsiders in juxtaposition to traditional party elites. Margaret Thatcher in the United Kingdom in the 1980s (King, 1987) or Michel Rocard in France between the 1980s and the 1990s (Elgie, 1993) are cases in point.

Similar to populism, technocracy ensues from the increasing gap between party responsiveness and responsibility. Technocracy is defined as 'a form of power in which decisions over the allocation of values are made by experts or technical elites based on their knowledge, independently and in the long-term interest of the whole society' (Caramani, 2020, p. 3). Technocracy and populism share some common features. First, they are both anti-pluralist: for populists, there is one 'people' whose will is 'right'; for technocrats, there is one 'optimal' solution to policy problems. Second, populism and technocracy pursue an unmediated relationship between leaders and citizens. In the case of technocracy, this does not imply any direct citizens' rule, but rather governmental policy's independence from contingent voters' opinions. Finally, populism and technocracy undermine the very idea of democratic accountability. For populists, acting politicians should simply implement the demands of the 'people'. If politics expresses the general will of the 'people', citizens cannot sanction politicians because it would end up with self-sanctioning. For technocrats, who consider themselves as being the trustees of citizens, common persons are not competent enough to sanction them and should therefore refrain from doing so (Caramani, 2017, p. 61).

Technocracy is even less party-based than populism. While the latter emphasizes the popular side of party government (i.e., the connection between citizens' preferences and policy outputs), technocracy promotes the efficiency of the governmental process and the effectiveness of its outcomes. Whereas populism is anti-elitist, technocracy is by definition elitist. Indeed, technocracy regards a political elite as being legitimized by its particular expertise rather than its representative capacity. In other words, technocratic experts in government are trusted because of their competence in specific policy sectors. Furthermore, while populism argues that their representatives mirror the represented, technocracy minimizes descriptive representation (Caramani, 2017, p. 62).

It is not surprising that most technocrats have become successful in the globalized world, where non-majoritarian institutions and supranational organizations have gained the upper hand in many aspects of policy-making (McDonnell & Valbruzzi, 2014). Once these technocrats enter government, politics becomes temporarily 'de-politicized' as political parties step back. Usually, this situation occurs in times of serious state crisis when traditional parties are unable to find rational and pragmatic answers to government complexity. A technocratic government is therefore considered as a viable solution for crisis management (e.g., Brunclík, 2015; Brunclík & Parízek, 2019).

For example, during the political and economic crisis of the early 1990s, the governor of the Bank of Italy, Carlo Azeglio Ciampi, was appointed as a non-partisan head of government in 1993. Moreover, Italy as well as Greece appointed a prime minister with a technical, expertise-oriented background, after facing severe economic repercussions following the 2008 financial crisis. Because Berlusconi's government could not protect Italy's state bond market from international speculation, the head of state appointed Mario Monti, president of a renowned private university in Milan and former member of enterprises and banks, to take over the government in November 2011. Monti formed a non-partisan cabinet with large support in parliament. In the same month, the two main Greek parties agreed to give their parliamentary confidence to a cabinet led by the academic economist Lucas Papademos, taking over for the socialist Prime Minister Papandreou, who resigned following the EU bailout program negotiations. Similarly, in May 2009, the Czech president of the republic appointed the then-president of the Statistical Office, Jan Fischer, as leader of a non-partisan cabinet which lasted until July 2010. In February 2021, amidst the COVID-19 pandemic, the Italian parliament gave its confidence to a new cabinet led by the former president of the European Central Bank, the non-partisan Prime Minister Mario Draghi (Garzia & Karremans, 2021).

In sum, populism and technocracy provide a holistic view of political representation, with no room for pluralism or contested viewpoints. The legitimizing principle of populism is the realization of the will of 'the people', while technocracy relies on 'rationality and efficiency' to guide its decisions (Caramani, 2017, 2020, p. 20). The more governments become distant from the traditional type of party government, the more they approach either the populist or the technocratic side, depending on the emphasis on one principle or the other.

Presidentialization

In addition to populism and technocracy the presidentialization of politics has emerged as another consequence of party government decline, in that it gives increasing political authority to individual leaders ('personal government'), who can—compared to political parties—directly respond to citizens' demands. Our definition of presidentialization builds on the seminal book by Poguntke and Webb (2005a) because it provides an excellent description about the recent, dynamic changes in the prime ministerial role and function across European democracies.[8] Their definition implies that these democratic 'regimes are becoming more presidential in their actual practice without, in most cases, changing their formal structure, that is, their regime-type' (Poguntke & Webb, 2005b, p. 1). This means that, even in 'pure' parliamentary systems, prime ministers can become—in the long run and under certain conditions—more 'presidential' in their actual characteristics.

According to Poguntke and Webb (2005b, pp. 4–5), presidential systems produce three effects for chief executives: first, the growth of leadership power resources, inasmuch as a president is not responsible to the parliament and can govern without interference. Second, leadership independence, because the president is autonomous from the party and owes her political success primarily to her electoral appeal. Third, electoral personalization, since candidates' personalities deeply affect electoral campaigns and outcomes. Partisan governments—so the argument—are operating essentially in the presidential logic in that the power and the autonomy of political leaders within political executives are increasing and that the electoral success of political parties are strongly dependent upon the performance of prime ministers in office. Thus, presidentialization is considered as being conducive to 'personal government', which diminishes the impact of parties relative to prime ministers and gives value to individual characteristics relative to *party* programs. Put differently, the trend toward presidentialization is interrelated with the personalization of politics in a way that presidentialized prime ministerial leadership is by definition also personalized, but personalization does not necessarily lead to presidentialization (Poguntke & Webb, 2018, pp. 194–195).

Webb et al. (2012, p. 93) furthermore argue that 'presidential' leaders may bypass the long and painstaking process of building a power base within the party by the sheer force of their electoral appeal. The party may cede powers to such a leader on the assumption that it will benefit electorally by hanging on to the individual's coattails, at least as long as the leader is an asset rather than a liability. This means that presidentialization produces a form of representation that enhances the chief executives' capacity to act autonomously from parties, yet making her somehow directly accountable to the voters whose personal support is crucial for remaining in the prime ministerial office. Manin's notion of 'audience' democracy, where reactive voting is more important than expressive support for parties based on partisan identification, well-portrays this situation. In his view, voters constitute an 'audience', which responds to the political views that individual leaders present on the political stage (Manin, 1997, p. 223).

The increasing trend of presidentialization is explained by four structural causes that interact with contingent political conditions as well as leaders' personality (Poguntke & Webb, 2005b, pp. 13–17). The first cause is the internationalization of politics. In the more globalized and interconnected world that resulted from the end of the Cold War in the 1990s, national governments have coordinated their actions to manage global issues, such as international economic exchange, migration, climate change, and pandemics. Since chief executives are leaders who represent their governments in international meetings, summits increase the chances for heads of government to act as key negotiators for their countries. Representative institutions such as parliaments, cabinets, and parties ratify decisions taken at these summits. This phenomenon is especially visible within the countries of the European Union, where the European Council gathers all heads of government or state to set priorities and guidelines for European policies. Political parties play a diminished role as agenda setters during these international negotiations.

The second structural cause for an increasing presidentialization of politics is the growth of the state, which is manifested in the complexity of bureaucratic processes, whose management requires new, technical competences. The increasing complexity of governmental tasks, paired with the delegation of policy-making to non-partisan agencies and authorities, undermines the partyness of policy. As a result, chief executives centralize their executive power and streamline decision-making through bilateral contacts between themselves and the relevant minister.

The third cause for the emergence of presidentialization is the erosion of social cleavages and their representation in European party systems. Until the early 1970s, party systems were clearly shaped along social divisions, whose roots can be traced back to the period ranging between the formation of modern nation-states and the early 1900s (Lipset & Rokkan, 1967). Christian Democratic parties, for example, have long represented religious interests against the state as well as the peripheries against political centers. Conservative and agrarian parties have spoken for the countryside against cities, while liberals have represented the growing productive bourgeoisie against representatives of the working class. In turn, the Bolshevik Revolution created divisions within the left-wing parties, between Social Democrats and radical revolutionary parties.

Parties resulting from old social cleavages have long dominated the European political scene (Bartolini & Mair, 1990; Karvonen & Kuhnle, 2001). However, in the 1970s, Europe started witnessing a value change from old left-right ideological positions to new emancipative values which eventually turned into a new social cleavage and shaped a new dimension of political competition (Inglehart, 1977; Inglehart & Welzel, 2005). The individualization of societies, the weakening of the links between parties and well-defined sectors of society, and the end of politics based on ideological doctrines have 'liberated' masses from previous party loyalties and favored electoral volatility. What follows are decreasing ties with traditional party organizations and an increasing attention to political personalities and leadership styles of prominent politicians. Thus, citizens' evaluation of the prime ministers' public performance becomes more important for their voting behavior than the electoral program of their political parties (Berz, 2020; Garzia et al., 2020).

Finally, the radical transformation in the structure of political communication has witnessed a pervasive impact on the rise of presidentialization. Key milestones include the increasing number of TV channels, available to the citizens and—most importantly—the advent of the internet, the fastest expanding communication technology of all time. It not only enables fast access to an enormous amount of information but also provides individuals who were hitherto largely passive consumers of political information with the opportunity of creating their own sources of information and communication networks (Mazzoleni, 2014). According to Chadwick (2017) these new communication technologies can be a powerful tool for increasing the personal influence of chief executives on voting behavior. This holds true especially when leaders use media for political announcements and for emphasizing the strategic salience of political issues. Put differently, several prime ministers adapt their behavior to the new communication environments and cultivate appropriate communicative skills in order to become politically successful.

According to Poguntke and Webb (2005b, pp. 7–11) these four structural factors have an indirect effect on the increasing political power resources of individual leaders in party governments, which defines three faces of presidentialization: a growth of autonomous control and political power of the chief executive (executive face), a growing leadership autonomy within political parties (party face), and a growing emphasis on leadership appeals in election campaigns (electoral face). For each of these three faces, a given political system can be closer to a pure presidential model or to a pure party government model. While presidential countries are posited to coincide with the former, the ideal-type of a parliamentary country should fit the latter; semi-presidentialism lies somewhere in between. With regard to parliamentary systems, one of Poguntke and Webb's major arguments states that their actual functioning is moving toward the presidential end of the spectrum. Thus, personal mandates, rather than the support from activists and party members, become the true basis of prime ministerial power. This shift is mirrored particularly in electoral campaigns, where personal standing and public appeal are more likely to determine voters' choice and attract media's interest (Garzia, 2014). In semi-presidential systems, prime ministers are also likely to benefit from presidentialization, depending, however, on the constitutional power that is given to presidents and prime ministers.

In sum, the development of presidentialization stems from the waning of party government. Although not all European countries have experienced the process of presidentialization at the same time and to the same extent, the theoretical argument remains very clear: the political power and the autonomy of prime ministers is increasing; thereby party governments are changing toward presidentialized democratic politics.

Declining Party Government and Prime Ministers' Careers

What are the implications of increasing populism, technocracy, and presidentialized politics on the political careers of prime ministers? We argue that these three alternative forms of political representation have an impact on the change in the level of political and technical experience and in the career profiles of prime ministers in Europe. This section extends our main argument and provides the major expectations for the empirical analysis in Chaps. 4 and 5.

The Impact of Populism and Technocracy

Over the past years, populism and technocracy have become more prominent as new forms of representation. They undermine the ability of established parties to constrain leaders and make long party apprenticeships less relevant when it comes to the selection of prime ministers. These developments have major implications for both the traditional patterns of political recruitment and the degree of career experiences among prime ministers in Europe.

It is well-known that the very notion of party government is deeply party-centered. In the party government model, parties are *the* political actors, which recruit and promote prime ministers. When party government functions appropriately, parties are the king-makers and ambitious politicians must satisfy the preferences of party gate-keepers to ascend to power. Long and clearly identifiable careers in the party and political institutions are the main indicators of prime ministers' reliability and loyalty toward their parties. Since 'the like usually attracts the like' it is highly inconceivable that gate-keepers in established political parties select a political outsider as prime minister, who is not well-socialized within the party organization or even hostile to the party itself.

As argued by Samuels and Shugart (2010, pp. 68–72), party 'insiders' are more likely to become chief executives when mainstream political parties keep the government formation under their control. These prime ministers are usually politicians who have spent some time in the national parliament, as cabinet ministers, and/or as party leaders before entering office. British prime ministers have, for instance, traditionally held these three positions sequentially (Rose, 2001, p. 72). Winston Churchill is a case in point of an 'insider': except for periods of military service, he dedicated most of his life to British politics, spending several years in parliament, in cabinet, and finally becoming prime minister for the first time at the age of 62 in 1940. The same is true for many other prime ministers in Europe who were in office between 1950 and 1980. The majority of these politicians went through a long period of 'party training' as parliamentarians and cabinet members. This 'recruitment channel' of prime ministers diminished in more recent decades (see Chap. 4).

While the recruitment structures of the established political parties have usually favored party 'insider' candidates, the 'political life' of populist leaders often starts outside of established political institutions. However, interestingly enough, populists do not reject the existence of political parties as a recruitment ground for political leaders, including prime ministers. Notwithstanding their common anti-establishment rhetoric, populist leaders are aware that, due to the institutional logic of parliamentarism, political parties are needed to control the premiership. Indeed, in parliamentary systems 'voters cannot vote *against* a party while voting *for* its leader—and it is impossible for a politician, no matter how personally popular, to ascend to the top executive post and remain there without the ongoing support from the legislative majority' (Samuels & Shugart, 2010, p. 17, emphasis in the original). However, as intermediate bodies between the citizens and the leader, political parties are discredited by the normative foundations of populism and, therefore, their primacy as recruiting agencies fades away. Populist leaders only recognize the instrumental utility of political parties as formal organizations to run for election.

In several countries, populist leaders use party brands to provide voters with heuristic shortcuts to choose among party alternatives. In fact, some populist politicians have taken over existing non-populist parties for their own political purposes and used them as a stepping stone for their individual political career as prime ministerial candidates. Barr (2009, p. 34) has labeled those politicians as mavericks

> who rises to prominence within an established, competitive party but then […] radically reshapes [… their] own party. […] Such unconventional or even rebellious behavior is notable not only with respect to the character of the party, but because it provides some basis for th[ose] politician[s] to make the same claims as outsiders often make.

This process describes, for instance, the case of the conservative *Fidesz* under Orbán's leadership in Hungary after 2003 and—to a lesser extent—the case of the left-wing *SYRIZA* under Alexis Tsipras in Greece. Similar situations were also witnessed outside Europe, for example, in Japan with the success of the former Prime Minister Koizumi (2001–2006) from the Liberal Democratic Party and in India, where Prime Minister Modi (2014–in office in 2021) reached the chief executive position through the established nationalist Bharatiya Janata Party.

Understanding that political parties remain pivotal vehicles for gaining the prime ministerial office, some populist leaders have also founded their own personal parties to win elections (Musella, 2018). Silvio Berlusconi, for instance, created *Forza Italia* in Italy (in 1994) and Andrej Babiš established ANO (Action of Unsatisfied Citizens) in the Czech Republic (in 2012). While both Berlusconi and Babiš entered politics as businessmen, the Bulgarian populist Prime Minister Simeon Saxe-Coburg-Gotha returned from exile as former king of the country (1943–1946) and founded his own party (National Movement for Stability and Progress) in 2001. Simeon Saxe-Coburg-Gotha resembles the ideal-type of the political 'outsider' depicted by Linz (1994, p. 26), as a political leader who becomes prime minister 'without any governmental or even political experience, on the basis of a populist appeal, often based on hostility to parties and "politicians"'.

Hence, populist prime ministers mostly belong to a political party but lack long-term political experience within representative institutions. Instead of presenting themselves as members of a reliable political party, their personal esteem and their linkage to the voters are their most important resources for achieving the prime ministerial office. In this sense, a populist prime minister is likely to present herself simply as the executor of the will of the people and as an outsider to the political system. One example is Giuseppe Conte, who was a non-partisan professor, but a close follower of the populist Five Star Movement before entering office as Italian prime minister in 2018. He introduced his mission as that of a 'defense attorney of the Italian people' (*avvocato difensore del popolo italiano*).[9] This concept of political representation does not require party reliability *per se* or any political experience, but the ability to listen to, and solve, citizens' list of grievances (*cahier de doléances*), irrespective of party goals.

Following this line of argument, we expect that—along with the increase of populist demands of representation—the level of political experience of prime ministers within representative institutions and parties has declined in several European countries over the past decades. Related to this, we expect that the rate of 'pure' outsider prime ministers, with no substantial political experience, has modestly increased, while still remaining relatively low among the total of all European chief executives.

If populism leads to less politically experienced prime ministers, then technocracy, in turn, should favor more technical, non-political expertise among prime ministers. In empirical terms, technocracy means 'government by technicians' (Putnam, 1977, p. 383). Put differently, technocratic governments are ruled by prime ministers with specialized expertise (Cotta, 2018, p. 272). They are predominantly selected because of their competence in specific policy fields, and not necessarily because of their political experiences.

Political and technical experiences are two different dimensions of one's career experience. Prime ministers with considerable political experience in their own parties are likely to lack technical competence, since they spend most of their professional life in politics. Technocratic prime ministers, in turn, usually have no (or only very little) political experience in representative institutions but extensive expertise in different policy domains as well as distinct managerial skills. One example of a technocratic prime minister is Tihomir Orešković from Croatia, who spent more than 20 years in finance and business for a pharmaceutical company in Canada, before entering the prime ministerial office without having gathered any party or government-based political experiences.

Although different in nature, political and technical experiences may also be combined, which occurs, for instance, when a policy expert becomes prime minister after having entered politics only for a short period of time. Carreras (2017) has defined these politicians as political 'newcomers' with technical background. A good example is the Swedish

Prime Minister, Stefan Löfven (2014–), who served as chairman of the powerful IF Metal trade union for seven years before being elected as leader of the Social Democratic Party in 2012. There are good reasons for arguing that Löfven's political responsibility in trade unions helped him to connect with powerful politicians. Thereby, he could establish a personal network, which supported his successful political career. As shown by Carreras (2017, p. 367), it is no coincidence that being a former leader of a trade union is one of the main background characteristics of 'newcomer' heads of government.

Other prime ministers in Europe gathered a combination of populist and technocratic traits. Buštíková and Guasti (2019) have labeled these politicians as 'technocratic populists'. The political experience of these prime ministers is usually low, while their populist origin and behavior as well as their technical experience are remarkable. Examples are Prime Ministers Václav Klaus (1992–1997) and Andrej Babiš (2017–in office in 2021) in the Czech Republic. Both have 'sweetened' their populist ideology by advocating technical expertise as an indicator of authenticity. The success of this kind of leaders indicates the rising of a new logic of democratic political competition, which results from the combination of populist and technocratic modes of political organization. Bickerton and Invernizzi Accetti (2021) have labeled this new trend as 'technopopulism'. According to the authors, citizens (populus) increasingly ask for politically competent prime ministers with expert knowledge (technocrats) who are expected to offer pragmatic political answers in times of political crisis. One example is the 'Get Brexit Done' campaign by politicians and voters in the United Kingdom. A similar development of 'technopopulism' exists in Italy (Vercesi, 2021).

In sum, the majority of all prime ministers still have substantial political experience before entering office. However, since the rise of populism and technocracy have become more prominent forms of political representation, we expect to see trends of slowly decreasing political experiences, as well as increasing technical experiences among prime ministers in several European countries.

The Impact of Presidentialization

The third main expectation of our study is derived from the discussion about the 'personal governing' of prime ministers in Europe. Under presidentialized politics, the electoral appeal of individual executive leaders becomes more important for winning elections than their party apprenticeship. Although voting for 'political personalities' already took place in the 1950s and 1960s (examples are, for instance, Konrad Adenauer in Germany and Winston Churchill in the United Kingdom), the change toward 'personal voting' became more prominent in the late 1970s and especially in the most recent decades.

Moreover, and as pointed out above, presidentialization has increased the political power of prime ministers within their parties and their policy expertise. Increasing power together with a 'personal mandate' has, in turn, created the conditions for substantial changes in the prime ministers' political role. In presidentialized governments, prime ministers are no longer 'chairs' but become 'chiefs' of cabinet government. They cease to be *primi inter pares* (first among equals) within the cabinet and adopt a monocratic (i.e., presidential) form of leadership.[10] This makes it possible for them to hire personally favored ministers (i.e., their political followers) and to unilaterally fire them when they drift from the policy guidelines set by the chief executive.

Furthermore, the increasing number of international summits influences the prime ministerial role substantially by providing an important legitimizing resource for the centralization of power in the hands of prime ministers. Since it is difficult for national, political institutions to renegotiate signed, international agreements, 'presidentialized' prime ministers can present them to their political parties, parliament, and cabinet as 'take it or leave it' decisions. In this situation, national political parties are usually willing to grant prime ministers' decisional autonomy, inasmuch as prime ministers are electoral assets. In the end, a presidentialized government does not proceed *through* parties (i.e., in the way suggested by the model of party government) but *past* parties (Poguntke & Webb, 2005b, p. 8ff).

One example of a prime minister bypassing her party in policy-making is Chancellor Angela Merkel in Germany. In 2015, she agreed with the Austrian government on the transit of several thousand Syrian refugees from Hungary to Germany without prior parliamentary debate. Moreover, during the pandemic crisis in 2020, Merkel (as well as many other chief executives in Europe) imposed several measures at the expense of fundamental democratic rights, such as placing limitations on citizens' freedom of movement, and on the freedom to associate and assemble, with little consultation of her own party or national parliament. Another example of 'personal governing' in a presidentialized parliamentary system is Prime

Minister Matteo Renzi's behavior in Italy. In April, 2016, he passed his package of constitutional reforms through parliament by building alternative voting coalitions against the opposition of major factions within his own party. It was only in December 2016 that these reform initiatives were rejected by a constitutional referendum (Poguntke & Webb, 2018).

That said, in presidentialized governments not all that glitters is gold for prime ministers. The drawback of their increased political autonomy is that they become more vulnerable to unstable public opinions. When power is rooted within a stable party organization, the prime minister can cope with political challenges, backed by the support of a party that ideally has its own resources for voters' mobilization. Personal leadership, however, may decline quickly when prime ministers make political mistakes and volatile groups of voters change their opinion on the chief executive. In that case, the retirement of prime ministers is prominent on the political agenda.

We find multiple empirical evidence for presidentialized governments in several European countries. Michael Foley (2000) showed, for instance, that the British premiership of Tony Blair was the epitome of a presidentialized government, whose origins can be traced back to the premiership of Margaret Thatcher. Around the same time, this trend was also visible in Italy and Germany, where strong leaders such as Silvio Berlusconi and Gerhard Schröder became prime ministers for the first time in 1994 and 1998, respectively. In the 2000s, 'best practice' cases of presidentialization emerged all over Western Europe. Webb and Poguntke (2005) found at least a moderate trend of presidentialization in 11 West and South European countries (Belgium, Denmark, Finland, France, Germany, Italy, the Netherlands, Portugal, Spain, Sweden, and United Kingdom).

Presidentialization has also developed in Central-Eastern Europe after the transition to democracy. In this region, the absence of a traditional cleavage structure, the weak institutionalization of parties and the party system, and high electoral volatility, as well as elites' influence on the media system have enhanced prime ministerial chances to shape leader-centered electoral campaigns and to produce a personal effect on the electoral outcome (Berz, 2019). Moreover, some established parties—such as the Czech Social Democrats and the Hungarian *Fidesz*—have adopted leader-centered structures in order to survive under new political conditions. Notwithstanding frequent coalitional constraints, cases of 'presidential' prime ministership in Central-Eastern Europe have been numerous. Slovak politics was dominated by Prime Minister Vladimir Mečiar for most of the 1990s and by Robert Fico (2006–2010 and 2012–2018). After the PiS's government of Jarosław Kaczyński, Poland experienced the presidentialized premiership of Donald Tusk from Civic Platform from 2007 to 2014. Finally, in Hungary, Victor Orbán since 2010 represents a clear case of personal leadership (Hloušek, 2015).

These examples show that the delegation of power has shifted within partisan governments. What has changed in presidentialized democracies is the principal-agent relationship of prime ministers within their parties. First, according to the 'principal-agent approach' (Strøm, 2000; Berlinski et al., 2012) political parties make the delegation from voters to members of parliament effective by structuring the elections. Second, parliamentary parties are the major actors that make and break political executives. Third, political parties are involved in the allocation of ministerialportfolios within government and also shape the intra-executive relations through partisan logics. Thus, under this classic party government model, parties control all aspects of the delegation of power while members of parliament and government are accountable through them. In this scenario, prime ministers are nothing but agents of their parties, who are socialized within party organizations, show a loyalty toward them, and implement party policies and guidelines once being in government.

In contrast, in times of presidentialized government, prime ministers with strong leadership skills for setting party strategies, centralizing policy-making, finding solutions to intra-party conflicts, and playing the part of the outstanding candidate during electoral campaigns become the most important persons for the political parties' electoral and policy success. In other words, political parties become dependent upon the public performance of prime ministers who, in turn, increase their impact on both governmental decision-making and the programmatic stands of their own party. In the language of the 'principal-agent approach' prime ministers become the principals of their parties.

Naturally, these two types of prime ministers are not mutually exclusive, but one can expect that the presidentialization of politics increases the demand for prime ministers of the principal rather than the agent type. Thus, with the increase of presidentialization, we expect that the career profile of prime ministers shifts from the type of *party-agent*—who have followed a traditional political career as members of national parliament and cabinet—to the type of *party-principal*—who have primarily held political leadership positions.

Conclusion

This chapter has provided a theoretical framework for studying prime ministers' career changes and presented a series of deductively derived expectations. Our core argument is that the decline of party government favors the emergence of populist, technocratic, and presidentializing drives in European democracies. These phenomena have been jointly conducive to a substantial reconfiguration of prime ministers' careers in two ways. First, the level of political and technical experience and, second, the career profiles of prime ministers have changed over time.

Due to the decline of party government and its political consequences, we expect the following implications on the changes of prime ministers' careers:

- first, the level of political experience has declined in prime ministers' political careers over the past decades;
- second, technical experience has increased as an important competence of prime ministers, particularly during the most recent decades;
- third, while the percentage of prime ministers who have acquired experience outside the traditional arenas of political careers ('outsider experiences') has increased, they still remain a minority compared to the prime ministers with experiences in major political positions ('insider experiences');
- fourth, the proportion of prime ministers with a party-principal career profile has increased over the past decades compared to the prime ministers with a party-agent profile.

The following two chapters explore these theoretical expectations in greater empirical depth.

Notes

1. It is worth noting that the selection of prime ministers also depends on factors other than previous political careers. For example, parties value the intra-party ideological position of possible prime ministers, their popularity within the party, or their relationship with other coalition partners (Bäck & Dumont, 2008).
2. For the conceptual distinction between mainstream and challenger/populist party, see De Vries and Hobolt (2020).

3. Countries are listed according to their general degree of partyness of government.
4. Moreover, testing David Easton's argument, Linde and Peters (2018, p. 301) find that, when voters perceive that governments are responsive to short-term demands, governing parties benefit from a 'responsiveness capital'. This capital allows governments to make non-responsive (and responsible) decisions, which citizens are more likely to accept.
5. Following Zulianello's (2018) revisited concept of anti-system party, a party is anti-systemic when it has no visible interactions with the system and presents meta-antipolitical ideological instances. As the author states, '[i]n contrast to the historical cases, the vast majority of contemporary anti-system parties do not question democracy as such' (Zulianello, 2018, p. 667).
6. Austria; Belgium; Czech Republic; Denmark; Finland; France; Germany; Greece; Hungary; Ireland; Italy; Netherlands; Norway; Portugal; Slovakia; Spain; Sweden; Switzerland; United Kingdom.
7. Before the 1970s, populist parties hardly existed in Europe. There were only cases such as the Common Man's Front (*Fronte dell'Uomo Qualunque*) in Italy between 1946 and 1949 and the French Poujadists in the 1950s.
8. We are aware that the concept of presidentialization as introduced by Poguntke and Webb has been heavily criticized in the literature. Yet, their analysis fits prominently with our empirical observations and theoretical assumptions. For a critical discussion, see Dowding (2013a) and Elgie and Passarelli (2020).
9. See 'A Conte l'incarico di Mattarella per il governo: "Sarò l'avvocato difensore del popolo italiano"'. *La Stampa*, 23 May 2018.
10. In this context Dowding (2013b) argued that prime ministers, who are free from the system of checks and balances of the presidential form of government, can even become stronger than (constrained) presidents.

References

Andeweg, R. B. (2020). Parties and Executives in Parliamentary Systems: From Party Government to Party Governance. In R. B. Andeweg, R. Elgie, L. Helms, J. Kaarbo, & F. Müller-Rommel (Eds.), *The Oxford Handbook of Political Executives* (pp. 460–480). Oxford University Press.

Bäck, H., & Dumont, P. (2008). Making the First Move: A Two-Stage Analysis of the Role of Formateurs in Parliamentary Government Formation. *Public Choice, 135*(3–4), 353–373.

Barr, R. R. (2009). Populists, Outsiders and Anti-Establishment Politics. *Party Politics, 15*(1), 29–48.

Bartolini, S., & Mair, P. (1990). *Identity, Competition, and Electoral Availability. The Stabilization of European Electorates 1885–1985*. Cambridge University Press.

Berlinski, S., Dewan, T., & Dowding, K. (2012). *Accounting for Ministers. Scandal and Survival in British Governments 1945–2007*. Oxford University Press.

Berman, S., & Snegovaya, M. (2019). Populism and the Decline of Social Democracy. *Journal of Democracy, 30*(3), 5–19.

Bertsou, E., & Caramani, D. (2020). People Haven't Had Enough of Experts: Technocratic Attitudes among Citizens in Nine European Democracies. *American Journal of Political Science*. https://doi.org/10.1111/ajps.12554

Berz, J. (2019). Potent Executives: The Electoral Strength of Prime Ministers in Central Eastern Europe. *East European Politics, 35*(4), 517–537.

Berz, J. (2020). All the Prime Minister's Glory? Leader Effects and Accountability of Prime Ministers in Parliamentary Elections. *Politics, 40*(4), 444–459.

Bickerton, C. J., & Invernizzi Accetti, C. (2021). *Technopopulism. The New Logic of Democratic Politics*. Oxford University Press.

Blondel, J., & Cotta, M. (1996). Conclusion. In J. Blondel & M. Cotta (Eds.), *Party and Government: An Inquiry into the Relationship between Governments and Supporting Parties in Liberal Democracies* (pp. 249–262). Palgrave.

Blondel, J., & Cotta, M. (Eds.). (2000). *The Nature of Party Government. A Comparative European Perspective*. Palgrave.

Blondel, J., & Thiébault, J.-L. (2010). *Political Leadership, Parties and Citizens: The Personalisation of Leadership*. Routledge.

Bordignon, F. (2014). Matteo Renzi: A 'Leftist Berlusconi' for the Italian Democratic Party? *South European Society and Politics, 19*(1), 1–23.

Brunclík, M. (2015). The Rise of Technocratic Cabinets. What We Know, and What We Should Like to Know. *Austrian Journal of Political Science, 44*(3), 57–67.

Brunclík, M., & Parízek, M. (2019). When Are Technocratic Cabinets Formed? *Comparative European Politics, 17*(5), 759–777.

Budge, I. (1984). Parties and Democratic Government: A Framework for Comparative Explanation. *West European Politics, 7*(1), 95–118.

Buštíková, L., & Guasti, P. (2019). The State as a Firm: Understanding the Autocratic Roots of Technocratic Populism. *East European Politics and Societies and Cultures, 33*(2), 302–330.

Campus, D. (2020). Political Executives and the Mediatization of Politics. In R. B. Andeweg, R. Elgie, L. Helms, J. Kaarbo, & F. Müller-Rommel (Eds.), *The Oxford Handbook of Political Executives* (pp. 588–607). Oxford University Press.

Caramani, D. (2017). Will vs. Reason: The Populist and Technocratic Forms of Political Representation and Their Critique to Party Government. *American Political Science Review*, 111(1), 54–67.

Caramani, D. (2020). Introduction. The Technocratic Challenge to Democracy. In E. Bertsou & D. Caramani (Eds.), *The Technocratic Challenge to Democracy* (pp. 1–26). Routledge.

Carreras, M. (2017). Institutions, Governmental Performance and the Rise of Political Newcomers. *European Journal of Political Research, 56*(2), 364–380.

Castles, F. G., & Wildenmann, R. (Eds.). (1986). *Visions and Realities of Party Government.* de Gruyter.

Chadwick, A. (2017). *The Hybrid Media System: Politics and Power.* Oxford University Press.

Chiaramonte, A., & Emanuele, V. (2017). Party System Volatility, Regeneration and De-Institutionalization in Western Europe (1945–2015). *Party Politics, 23*(4), 376–388.

Cotta, M. (2018). Technocratic Government Versus Party Government? Non-Partisan Ministers and the Changing Parameters of Political Leadership in European Democracies. In A. Costa Pinto, M. Cotta, & P. Tavares de Almeida (Eds.), *Technocratic Ministers and Political Leadership in European Democracies* (pp. 267–288). Palgrave Macmillan.

Dalton, R. J. (2000). The Decline of Party Identifications. In R. J. Dalton & M. P. Wattenberg (Eds.), *Parties without Partisans. Political Change in Advanced Industrial Democracies* (pp. 19–36). Oxford University Press.

Dalton, R. J. (2016). Party Identification and Its Implications. *Oxford Research Encyclopedia of Politics.* https://doi.org/10.1093/acrefore/9780190228637.013.72

Dalton, R. J., Farrell, D., & McAllister, I. (2011). *Political Parties & Democratic Linkage. How Parties Organize Democracy.* Oxford University Press.

De Vries, C. E., & Hobolt, S. B. (2020). *Political Entrepreneurs: The Rise of Challenger Parties in Europe.* Princeton University Press.

Dowding, K. (2013a). Beneath the Surface: Replies to Three Critics. *Parliamentary Affairs, 66*(4), 663–672.

Dowding, K. (2013b). The Prime Ministerialisation of the British Prime Minister. *Parliamentary Affairs, 66*(3), 617–635.

Elgie, R. (1993). *The Role of the Prime Minister in France, 1981–91.* St. Martin's Press.

Elgie, R., & Passarelli, G. (2020). The Presidentialization of Political Executives. In R. B. Andeweg, R. Elgie, L. Helms, J. Kaarbo, & F. Müller-Rommel (Eds.), *The Oxford Handbook of Political Executives* (pp. 359–381). Oxford University Press.

Foley, M. (2000). *The British Presidency. Tony Blair and the Politics of Public Leadership.* Manchester University Press.

Franklin, M. N. (2004). *Voter Turnout and the Dynamics of Electoral Competition in Established Democracies since 1945.* Cambridge University Press.

Frognier, A.-P. (2000). The Normative Foundations of Party Government. In J. Blondel & M. Cotta (Eds.), *The Nature of Party Government. A Comparative European Perspective* (pp. 21–37). Palgrave.

Garzia, D. (2014). *Personalization of Politics and Electoral Change*. Palgrave Macmillan.

Garzia, D., Ferreira da Silva, F., & De Angelis, A. (2020). Partisan Dealignment and the Personalisation of Politics in West European Parliamentary Democracies, 1961–2018. *West European Politics*. https://doi.org/10.1080/01402382.2020.1845941

Garzia, D., & Karremans, J. (2021). Super Mario 2: Comparing the Technocrat-Led Monti and Draghi Governments in Italy. *Contemporary Italian Politics, 13*(1), 105–115.

Heinisch, R., & Werner, A. (2019). Who Do Populist Radical Right Parties Stand for? Representative Claims, Claim Acceptance and Descriptive Representation in the Austrian FPÖ and German AfD. *Representation, 55*(5), 475–492.

Hloušek, V. (2015). Two Types of Presidentialization in the Party Politics of Central Eastern Europe. *Italian Political Science Review, 45*(3), 277–299.

Inglehart, R. (1977). *The Silent Revolution. Changing Values and Political Styles Among Western Publics*. Princeton University Press.

Inglehart, R., & Welzel, C. (2005). *Modernization, Cultural Change, and Democracy. The Human Development Sequence*. Cambridge University Press.

Johansson, K. M., & Tallberg, J. (2010). Explaining Chief Executive Empowerment: EU Summitry and Domestic Institutional Change. *West European Politics, 33*(2), 208–236.

Karremans, J. (2021). This Time Wasn't Different: Responsiveness and Responsibility in the Eurozone between 2007 and 2019. *Journal of Common Market Studies, 59*(6), 1536–1554.

Karvonen, L., & Kuhnle, S. (Eds.). (2001). *Party Systems and Voter Alignments Revisited*. Routledge.

Katz, R. S. (1986). Party Government: A Rationalistic Conception. In F. G. Castles & R. Wildenmann (Eds.), *Visions and Realities of Party Government* (pp. 31–71). de Gruyter.

Katz, R. S. (1987). Party Government and Its Alternatives. In R. Katz (Ed.), *Party Governments: European and American Experiences* (pp. 1–26). de Gruyter.

Katz, R. S., & Mair, P. (2009). The Cartel Party Thesis: A Restatement. *Perspectives on Politics, 7*(4), 753–766.

Keman, H. (2017). Responsible Responsiveness of Parties in and out of Government. In P. Harfst, I. Kubbe, & T. Poguntke (Eds.), *Parties, Governments and Elites. The Comparative Study of Democracy* (pp. 25–52). Springer.

Keman, H., & Müller-Rommel, F. (2012). The Life Cycle of Party Government across the New Europe. In H. Keman & F. Müller-Rommel (Eds.), *Party Government in the New Europe* (pp. 3–24). Routledge.

King, A. (1987). The Outsider as Political Leader: The Case of Margaret Thatcher. *British Journal of Political Science, 32*(3), 435–454.

Kölln, A.-K. (2016). Party Membership in Europe: Testing Party-Level Explanations of Decline. *Party Politics, 22*(4), 465–477.

Kostelka, F. (2017). Does Democratic Consolidation Lead to a Decline in Voter Turnout? Global Evidence Since 1939. *American Political Science Review, 111*(4), 653–667.

Kriesi, H., Bochsler, D., Matthes, J., Lavenex, S., Bühlmann, M., & Esser, F. (2013). *Democracy in the Age of Globalization and Mediatization.* Palgrave Macmillan.

Leininger, A., & Meijers, M. J. (2021). Do Populist Parties Increase Voter Turnout? Evidence From Over 40 Years of Electoral History in 31 European Democracies. *Political Studies, 69*(3), 665–685.

Linde, J., & Peters, Y. (2018). Responsiveness, Support, and Responsibility: How Democratic Responsiveness Facilitates Responsible Government. *Party Politics, 26*(3), 291–304.

Linz, J. J. (1994). Presidential or Parliamentary Democracy: Does It Make a Difference? In J. J. Linz & A. Valenzuela (Eds.), *The Failure of Presidential Democracy, Volume 2: The Case of Latin America* (pp. 3–90). John Hopkins University.

Lipset, S. M., & Rokkan, S. (1967). Cleavage Structures, Party Systems, and Voter Alignments: An Introduction. In S. M. Lipset & S. Rokkan (Eds.), *Party Systems and Voter Alignments: Cross-National Perspectives* (pp. 1–64). The Free Press.

Mair, P. (2002). Populist Democracy vs. Party Democracy. In Y. Mény & Y. Surel (Eds.), *Democracies and the Populist Challenge* (pp. 81–98). Palgrave.

Mair, P. (2008). The Challenge to Party Government. *West European Politics, 31*(1–2), 211–234.

Mair, P. (2009). *Representative versus Responsible Government.* MPIfG Working Paper 09/8. Cologne: Max Planck Institute for the Study of Societies.

Mair, P. (2013). *Ruling the Void. The Hollowing of Western Democracy.* Verso Books.

Manin, B. (1997). *The Principles of Representative Government.* Cambridge University Press.

Mazzoleni, G. (2014). Mediatization and Political Populism. In F. Esser & J. Strömbäck (Eds.), *Mediatization of Politics. Understanding the Transformation of Western Democracies* (pp. 42–56). Palgrave Macmillan.

McDonnell, D., & Valbruzzi, M. (2014). Defining and Classifying Technocrat-Led and Technocratic Governments. *European Journal of Political Research, 53*(4), 654–671.

Mudde, C. (2004). The Populist Zeitgeist. *Government and Opposition, 39*(4), 541–563.

Musella, F. (2018). *Political Leaders beyond Party Politics.* Palgrave Macmillan.

Pastorella, G. (2016). Technocratic Governments in Europe: Getting the Critique Right. *Political Studies, 64*(4), 948–965.

Plescia, C., Kritzinger, S., & De Sio, L. (2019). Filling the Void? Political Responsiveness of Populist Parties. *Representation, 55*(4), 513–533.

Poguntke, T., & Webb, P. (Eds.). (2005a). *The Presidentialization of Politics. A Comparative Study of Modern Democracies*. Oxford University Press.

Poguntke, T., & Webb, P. (2005b). The Presidentialization of Politics in Democratic Societies: A Framework for Analysis. In T. Poguntke & P. Webb (Eds.), *The Presidentialization of Politics. A Comparative Study of Modern Democracies* (pp. 1–25). Oxford University Press.

Poguntke, T., & Webb, P. D. (2018). Presidentialization, Personalization and Populism. The Hollowing out of Party Government. In W. P. Cross, R. S. Katz, & S. Pruysers (Eds.), *The Personalization of Democratic Politics and the Challenge for Political Parties* (pp. 181–196). Rowman & Littlefield.

Putnam, R. D. (1977). Elite Transformation in Advanced Industrial Societies. An Empirical Assessment of the Theory Technocracy. *Comparative Political Studies, 10*(3), 383–412.

Rooduijn, M., de Lange, S. L., & van der Brug, W. (2014). A Populist *Zeitgeist*? Programmatic Contagion by Populist Parties in Western Europe. *Party Politics, 20*(4), 563–575.

Rose, R. (1969). The Variability of Party Government: A Theoretical and Empirical Critique. *Political Studies, 17*(4), 413–445.

Rose, R. (1974). *The Problem of Party Government*. Macmillan.

Rose, R. (2001). *The Prime Minister in a Shrinking World*. Polity Press.

Samuels, D. J., & Shugart, M. S. (2010). *Presidents, Parties, and Prime Ministers. How the Separation of Powers Affects Party Organization and Behavior*. Cambridge University Press.

Schattschneider, E. E. (1945). Party Government and Employment Policy. *American Political Science Review, 39*(6), 1147–1157.

Siavelis, P., & Morgenstern, S. (Eds.). (2008). *Pathways to Power. Political Recruitment and Candidate Selection in Latin America*. The Pennsylvania State University Press.

Sikk, A. (2005). How Unstable? Volatility and the Genuinely New Parties in Eastern Europe. *European Journal of Political Research, 44*(3), 391–412.

Strøm, K. (2000). Delegation and Accountability in Parliamentary Democracies. *European Journal of Political Research, 37*(3), 261–290.

Thatcher, M., & Stone Sweet, A. (2002). Theory and Practice of Delegation to Non-Majoritarian Institutions. *West European Politics, 25*(1), 1–22.

Thomson, R., Royed, T., Naurin, E., Artés, J., Costello, R., Ennser-Jedenastik, L., Ferguson, M., Kostadinova, P., Moury, C., Pétry, F., & Praprotnik, K. (2017). The Fulfillment of Parties' Election Pledges: A Comparative Study on the Impact of Power Sharing. *American Political Science Review, 61*(3), 527–542.

Van Biezen, I., Mair, P., & Poguntke, T. (2012). Going, Going, …Gone? The Decline of Party Membership in Contemporary Europe. *European Journal of Political Research, 51*(1), 24–56.

Vercesi, M. (2021). Society and Territory: Making Sense of Italian Populism from a Historical Perspective. *Journal of Contemporary European Studies.* https://doi.org/10.1080/14782804.2021.1939664

Webb, P. (2000). Political Parties in Western Europe: Linkage, Legitimacy and Reform. *Representation, 37*(3–4), 203–214.

Webb, P., & Poguntke, T. (2005). The Presidentialization of Contemporary Democratic Politics: Evidence, Causes and Consequences. In T. Poguntke & P. Webb (Eds.), *The Presidentialization of Politics. A Comparative Study of Modern Democracies* (pp. 336–356). Oxford University Press.

Webb, P., Poguntke, T., & Kolodny, R. (2012). The Presidentialization of Party Leadership? Evaluating Party Leadership and Party Government in the Democratic World. In L. Helms (Ed.), *Comparative Political Leadership* (pp. 77–98). Palgrave Macmillan.

Webb, P., & White, S. (2007). Political Parties in New Democracies: Trajectories of Development and Implications for Democracy. In P. Webb & S. White (Eds.), *Party Politics in New Europe* (pp. 345–370). Oxford University Press.

Werner, A., & Giebler, H. (2019). Do Populists Represent? Theoretical Considerations on How Populist Parties (Might) Enact their Representative Function. *Representation, 55*(4), 379–392.

Zulianello, M. (2018). Anti-System Parties Revisited: Concept Formation and Guidelines for Empirical Research. *Government and Opposition, 53*(4), 653–681.

CHAPTER 4

Changing Career Experiences: Less Political, More Technical

In the previous chapter, we argued that the decline of party government will lead to changes in prime ministers' career experiences and career profiles. In this chapter, we provide empirical evidence for the first part of our theoretical argument by conceptualizing and measuring the different political and technical experiences of European prime ministers. We first summarize the varieties of prime ministers' career experiences. In a second step, we examine the longitudinal changes in the political and technical experiences of prime ministers in the three major European regions over a period of more than 70 years (1945–2020) and discuss the observed changes in light of our theoretical expectations.

VARIETIES OF CAREER EXPERIENCES

As noted in Chap. 2, each prime minister's career is determined by several factors, such as age, sex, and educational and occupational background, but also—and more importantly—by their specific professional experiences acquired during their lifetime. In very general terms, we observe two different forms of prime ministerial career experiences: *political* and *technical* experiences.

Comparative studies of parliamentary and executive elites have always been particularly interested in the impact of career trajectories on the *political experiences* of politicians because each political office enables the holder to acquire specific knowledge and skills that also help her to perform well in future career positions (Blondel, 1991). Although the political experiences of European cabinet ministers received some attention in the literature (Bright et al., 2015; Fischer et al., 2012), systematic research on the political experiences of prime ministers is still missing in comparative research.

The political experiences of individual prime ministers vary substantially. They range from no experience at all to multiple political experiences. Obviously, prime ministers who have served in many political positions within the party organization and other political institutions have developed a deeper knowledge about the activities that characterize the prime ministerial job than those who never held a political post. In this context, the literature has distinguished between *political insiders* and *political outsiders* (De Winter, 1991; Verzichelli, 1998; Martocchia Diodati & Verzichelli, 2017; Costa Pinto et al., 2018). The career path of insider prime ministers is more political than the one by outsiders in a sense that they held major political positions prior to becoming prime minister. In these positions, they accumulate a considerable amount of political experience on national, subnational, and supranational level.

Prime ministers with political experiences on national level held one or more of the following political offices: member of parliament, cabinet minister, and national party head. Membership in parliament provides prime ministers with detailed knowledge of the formal and informal procedures of the legislative processes. Usually, prime ministers with parliamentary experiences are also party members,[1] who provide skills in generating political support of the parliamentary majority for government policy-making (Grotz et al., 2021). Prime ministers with cabinet experiences have first-hand expertise in dealing with intra-cabinet conflict and in managing the formal and informal processes of cabinet decision-making (Thiébault, 1991; De Winter, 1993; Baturo & Elkink, 2021). A previous position as party head, in turn, provides a prime minister with important political experiences that are not supplied by the two other posts. Party heads, for instance, develop more leadership skills in intra-party decision-making. Therefore, the office of party head also bears some resemblance to the office of prime minister. Just like the head of government, a party leader needs to know how to resolve political conflicts, set the policy agenda, coordinate the decision-making in various policy arenas, and enlist the support of various interested individuals and groups.

While insider prime ministers accumulate remarkable political experience in different political positions, outsider prime ministers can be a member of a political party but never hold any of the three major political posts before being appointed. They become politically prominent outside of the national party system and often enter politics because of their special knowledge in certain policy fields and/or because of their technical and managerial experiences, for instance, as former directors of private enterprises or international organizations. Overall, it seems reasonable to state that the career experiences of insider prime ministers are more likely 'party-based' while the ones by outsiders are more 'technical knowledge-based'.

Prime ministers with political experiences at the subnational and the supranational level held positions in local, regional, and European parliaments and executives. Former local or regional experience provides prime ministers, for instance, with the political skills necessary for organizing majorities within their own party and dealing with nation-wide decisions that affect their regional constituencies. Political knowledge at the subnational level is particularly important for prime ministers in federal systems such as Germany and Austria, but also in countries with regional, autonomous governments such as Italy, Spain, and the United Kingdom. Moreover, executive political experience at the subnational level, that is, as former mayors of large cities or regional presidents, often provides prime ministers with considerable political skills, for instance, by organizing political support among the councilors. Political experience at the supranational level, that is, as former member of the European Parliament, supplies prime ministers with detailed knowledge about the functioning of the European Union as a collective political actor, in particular the way political decision-making is organized. It is therefore most likely that political experiences gathered at the European level influence prime ministers' political behavior in European summit meetings.

Aside from political experiences, prime ministers can also hold technical experiences from their previous occupational positions outside of party politics. Among the group of prime ministers with technical experience, there are, for instance, those who have been employed as heads of private and/or public enterprise,[2] heads of interest groups, senior civil servants, diplomats, as well as members of international organizations. Having formerly worked in one of these 'non-political sector' institutions or organizations provides prime ministers with crucial technical experience, which helps in negotiating governmental policy decisions with social actors outside of party politics.

In sum, we observe a variety of experiences gained by prime ministers prior to entering office. They may have extensive and important insider experience which they gather within parliament, cabinet, and/or within their political party. Prime ministers with this background usually lack technical know-how with respect to specific policy areas (Bakema & Secker, 1988, p. 157). They acquired, however, deep knowledge and political skills particularly when serving in several of the three career positions for longer periods. Prime ministers can also be political outsiders, in which case they gain no experience in any of the three political positions on national level but often acquire highly developed technical skills and specialized knowledge in non-political sectors prior to their investiture (Cotta, 2018). Finally, we find prime ministers who obtained a combination of both political and technical experiences before entering office. Some of these prime ministers developed more technical skills than political experiences in their previous occupation. These politicians are in the first instance experts in certain policy areas, but they might also have a party affiliation and thereby gathered some political experiences (Lavezzolo et al., 2021, p. 1511). Finally, although very rare in reality, prime ministers may have neither held a political position at national level nor acquired technical competence.

In the following analysis, we examine the varieties of these political and technical experiences among European prime ministers. Thereby, we first expect that these experiences have changed over time and across the European regions. Due to a decline of party government in liberal democracies, we expect to see a moderate decrease in prime ministers' political experiences and a relative increase in their technical expertise. Put differently, we claim that the demand for technical experiences among prime ministers has increased over the past decades, although political experience and knowledge of political institutions remain crucial assets for entering the pool of eligible prime minister candidates. Therefore, the appointment of prime ministers with neither political nor technical experience is an exception in European political executives.

Second, we expect prime ministers' experiences to vary substantially across three European regions. Although the decline of party government took place all over Europe, countries in Southern and Central-Eastern Europe are among the least 'partified'. This is because countries in these two regions democratized at a time when party government was already in decline in 'old' Western Europe. A well-functioning party government—as observed in Western Europe before the 1980s—never fully developed in these countries. Central-Eastern Europe in particular lacks strong political parties, voters with party identification, and stable social cleavages to an even greater extent than many West European countries. We therefore expect that prime ministers in these two regions gather less political experiences in traditional political institutions and more technical experiences from outside of party politics.

POLITICAL EXPERIENCES OF PRIME MINISTERS

As mentioned above, European prime ministers tend to gain their political experiences in political positions on national, subnational, and supranational level. This section therefore examines the different political posts that prime ministers held before their investiture, covering the past seven decades and the three European regions.

National Political Experiences

Several scholars consider former political experiences as member of the parliament and cabinet, and/or as national party leader as necessary conditions for becoming prime minister (e.g., Blondel, 1980; Müller & Philipp, 1991; Rose, 2001; Helms, 2020). Although this statement generally reflects the empirical reality, prime ministers' previous political experience varies considerably over time and across the European regions. There are seven main patterns of 'insider experiences' in national political institutions. Prime ministers may have held all three major positions subsequently or at the same time (i.e., member of parliament, cabinet member, and party head). Alternatively, they may have experiences in only two positions (i.e., as member of parliament and head of party; as cabinet member and party head; or as cabinet minister and member of parliament). Finally, prime ministers may have held only one position (i.e., as party head or as member of parliament or as cabinet minister).

As Table 4.1 shows, nearly one-third of all prime ministers (29 percent) gained political experiences in all three major positions while 45 percent held two positions during their preceding career; among them, the combination of a parliamentary seat and a post as cabinet minister (25 percent) and the combination of a seat in parliament with the party leadership (18 percent) are the most common. Thus, the vast majority of prime ministers

Table 4.1 Insider and outsider experience of prime ministers

	N	%	Cumulative %
'Insider' experience			
Party head & member of parliament & cabinet minister	101	29	28.86
Party head & member of parliament	64	18	47.14
Party head & cabinet minister	7	2	49.14
Cabinet minister & member of parliament	87	25	74.0
Party head	7	2	76.0
Member of parliament	23	6	82.57
Cabinet minister	34	10	92.29
'Outsider' experience	27	8	100
Total	*350*	*100*	

(74 percent) held two or three political positions on national level while a minority (18 percent) held only one post prior to entering office. While 92 percent of all prime ministers in the past seven decades held 'insider experiences' in at least one of the three positions, there are only 8 percent of the prime ministers who show 'outsider experience': that is, they entered office with no direct experience in one of the three major national political positions. Several of these political outsiders were prime ministers of short-lived, caretaker cabinets. Most recently, for instance, two prominent judges followed this path. In 2015, after Alexis Tsipras requested the formation of an interim government to lead Greece to the next general election, the President of the Greek Court of Cassation, Vassiliki Thanou-Christophilou, was appointed as head of a caretaker cabinet. Similarly, the president of the Austrian constitutional court, Brigitte Bierlein, was appointed chancellor in June 2019, following the defeat of the first Kurz cabinet in a parliamentary vote of no-confidence.

In a second step, we examine the continuities and changes of prime ministers' political experiences on national level over the past seven decades. Thereby, we look at the aggregated shares of prime ministers' experiences as member of parliament, member of cabinet, and head of the party for each decade (Fig. 4.1). Overall, we find more continuities than changes among the political experiences of prime ministers over the past 70 years. Political experiences as former member of parliament and as former head of the party tend to be rather stable over the decades. The average share of prime ministers with parliamentary experiences ranges between 70 and 90 percent in all seven decades. Similarly, political experiences as head of the party score on average between 40 and 60 percent

4 CHANGING CAREER EXPERIENCES: LESS POLITICAL, MORE TECHNICAL 107

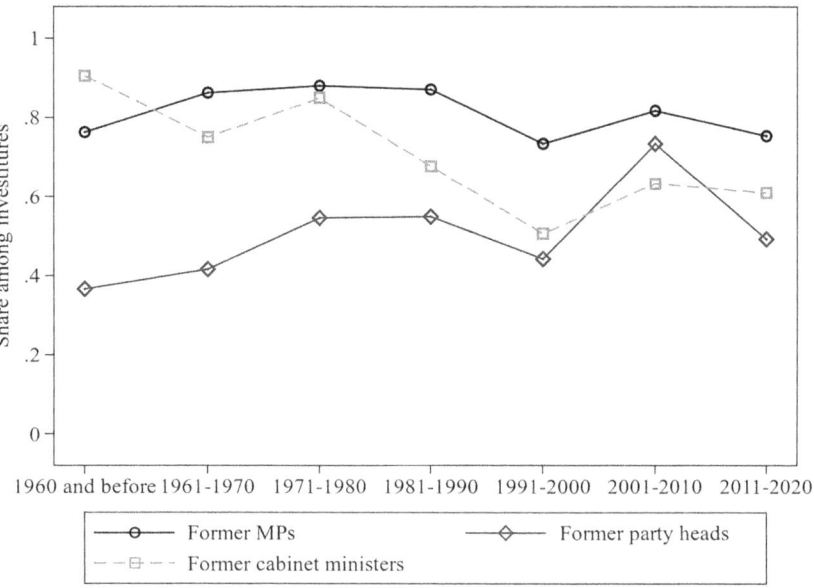

Fig. 4.1 Political experiences of prime ministers by decades (aggregated share, in percent)

over the past 70 years. Thus, the 'party-cum-parliamentary career' (Blondel, 1985, p. 55) was the essential channel in the prime ministers' pathway to power for many years. These results accord with our expectations. Prime ministers generally navigate through party careers before being elevated to the highest office. Some change emerges, however, among prime ministers with cabinet experience: their proportion is clearly declining over time, particularly since 1981. While around 90 percent of all prime ministers held a ministerial portfolio before the 1960s, only about 60 percent of them gathered cabinet experiences over the last ten years.

The data also show two additional discontinuities in prime ministers' political experiences. First, we observe a remarkable increase in former heads of parties among the prime ministers in the period from 2001 to 2010. Second the political experiences in all three positions decreased in the period from 1991 to 2000. These turning points correspond with the introduction of the Central-East European countries into the data set.

Most prime ministers in the newly founded democracies did not have any parliamentary or ministerial experiences in the former authoritarian regime. Moreover, new political parties in these countries were only formed after 1990. This is why the proportion of prime ministers with political experiences as head of a party was rather low in the early years of the democratic transition and increased after the institutionalization of the party systems in the phase of democratic consolidation (2001–2010). Thus, the discontinuity in the period from 1991 to 2000 might be an artifact of the data, not a significant change in career experiences of prime ministers in Europe.

Do we find any variation among the political experiences of prime ministers across Europe? The changing patterns of prime ministers' 'insider experiences' in the three European regions are shown in Fig. 4.2. and support our general conjecture.

First, the results show that the proportion of prime ministers with 'insider experiences' (i.e., those with political experiences in parliament, cabinet, and/or as party head) is effectively decreasing in Europe over the past 70 years, particularly since 1991. While in the 1960s nearly all prime ministers held at least one of the three political posts, the proportion of prime ministers with insider experiences reached the lowest share between 2011 and 2020.

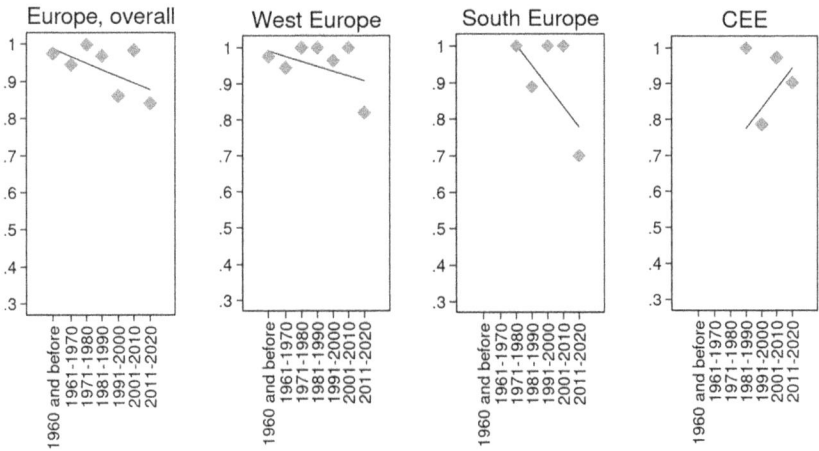

Fig. 4.2 'Insider experience' of prime ministers by region and decade (in percent)

Second, Fig. 4.2 illustrates substantial variations among prime ministers' political experiences between the three European regions. We find decreasing trends of political experiences in Western and Southern Europe, which supports our general expectations. Yet, interestingly enough this trend is fairly moderate in West European countries and more pronounced in Southern Europe. Contrary to our initial assumption the rate of West European prime ministers with insider political experiences remained fairly stable until 2010, although the decline of party government already started in the 1980s. However, in accordance with our expectations, the trends for Western and Southern Europe show a decrease of insider experiences among prime ministers over the past ten years. For Southern Europe, this finding reflects the appointment of three non-partisan prime ministers in Greece who had to manage periods of financial crises and parliamentary gridlock (Papademos in 2011, Pikrammenos in 2012, and Thanou-Christophilou in 2015). The decrease of insider experience among West European prime ministers is to a certain extent due to similar developments in Italy, which is included in our sample as a country of the 'old' Europe due to its early democratization. In 2011, the non-partisan Prime Minister Monti was appointed to deal with the crisis of sovereign debt, while the non-partisan Prime Minister Giuseppe Conte was selected in 2018 as 'guarantor' of a heterogeneous government coalition. Thus, the rate of 'outsiders' among prime ministers is particularly high in the four South European 'old' and 'new' democracies.[3]

Unlike Western and Southern Europe, the proportion of prime ministers with 'insider experience' increased in Central-Eastern Europe from 1991 to 2020. As suggested before, this observation can be interpreted in light of the democratic transition and the subsequent consolidation which took place in the 1990s, together with the take-over of a new party elite. Most prime ministers of the first and second cohort after the transition could not look back at any political experiences in political parties, parliaments, and governments of democratic regimes, which is why the share of insider experiences is rather low. The exceptionally high percentage of political insiders among the prime ministers in Central-Eastern Europe in the first period after the transition is misleading because the aggregated share for that decade is only based on the political experience of two prime ministers (József Antall in Hungary and Ivars Godmanis in Latvia) who entered office in 1990. However, their political experiences in democratic institutions were rather limited: Antall had been party leader for five months and, like Godmanis, member of parliament for two months. Thus, if we ignore the political experiences of these two prime ministers for obvious reasons, we find an increasing trend of insider experience among the prime ministers in Central-Eastern Europe.

In a third step, we look at the internal changes within the three 'insider' posts in more detail. Table 4.2 provides longitudinal information about the percentage of prime ministers who gained political experiences in the three positions. Two major empirical findings are worth highlighting: on the one hand, the percentage of prime ministers with parliamentary experiences scores 86 percent in Western and only 68 percent in Central-Eastern Europe. The difference is even higher in cabinet experiences (77 percent in Western and 53 percent in Central-Eastern Europe). The parliamentary and cabinet experiences of prime ministers from the three

Table 4.2 Experience of prime ministers by political post, region, and decade (in percent)

	Member of parliament	*Cabinet member*	*Party head*	*N*
Western Europe				
1960 and before	76	90	36	42
1961–1970	86	75	42	36
1971–1980	92	85	58	26
1981–1990	90	75	55	20
1991–2000	93	66	62	29
2001–2010	89	74	74	19
2011–2020	82	64	54	28
Regional average	*86*	*77*	*52*	*200*
PDI (2020–1960)	+6	−36	+18	
Southern Europe				
1980 and before	71	86	43	7
1981–1990	78	67	56	9
1991–2000	100	33	67	3
2001–2010	100	50	100	6
2011–2020	70	40	70	10
Regional average	*80*	*57*	*66*	*35*
PDI (2020–1976)	−1	−46	+27	
Central-Eastern Europe				
2000 and before	61	41	33	49
2001–2010	74	60	69	35
2011–2020	71	65	39	31
Regional average	*68*	*53*	*45*	*115*
PDI (2020–1990)	+10	+24	+6	

Note: PDI = Percent difference index

South European countries range between these two regions. Relative to their counterparts in both other regions, prime ministers in Southern Europe show a higher rate of political experience as former head of a party (66 percent versus 52 percent in Western and 45 percent in Central-Eastern Europe).

On the other hand, we find major changes of prime ministers' political experiences in the three political posts over time and across the three regions. These changes are measured by a percent different index (PDI), which subtracts the values of the single political experience (member of parliament, cabinet member, party head) in the first period (i.e., 1960 and before in Western Europe; 1980 and before in Southern Europe, and 2000 and before in Central-Eastern Europe) from the values of the last period (2011–2020). The results of the PDI show that the proportion of prime ministers with cabinet experiences has substantially decreased in Western and Southern Europe. In the latter region, prime ministers' parliamentary experiences remained rather stable, while the political experiences as head of the party increased in both regions over time. By contrast, the proportion of prime ministers' political experiences in all three posts expanded in Central-Eastern Europe, which explains the positive linear fit illustrated in Fig. 4.2 for this region. It is also evident that the largest increase among the percentages of prime ministers with cabinet experiences took place in Central-Eastern Europe, whereas the political skills of their counterparts in Western and Southern Europe are based predominantly on their legislative and partisan experiences.

While previous position holding in parliament, in cabinet, and as head of the party has an effect on the political experience of prime ministers, much also depends on the time they spend in these three positions. In fact, the duration of prime ministers in these three positions stands as an even more convincing proxy of their political experience. The longer the prime ministers stay in these offices, the more opportunities they find to 'learn the job' and to gain more experience. In the following analyses, we therefore measure the time a prime minister spent in one of the three major political offices by the duration in years. Thereby, we count a duration of more than 15 days in a position as one month, while a total duration of less than 15 days is classified as 'no political experience'.

The following three figures provide detailed information about the tenure of prime ministers in all three political positions. The analysis first examines the duration of prime ministers in national parliaments (i.e., in the lower chamber) (Fig. 4.3). As stated above, a position in the national legislature is the most common national political experience that prime ministers acquire prior to their investiture. Overall, the data underline our general expectation: the duration of prime ministers in national parliaments across Europe has declined slightly over the past decades. The median tenure moved from more than ten years in the 1960s to about five years in the last decade. There are, however, major differences of prime ministers' parliamentary duration across the three regions. In Western Europe, for instance, we observe rather stable values, with a median tenure greater than five years in all seven decades and almost 15 years in the period from 2001 to 2010. In the other two regions, the prime ministers' duration in parliament was—for reason mentioned above—rather low during the first decade after the transition to democracy. In Southern Europe, for instance, it was not until 1991 that prime ministers stayed in parliament for more than ten years. The parliamentary duration of prime

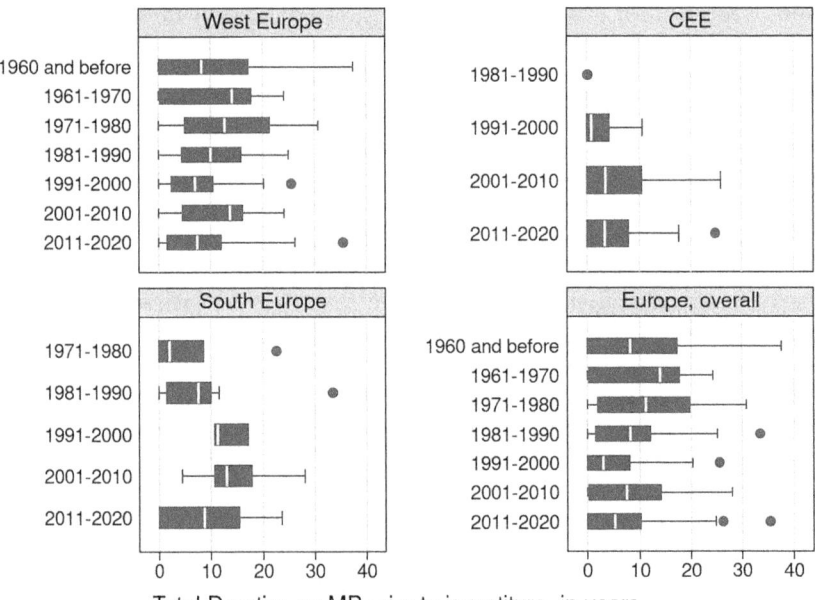

Fig. 4.3 Duration of prime ministers' parliamentary experience by region and decade

ministers in this region is on average 9.8 years over the past three decades. Their counterparts' parliamentary duration in Central-Eastern Europe is even lower, with an average of four years and a median value of 3.5 years.

The first two prime ministers with the longest duration in parliament were both appointed in the 1940s. The first is Winston Churchill[4] from the United Kingdom, who became head of government in 1940 after serving in the British House of Commons for about 38 years (with an interruption between 1922 and 1924). The second is Camille Huysmans, who became member of the Belgium parliament in 1910 and continuously remained member of the lower house for 36 years before his appointment as prime minister in 1946. Enda Kenny from Ireland held the third longest duration in parliament prior to becoming prime minister. He was only 24 years old when entering the Irish lower house in 1975, where he stayed, without interruptions, until his investiture as *Taoiseach* in 2011 (almost 36 years later). Kenny held the prime ministerial office from 2011 to 2017 and then returned to the national parliament. In contrast, ten prime ministers stayed in parliament for just one month before being appointed for the first time (Figl from Austria; Dimitrov from Bulgaria; Parts from Estonia; Couve de Murville and Messmer from France; Berlusconi and Prodi from Italy; Skvernelis from Lithuania; Buzek from Poland; Löfven from Sweden).

In sum, the overall parliamentary duration of prime ministers in all three regions is below ten years in the period from 2011 to 2020 and thereby lower than in the previous time period. Furthermore, the consolidation of the party and the democratic system in Southern and Central-Eastern Europe in the 1980s and 1990s is followed by an increase of prime ministers' parliamentary duration in both regions between 2001 and 2010.

The duration of ministerial experiences among European prime ministers provides similar declining trends (Fig. 4.4). Although fluctuations across the three regions are evident, the median ministerial duration decreased substantially from the first decade until the most recent one (2011–2020). In particular, this is true for Western Europe. In the first three decades after the Second World War, the ministerial median duration lasted around three to four years. Since the 1980s, the median duration dropped down to around two years. In contrast, the median duration of prime ministers' ministerial experience in Southern and Central-Eastern Europe was never above two years. Thus, compared to these two regions, ministerial experience was fairly high among prime ministers in Western Europe.

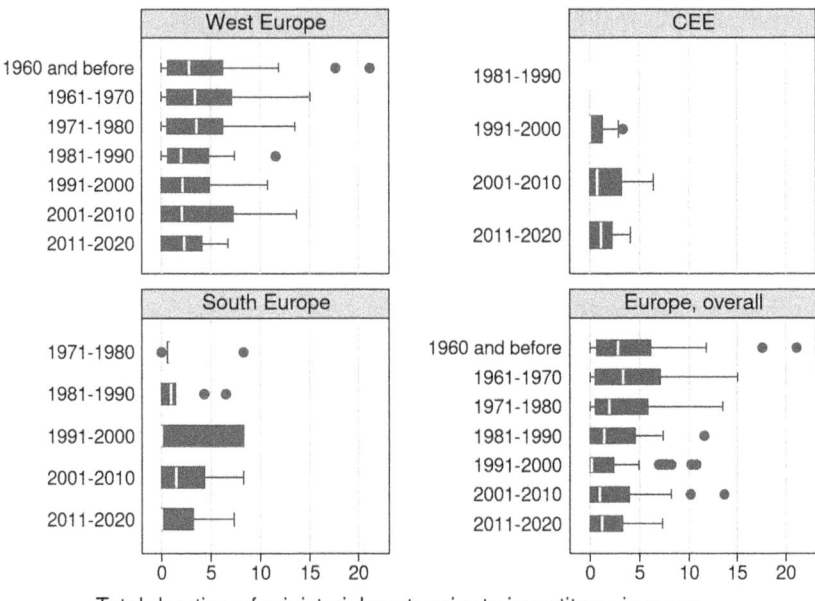

Fig. 4.4 Duration of prime ministers' ministerial experience by region and decade

Those prime ministers with the longest political experience as former cabinet minister are all located in Western Europe and entered office between 1940 and 1970. Seán Lemass has the highest record of ministerial tenure: before being Irish *Taoiseach* from 1959 to 1966, he served for about 21 years as minister, both before and after the Second World War. Winston Churchill in the United Kingdom became prime minister for the first time in 1940, after 18 years of ministerial service, starting in 1908. With a ministerial career of about 15 years, the Italian Prime Minister Emilio Colombo (1970–1972) ranks third. In contrast, Andris Šķēle and Matti Vanhanen share the record for the shortest time in office with only two months. However, their career trajectories differ substantially. Vanhanen became Finnish prime minister in 2003 after a long career in politics and serving as minister of defense in the short-lived Anneli Jäätteenmäki's cabinet, which lasted from April to June 2003. By contrast, when Andris Šķēle was chosen as Latvian chief executive in 1995, he was a business magnate who had only briefly served as interim minister of agriculture in 1993.

4 CHANGING CAREER EXPERIENCES: LESS POLITICAL, MORE TECHNICAL

A prime ministers' duration as head of the national party is a third potentially important factor for receiving extended political experience. The data in Fig. 4.5 show that the overall duration of prime ministers as party head is fairly low, although there are some variations across the three regions. Prime ministers in Southern Europe tended to hold the national party leader's office for longer periods compared to their counterparts in Western and Central-Eastern Europe. Since 1991, half of all prime ministers in Southern Europe spent at least two years as party heads before entering the prime ministerial office (among them, in Greece: Karamanlis, Papandreou, Samaras, Tsipras, and Mitsotakis; in Portugal; Guterres and Barroso; in Spain: Aznar, Rodríguez Zapatero, Rajoy, and Sanchez in Spain). In contrast, nine prime ministers held no experience as party leaders at all: those were Rallis, Tzannetakis, Grivas, and Zolotas in Greece; Nobre da Costa, Mota Pinto, and Pintasilgo in Portugal; and Suárez and Calvo-Sotelo in Spain.

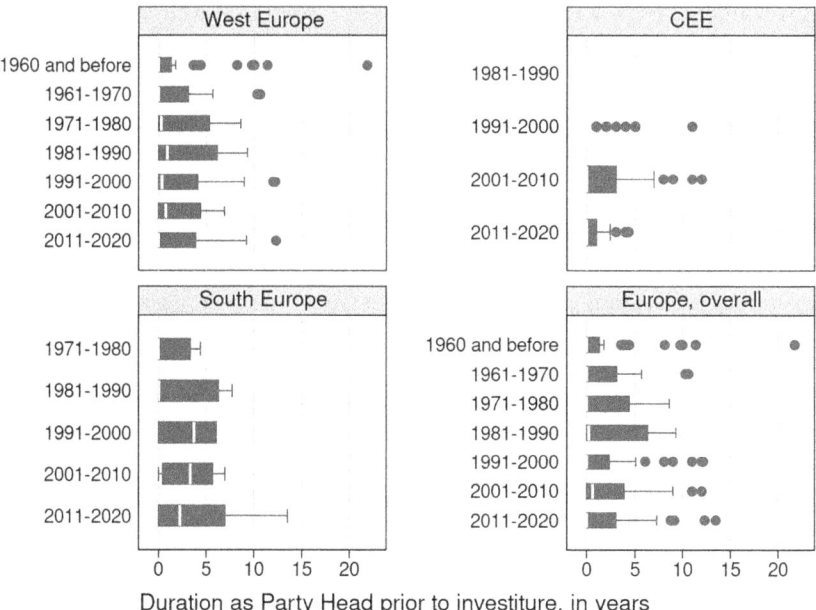

Fig. 4.5 Duration of prime ministers' experience as party leader by region and decade

In Western Europe, about half of the prime ministers held the office of party leader for considerable periods prior to their investiture, the other half spent only very little or no time as heads of the national party. The range of those who occupied the position varies from a short duration of a few weeks, for example, by Jan de Quay (1959–1963) in the Netherlands, to the exceptionally long duration of almost 22 years by Oscar Torp (1951–1955) in Norway. Torp was already elected as leader of the Norwegian Labour Party in 1923 and led the party without interruptions until 1945. The second longest duration as former party head is that of Elio Di Rupo, prime minister of Belgium (2011–2014), who spent over 12 years as leader of the Belgian French Community's Socialist Party prior to investiture.

In Central-Eastern Europe, most prime ministers have not been party leaders before entering office. Only six out of 115 gained political experience as former leader of their national party with a duration in office of more than five years. Among them, three prime ministers led their political party for more than ten years before they were first appointed as heads of government: Ivica Račan (2000–2003) in Croatia, as well as Janez Janša (2004–2008) and Borut Pahor (2008–2012), both in Slovenia.

Subnational and Supranational Political Experiences

Political experiences acquired in local and regional politics, as well as in EU politics, can also be a beneficial resource for managing national decision-making in government. In several European countries, local and regional institutions have a large political influence in national policy-making. In Germany and Austria, for instance, the federalist state organization frequently challenges prime ministers to manage subnational constraints and opportunities. Particularly in times of national political crises, it is essential for prime ministers to know and understand the working mode of local and regional councils. This became particularly evident during the management of the COVID-19 pandemic crisis by prime ministers Angela Merkel in Germany and Sebastian Kurz in Austria, who had to define the most important, national containment measures while coordinating federal policy initiatives with their countries' constituent units (Hegele & Schnabel, 2021).

Several prime ministers developed their political career on the subnational level. In Germany, for instance, former Prime Ministers Kurt Georg Kiesinger (1966–1969) and Gerhard Schröder (1998–2005) were recruited directly into the prime ministerial office as former chiefs of regional governments in Baden-Württemberg and Lower Saxony, respectively. In Belgium, both Yves Leterme (2008, 2009–2011) and Elio Di Rupo (2011–2014) were regional presidents of Flanders and Wallonia, respectively, before being invested as prime ministers. Other former prime ministers were members of municipal councils, such as the long-serving Swedish Prime Minister Tage Erlander (1946–1969) and Italian Prime Minister Massimo D'Alema (1998–2000), or former mayors of large cities. Among them Konrad Adenauer, who was first prime minister of West Germany (1949–1963) and mayor of the city of Cologne (1917–1933) during the Weimar Republic; Willy Brandt, German prime minister from 1969 to 1974, who was mayor of the city of Berlin for nine years (1957–1966); and the Bulgarian prime ministers and former mayors of Sofia, Stefan Sofiyanski and Boyko Borisov.

As Fig. 4.6 shows, several European prime ministers held political posts at the subnational level. For reasons of simplicity, we consider municipal,

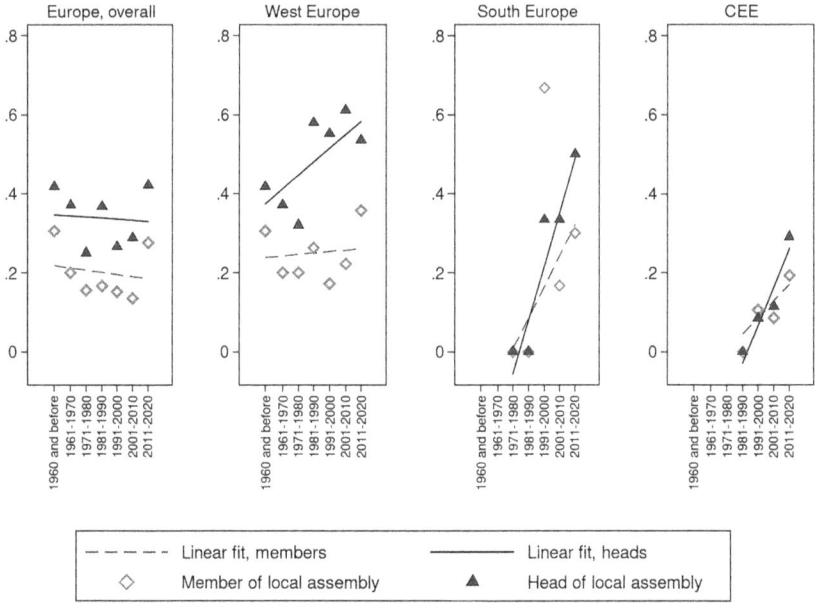

Fig. 4.6 Prime ministers' subnational political experience by region and decade. (Note: The label 'local assembly' comprises all levels of government and both legislative and executive institutions)

county, or regional office-holding as subnational experience and operationalize this notion by focusing on whether or not the candidate held one of two positions: membership in, or head of, a local assembly. The results show that the previous experiences of European prime ministers in both subnational positions have remained relatively constant over the past 70 years. This finding can be attributed to the very low rate of subnational experiences prime ministers held during the transitional period in Southern and Central-Eastern Europe. In both regions, the subnational experience of prime ministers increased over time, whereas the trend line for members of local assemblies is almost flat for Western Europe. While the subnational experience of prime ministers in Western Europe was relatively low in the early decades after the Second World War, it increased considerably since the 1980s: over the past 40 years, the majority of prime ministers in Western Europe entered office after having gained political experience as heads of a subnational institution. These findings are in line with studies that have identified the increasing importance of subnational political careers for ambitious politicians interested in achieving political prestige, higher visibility, and increased influence over policy-making at the national level (Tronconi, 2018).

In a further step, we examine the former political experiences of prime ministers at the supranational level by measuring their membership in the European Parliament (Fig. 4.7). Obviously, not all European prime ministers had the same chance to gain supranational experiences, since the countries under consideration became EU members at different points in time.[5]

As Fig. 4.7 shows, the number of European prime ministers who were previously members of the European Parliament is low, but increased slightly over the past 70 years. This is likely due to EU enlargement and the increase in the number of parliamentary seats which followed those expansion. Overall, prime ministers with experience in the European Parliament remain statistical outliers, regardless of the time they spent in parliament. Even in the most recent decade (2011–2020), only 10 prime ministers gained experience in the European Parliament, making them a minority among all 69 prime ministers who were invested and ran cabinets in Europe in this decade. Moreover, only 7 percent of all prime ministers in all seven decades were members of the European Parliament and only 17 percent of those stayed in office for a full, five-year term. Among the most recent examples of prime ministers who were former members of the European Parliament are Viorica Dăncilă (Romania), Enrico Letta (Italy),

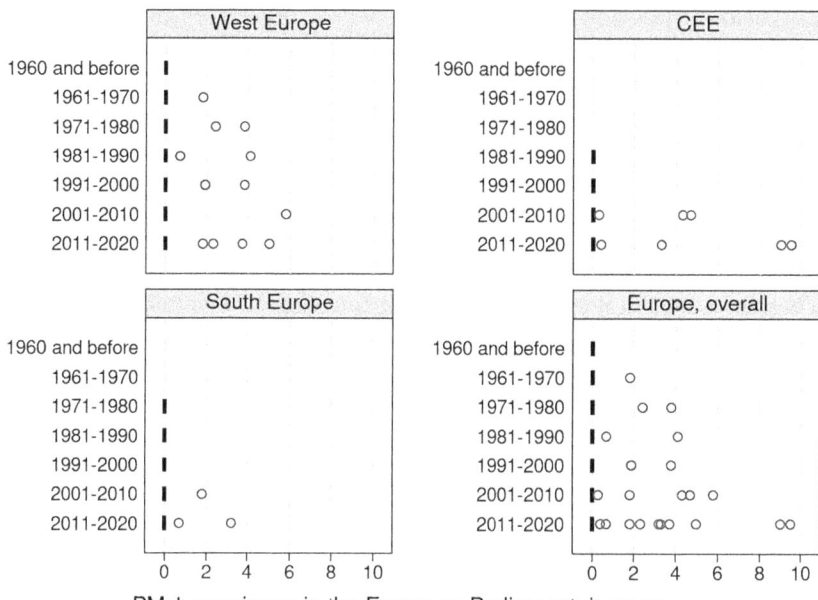

Fig. 4.7 Prime ministers' experience in the European Parliament by region and decade. (Note: Thick black bars represent the quartiles and median; hollow circles represent outliers)

Andrej Plenković (Croatia), and Helle Thorning-Schmidt (Denmark). Two German chancellors, Kurt Georg Kiesinger and Helmut Schmidt, as well as a Dutch prime minister, Barend Biesheuvel, were appointed members of the European Parliament prior to the first popular European election in 1979.

Aside from being a member of the European parliament, there is another source for gaining political experience at the European level, which is associated with wider knowledge of international governance. The growing politicization of the EU integration process and the economic policy at the European level have given higher political visibility to EU commissioners (Smith, 2003; Wille, 2012). Among prime ministers with this background are Raymond Barre, who served as commissioner for economic and financial affairs from 1966 to 1973 and then became French prime minister in 1976; Mario Monti who held ten years of experience as former EU commissioner of 'internal market' and 'competition' prior to becoming Italian prime minister in 2011; Dacian Cioloș from Romania, who held the position of EU commissioner for agriculture and rural development from 2010 to 2014, before becoming prime minister in 2015. Yet, this 'supranational turn' in the political experiences is still absent for most prime ministers in Europe.

Technical Experiences of Prime Ministers

As noted in Chap. 3, we expect that the decline of party government fosters the appointment of executive leaders with more technical skills. Therefore, technical experiences among European prime ministers should increase over time. Technical experience is defined by having expertise of the economic market, having managerial skill, and/or having knowledge about complex decision-making and bargaining processes in the 'non-political' sector. In the following analysis, we measure the technical experience of prime ministers by their occupational position outside of party politics prior to entering office. Thereby, we differentiate between five occupational groups: first, prime ministers who have been employed as heads of public and private enterprises; second, those who have been heads of national interest groups; and third to fifth, those who have formerly worked as civil servants, diplomats, and/or members of international organizations.

Obviously, prime ministers may have occupied one or more of these five positions at different points in time before entering office. This means that the occupational positions listed above are not to be understood as mutually exclusive categories. In the remaining tables and figures of this section, we will therefore first present the proportion of those prime ministers who held one or more of the five positions in the three regions over the past decades. Second, we combine this information and provide an index of prime ministers' technical experience, which aggregates the number of technical positions that each prime minister held on their path to power.

The first observation is related to prime ministers' experiences as former head of public and private enterprises, which provide managerial skills and first-hand knowledge of the market economy. As illustrated in Table 4.3, the proportion of prime ministers with these experiences varies notably between the regions and the decades. While in Western and Southern Europe about one-third of all prime ministers have been heads of a private and/or a public enterprise before entering office, the proportion among their counterparts in Central-Eastern Europe reaches almost 40 percent. Moreover, in Western Europe, the personal experiences of

Table 4.3 Prime ministers with experience in enterprises by region and decade (in percent)

Decade	Region		
	Western Europe (N = 200)	Southern Europe (N = 35)	Central-Eastern Europe (N = 115)
1960 and before	26	–	–
1961–1970	36	–	–
1971–1980	27	29	–
1981–1990	30	44	0
1991–2000	41	33	34
2001–2010	47	33	43
2011–2020	29	10	42
Mean	*33*	*29*	*38*
PDI	+3	–19	+8

Note: PDI = Percent difference index. PDI is calculated for each region with the decades' values as follows: Western Europe, 2020–1960; Southern Europe, 2020–1980; Central-Eastern Europe, 2020–2000

prime ministers as former business leaders ranged from 26 percent (in 1960 and before) to 47 percent (in 2001–2010) and back to 29 percent in the most recent decade. A similar fluctuation took place in Southern Europe (from 29 percent in the 1970s, to 44 percent in the 1980s, and down to 10 percent in the most recent decade), while in Central-Eastern Europe the proportion of prime ministers with these experiences increased since the 1990s and remained stable above 40 percent until 2020. Overall, the percent different index (PDI) shows that the rate of prime ministers with personal experiences in public and private enterprises moderately increased in Western and Central-Eastern Europe (+3 and +8 percent points respectively) while it decreased remarkably in Southern Europe (-19 percent points).

A second major source for collecting technical experiences is the post of former heads of interest groups. Prime ministers with this occupational background are former heads of trade unions, employers' organizations, and any other type of interest groups. In these positions, they have gained numerous experiences in coordinating political demands and pressuring parties or governments to obtain their preferred policy outcomes. The results about prime ministers' former experiences as chiefs of the various interest groups are presented in Table 4.4 and can be summarized as

Table 4.4 Prime ministers' technical experience in interest groups by region and decade (in percent)

Decade	Region		
	Western Europe (N = 200)	Southern Europe (N = 35)	Central-Eastern Europe (N = 115)
1960 and before	26	–	–
1961–1970	8	–	–
1971–1980	15	0	–
1981–1990	10	0	(50)
1991–2000	10	0	17
2001–2010	5	0	9
2011–2020	14	10	3
Mean	14	3	11
PDI	–12	(0)	–14

Note: PDI is calculated as in Table 4.3

follows: first, the proportion of prime ministers with experiences as former head of interest groups is smaller than the one of business leaders (see Table 4.3). Second, their percentage decreased over time in Western Europe from 26 percent (1960 and before) to 14 percent in the most recent decade (PDI = –12) and in Central-Eastern Europe from 17 percent in the 1990s to only 3 percent until 2020 (PDI = –14). The percentage of the first decade (1981–1990) was neglected since only two prime ministers were appointed during this period; among them only József Antall (50 percent) from Hungary served as head of an interest group prior to entering office. In Southern Europe, prime ministers never really brought any interest group-related technical experience to office, with the exception of Alexis Tsipras (prime minister of Greece), who gained experience as former head of the National Students Union.

Third, prime ministers gathered technical experience as senior civil servants in state bureaucracies (i.e., in national banks, ministries, and other governmental agencies) and/or as diplomats, and/or as official members of international organizations, including national delegations to international organizations. The proportion of prime ministers coming from these three career backgrounds are calculated in Table 4.5. It should be noted in this context that prime ministers may have held one or more of these three positions before entering office. Therefore, the percentages for each decade within one region do not add up to 100 percent.

In a nutshell, Table 4.5 provides three major findings. First, a former background as senior civil servant is more common among prime ministers in all three regions than their previous experience as diplomat or member of international organizations. However, the proportion of prime ministers with personal experiences as civil servants decreased over time in Western Europe and increased in the newly established democracies. Second, prime ministers' experiences as former member of an international organization declined in all three regions over the past 30 years. In Western Europe, in particular, the value decreased from 31 percent in the 1960s to 14 percent in the most recent decade. In Southern Europe, it decreased over five decades from 29 to 10 percent and in Central-Eastern Europe from 26 to 19 percent. Third, the proportion of diplomats among the three occupational groups remained comparatively low over the decades and across the regions. Only one prime minister in Southern Europe (Pintasilgo from Portugal), 5 percent of the prime ministers in Western Europe, and 6 percent of their counterparts in Central-Eastern Europe held experiences as former diplomats of their countries.

Table 4.5 Prime ministers' technical experience as senior civil servant, diplomat, and member of international organizations by region and decade (in percent)

Decade	Region								
	Western Europe (N = 200)			Southern Europe (N = 35)			Central-Eastern Europe (N = 115)		
	Sen. civil servant.	Diplomat	Intern org.	Sen. civil servant.	Diplomat	Intern org.	Sen. civil servant	Diplomat	Intern. org.
1960 and before	35	5	17						
1961–1970	39	14	31						
1971–1980	27	0	31	14	17	29			
1981–1990	10	0	21	50	0	13	0	0	0
1991–2000	34	3	28	0	0	33	32	6	26
2001–2010	33	5	26	0	0	17	43	3	20
2011–2020	26	4	14	22	0	10	35	10	19
Mean	31	5	24	22	3	18	36	6	22
PDI	−9	−1	−3	+8	(0)	−19	+3	+4	−7

Note: PDI is calculated as in Table 4.3. Percentages in the rows of each region should not be added up because of multiple position holding

How Prime Ministers' Career Experience Has Changed

According to our theoretical framework (see Chap. 3), political experience among prime ministers should decrease while technical experience should increase. Moreover, in relating the relative strength of both types of experiences, we expect political experience to be more dominant among prime ministers than technical experience. In order to prove the validity of these expectations, we first introduce an index for each of the two career experiences, including all European prime ministers over the past 70 years. Second, we identify and compare the changes in these two indexes over seven decades. Third, we suggest a typology of prime ministers' career experiences based on these empirical findings.

Measuring the relative strength of political experiences in an index is fairly easy compared to constructing an index of technical experience. Our *political career index* simply consists of a standardized measure covering the national political experience of prime ministers by aggregating the duration values for each of the three major political positions (member of parliament, cabinet member, and head of the national party) and dividing them by their standard deviation (see Figs. 4.3, 4.4, and 4.5 for the descriptive data on these three positions). Our *technical career index*, in turn, comprises an aggregated ordinal measure of the five technical experiences that prime ministers gained prior to entering office (i.e., experiences in private and/or public enterprise; head of interest group; senior civil servant; diplomat; member of international organization). This ordinal scale is a good proxy of the overall 'stockpile' of technical experiences that a prime minister collected in different sectors outside of politics. We count each type of experience once, thus, each prime minister can score a maximum of 'five' technical experiences (highest value). A prime minister with no technical experience scores zero. We confer the same weight to each variable on the assumption that each position is a significant source of technical experience in itself. The use of this additive index to calculate technical experience is due to lack of data about the duration of prime ministers in state administrations, interest groups, and international organizations. Unlike the transparency in the duration of the previous political posts that prime ministers held, publicly available information about the duration of prime ministers in leading positions outside of politics is incomplete, scattered, and often hard to identify.

Although we do not expect that any prime minister will hold all five technical experiences in their career, we do include the highest theoretical value in our ordinal measure of the technical index for two reasons: first, the theoretical maximum score of five allows us to avoid the creation of a 'ceiling effect', with many prime ministers reaching the highest technical experience score of the ordinal measure. Second, the variety of different technical categories summarized in our ordinal measure avoids a 'floor effect', with many prime ministers scoring in the lowest possible category. Thus, our measure provides a variation, through which we can differentiate the technical experiences of prime ministers appropriately.

The ordinal measure of prime ministers' technical experiences in Table 4.6 shows that two-thirds of all prime ministers held at least some technical experiences before entering office. Sixty percent obtained a low (1) to medium-low (2) level of technical skill, while less than 7 percent of all prime ministers obtained a medium-high (3) to high (4) level. The only prime minister who held four technical positions before his investiture is Siim Kallas, who entered the prime ministerial office in Estonia in 2002. Among others, he was chairman of Central Union of the Estonian Trade Unions, head of the Umbrella Organization of the Estonian Savings Banks during the Soviet period, chairman of the Committee of Ministers of the Council of Europe, as well as senior civil servant in the finance sector of the state.

How do these technical experiences of prime ministers relate to their political experience? Figure 4.8 summarizes the changes in both types of career experiences over time. The data shows that the bulk of prime ministers have gained only little technical experiences in all seven decades

Table 4.6 Ordinal measure of technical experience and prime ministers' distribution

Technical experience	N	Percent	Cum. %
0, No	115	32.86	32.86
1, Low	135	38.57	71.43
2, Medium-low	76	21.71	93.14
3, Medium-high	23	6.57	99.71
4, High	1	0.29	100
5, Highest	0	0.0	–
Total	350	100	

Note: Cum. % is the cumulative percentage

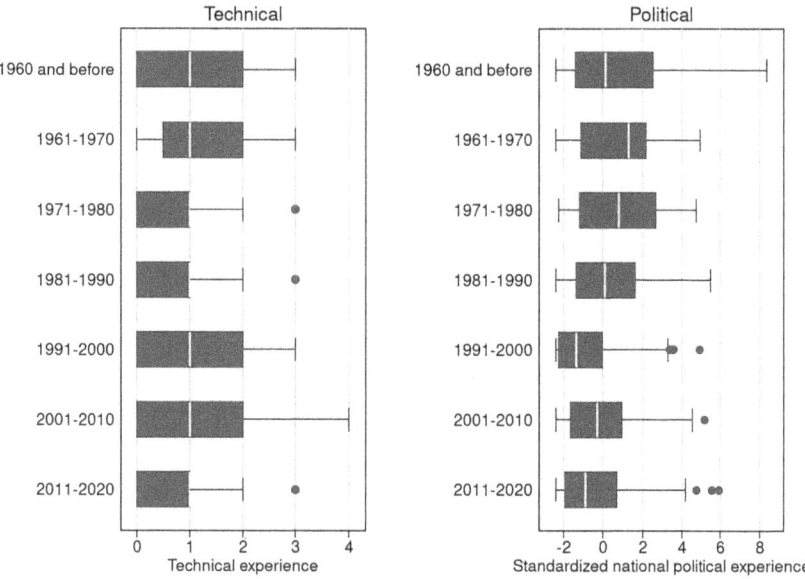

Fig. 4.8 Levels of prime ministers' technical and political experience by decade

(ranging between zero and two on the technical dimension) and that the level of technical experience remains stable over time. In contrast, the standardized measure of prime ministers' national political experience provides a clearer picture: the political experiences of prime ministers were higher in the pre-1990 period when compared to the last three decades, which are considered as the time period when European party governments faced a considerable declining.

Did both career experiences of prime ministers change over time and across the three regions? Figure 4.9 pools all the information. It first shows that prime ministers' technical experience displays an undulatory trend in Western Europe over the past 70 years, while it remained rather stable in Central-Eastern Europe since the 1990s. In contrast, in Southern Europe, technical experience declined over time. This finding indicates that the observed higher proportion of political outsiders in the most recent decade (see Fig. 4.2) does not correspond to an increase of technical experiences. Moreover, the technical background of prime ministers in Western and Southern Europe has converged on a fairly low level over the past ten

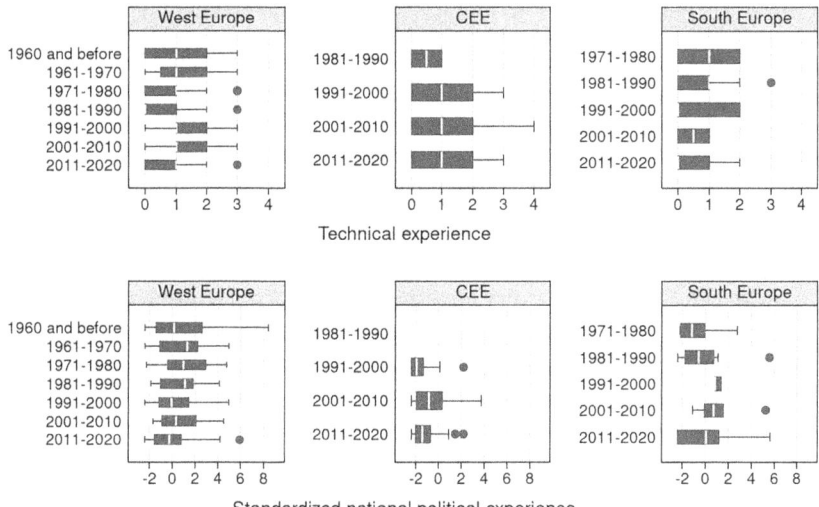

Fig. 4.9 Levels of prime ministers' technical and political experience by decade and region

years, while prime ministers in Central-Eastern European countries of the same period have—on average—gained more technical experiences. Second, Fig. 4.9 confirms a decline of political experiences among prime ministers in Western Europe over the past 70 years. Thus, our major expectation about trends of political experience is confirmed for this region and—to a certain extent—also for Southern and Central-Eastern Europe. In Southern Europe, in particular, political experience declined in the last 20 years after an initial period of increase. However, our expected increase in the technical experiences of prime ministers did not materialize for any of the three regions.

So far, we have constructed two indexes for measuring career experiences of prime ministers. We have also identified the levels of prime ministers' political and technical experience based on these indexes across the three European regions over time. Finally, we suggest to combine both indexes of prime ministers' career experiences and offer a classification of prime ministerial career types that are based on the level of their political and technical experiences. This classification consists of four types: *political veterans, technopols, technicians,* and *novices* (see Table 4.7).

Table 4.7 Prime ministers' technical and political experiences: a typology

		Technical experience	
		Low	High
Political experience	High	Political veteran	Technopol
	Low	Novice	Technician

A *political veteran* is defined as a prime minister who gathered extensive political experience as former member of parliament, government, and party head ('insider experience'). This career type held no, or only very limited, technical experience outside of politics and is the 'proto-type' of the traditional ('old school') prime minister in Europe.

The *technopol* type differs from political veterans in one major respect: this type of prime minister accumulated political experience in several major political posts, but also acquired extensive technical skills in non-political sectors before entering office. A *technopol*'s career path is therefore defined as a mix between political and the technical experiences (Joignant, 2011). For example, in Portugal Pedro Passos Coelho was appointed prime minister in 2011. At the time of his investiture, he had already experienced a long political career in the Social Democratic Party (first as member and later as national party head) and in the national parliament (as well as in two local assemblies as councilor). Yet, he also worked for several companies and for the NATO Parliamentary Assembly from 1991 to 1995.

The type of *technician*, in turn, is the opposite of the political veteran: this type consists of prime ministers whose career mostly focused on the acquisition of technical knowledge at the expense of political experiences. One example is the Portuguese Prime Minister Maria de Lourdes Pintasilgo (1979–1980), who enjoyed a successful career in a private chemical corporation (*Companhia União Fabril*) before acting as liaison for the Catholic Church in the World Council of Churches (WCC) and Portuguese Ambassador to UNESCO (United Nations Educational, Scientific and Cultural Organization). These activities provided her with the necessary technical background to become, first, minister for social affairs and, finally, prime minister. Similarly, former university professor and eventual Italian Prime Minister Romano Prodi (1996–1998, 2006–2008) was elected in 1963 to be a local councilor in the city of Reggio Emilia. In the 1970s, he managed two private companies (*Maserati* and *Callegari e*

Ghigi) and, from 1982 to 1989, he was the president of the Institute for the Industrial Reconstruction (IRI), a public authority overseeing industrial policy. Before being appointed prime minister for the first time, he had served as minister for industry, commerce, and craftsmanship for about four months.

Finally, the *novice* type of prime minister holds neither political nor technical experience and—in most cases—consist of pure political outsiders who, unlike technicians, have not developed a detailed expertise in any specify policy area. Giuseppe Conte from Italy is a case in point. Before entering office, he had worked as a lawyer and university professor of Private Law. In 2013, he was elected by the Chamber of Deputies as member of the Council of the Presidency of the Administrative Justice, which is the authority for the self-government of the administrative magistrature in Italy. During his academic career, he did not show any political activity, excluding his public support for the Five Star Movement party, which proposed him as prime minister in 2018.

In the final part of our analysis on the career experiences of prime ministers, we try to answer two questions: first, to what extent do these four types of prime ministers' career experiences exist in European liberal democracies? Second, do we find any changes among the relative strength of these four types over time? Figure 4.10 provides answers to both questions. In each of the seven decade boxes, we find *political veterans* to be located in the upper-left of the box, having high political and low technical experiences. In the upper-right corner of each box, we find the *technopols*, who combine relatively high levels of both types of experiences. The *technicians*, whose career experience is mostly technical and hardly never political, are placed in the lower-right-corner, while the *novice* with low political and technical experiences are located in the lower-left corner of each box.

In sum, the findings in Fig. 4.10 prove our general expectation: from the 1990s onward, the number of *political veterans* and of the *technopols* among European prime ministers decreased (the latter particularly in the last decade), while the number of *technicians* and the ones of the *novice* type increased. However, the *technopols* and the *novice* types are in the minority compared to the type of *political veterans* or *technicians*. More precisely, we find an increasing number of prime ministers who move from the type of '*technopol*' to the type of '*technician*' because the proportion of prime ministers with high political experiences decreased over time while the one with technical experiences remained stable. Moreover, as shown in

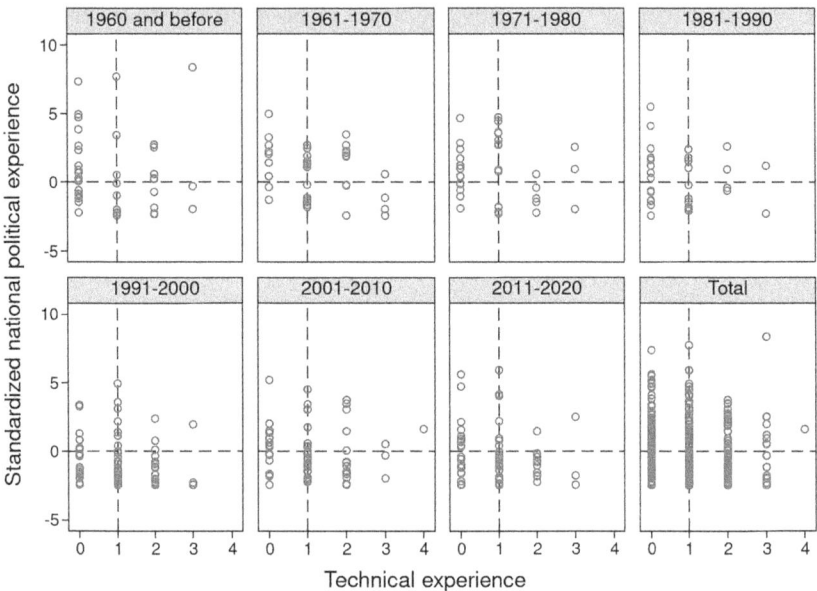

Fig. 4.10 Relationship between prime ministers' technical and political experience by decade. (Note: Dashed horizontal and vertical lines represent the average value of political and technical experiences)

Fig. 4.10, between 1960 and 1990, the number of *technopol* and *technician* prime ministers was basically on the same level, whereas from 1991 to 2020 the *technicians* became more numerous than the *technopols*.

Conclusion

Governmental policy-making in parliamentary and semi-presidential systems depends to a great deal on the experiences that prime ministers made on their way into the office. Scholars have long suggested that various political experiences within the parliament, the government, and the party make it easier for prime ministers to govern. This chapter therefore examined the level of political and technical experiences that European prime ministers acquired prior to entering office.

Although our findings prove the conventional wisdom that prime ministers are usually 'political insiders' and only rarely 'outsiders', prime ministers are not always 'pure' insiders. Instead, many of them achieved substantial political and technical experiences prior to entering office. Despite some regional variations, our data confirm that the ratio of European prime ministers who held national, political positions prior to entering office has indeed declined over the past decades. The same holds true for their duration in these political offices. There is, however, some variation: while the duration in parliament, and in particular in cabinet, decreased over time, the experiences as party leader remained rather stable. Our data also show that the proportion of prime ministers with political experiences at the subnational level slightly increased in all three European regions and may become a more common career pattern for prime ministers in the forthcoming decades. The results on technical experiences of prime ministers reveal only little change over the past decades. Moreover, prime ministers with high technical experiences are still in the minority compared to those with political experiences.

Since the level of technical experiences among prime ministers remained rather constant over time while political experiences decreased, we find a proportional increase of technical experiences in relation to political experiences in the careers of prime ministers. These results confirm our general theoretical argument that the career experiences of European prime ministers became relatively 'less political' and 'more technical'.

Notes

1. Exceptions are Godmanis (Latvia), Oresharski (Bulgaria), Prodi (Italy), Tarand and Vähi (Estonia), and Vagnorius (Lithuania), who entered office without party affiliation, after being independent members of parliament. Overall, at the time of investiture, 24 prime ministers with no party affiliation had some experiences in cabinet and/or parliament.
2. We count apical positions in general, including heads, CEOs, and executive board members.
3. This finding is in line with the research on technocratic ministers in the Mediterranean countries by Costa Pinto et al. (2018), according to whom non-partisan appointments of cabinet members have recently increased in South European executives.
4. See the Appendix for the criteria of his inclusion in the universe of analyzed prime ministers.
5. Five West European countries joined the European Union or one of its former forms since the very beginning (Belgium, France, Italy, the Netherlands, and West Germany in 1951); three (Denmark, Ireland, and the United Kingdom) in 1973; three (Austria, Finland, Sweden) in 1995, Greece in 1981, while Portugal and Spain in 1986. Eight Central-East European

countries (Czech Republic, Estonia, Hungary, Latvia, Lithuania, Poland, Slovakia, and Slovenia) became member states in 2004; two (Bulgaria and Romania) in 2007; and one (Croatia) in 2013. All prime ministers from Norway are excluded because the country has never been an EU member.

REFERENCES

Bakema, W. E., & Secker, I. P. (1988). Ministerial Expertise and the Dutch Case. *European Journal of Political Research, 16*(2), 153–170.

Baturo, A., & Elkink, J. A. (2021). What Countries Select More Experienced Leaders? The PolEx Measure of Political Experience. *British Journal of Political Science*.https://doi.org/10.1017/S0007123421000107

Blondel, J. (1980). *World Leaders: Heads of Government in the Postwar Period.* SAGE.

Blondel, J. (1985). *Government Ministers in the Contemporary World.* SAGE.

Blondel, J. (1991). Introduction. In J. Blondel & J.-L. Thiébault (Eds.), *The Profession of Government Minister in Western Europe* (pp. 1–4). Macmillan.

Bright, J., Döring, H., & Little, C. (2015). Ministerial Importance and Survival in Government: Tough at the Top? *West European Politics, 38*(3), 441–464.

Costa Pinto, A., Cotta, M., & Tavares de Almeida, P. (Eds.). (2018). *Technocratic Ministers and Political Leadership in European Democracies.* Palgrave Macmillan.

Cotta, M. (2018). Technocratic Government Versus Party Government? Non-Partisan Ministers and the Changing Parameters of Political Leadership in European Democracies. In A. Costa Pinto, M. Cotta, & P. Tavares de Almeida (Eds.), *Technocratic Ministers and Political Leadership in European Democracies* (pp. 267–288). Palgrave Macmillan.

De Winter, L. (1991). Parliamentary and Party Pathways to the Cabinet. In J. Blondel & J.-L. Thiébault (Eds.), *The Profession of Government Minister in Western Europe* (pp. 44–69). Macmillan.

De Winter, L. (1993). The Links between Cabinet and Parties and Cabinet Decision-Making. In J. Blondel & F. Müller-Rommel (Eds.), *Governing Together. The Extent and Limits of Joint Decision-Making in Western European Cabinets* (pp. 153–178). Macmillan.

Fischer, J., Dowding, K., & Dumont, P. (2012). The Duration and Durability of Cabinet Ministers. *International Political Science Review, 33*(5), 505–519.

Grotz, F., Müller-Rommel, F., Berz, J., Kroeber, C., & Kukec, M. (2021). How Political Careers affect Prime-Ministerial Performance: Evidence from Central and Eastern Europe. *Comparative Political Studies, 54*(11), 1907–1938.

Hegele, Y., & Schnabel, J. (2021). Federalism and the Management of the COVID-19 Crisis: Centralisation, Decentralisation and (Non-)Coordination. *West European Politics, 44*(5–6), 1052–1076.

Helms, L. (2020). Heir Apparent Prime Ministers in Westminster Democracies: Promise and Performance. *Government and Opposition, 55*(2), 260–283.

Joignant, A. (2011). The Politics of Technopols: Resources, Political Competence and Collective Leadership in Chile, 1990–2010. *Journal of Latin American Studies, 43*(3), 517–546.

Lavezzolo, S., Ramiro, L., & Fernández-Vázquez, P. (2021). The Will for Reason: Voter Demand for Experts in Office. *West European Politics, 44*(7), 1506–1531.

Martocchia Diodati, N., & Verzichelli, L. (2017). Changing Patterns of Ministerial Circulation: The Italian Case in a Long-Term Perspective. *West European Politics, 40*(6), 1352–1372.

Müller, W. C., & Philipp, W. (1991). Prime Ministers and other Government Heads. In J. Blondel & J.-L. Thiébault (Eds.), *The Profession of Government Minister in Western Europe* (pp. 31–43). Macmillan.

Rose, R. (2001). *The Prime Minister in a Shrinking World*. Polity Press.

Smith, A. (2003). Why European Commissioners Matter. *Journal of Common Market Studies, 41*(1), 137–155.

Thiébault, J.-L. (1991). The Social Background of Western European Ministers. In J. Blondel & J.-L. Thiébault (Eds.), *The Profession of Government Minister in Western Europe* (pp. 31–43). Macmillan.

Tronconi, F. (2018). Sub-National Elites. In H. Best & J. Higley (Eds.), *The Palgrave Handbook of Political Elites* (pp. 611–624). Palgrave Macmillan.

Verzichelli, L. (1998). The Parliamentary Elite in Transition. *European Journal of Political Research, 34*(1), 121–150.

Wille, A. (2012). The Politicization of the EU Commission: Democratic Control and the Dynamics of Executive Selection. *International Review of Administrative Sciences, 78*(3), 383–402.

CHAPTER 5

Changing Career Profiles: From Party-Agents to Party-Principals

In the previous chapter, we described the political and technical dimensions of career experiences among prime ministers and how these have changed over time and across European regions. We found a decrease in the level of political experience and—at the same time—a steady level of technical experience. Although gaining technical experience is becoming relatively more important for prime ministers, political experience remains *the* crucial experience brought into office by prime ministers. Holding one or more positions in the party or in government still characterizes the career profile of most prime ministers in Europe.

In this chapter, we argue that the increasing political influence of prime ministers in Europe—as described in Chap. 1—has produced a relative shift in the prime ministers' profile from *party-agent* toward *party-principal*. In the 'golden age' of party government from the 1950s to the 1970s, political parties usually selected loyal agents for the prime ministerial office, that is, those party members who had proven their commitment to the party during their parliamentary or cabinet service. Yet, under the pressure of the increasing presidentialization of politics (Poguntke and Webb 2005a) in the 1980s and 1990s, intra-party preferences in the selection of prime ministers have changed, making leadership skills more valuable than party loyalty when choosing prime ministers (see Chap. 3).

In the following sections, we first define and measure the dimensions of the party-agent and party-principal career profiles using an exploratory

© The Author(s), under exclusive license to Springer Nature Switzerland AG 2022
F. Müller-Rommel et al., *Prime Ministers in Europe*, Palgrave Studies in Political Leadership,
https://doi.org/10.1007/978-3-030-90891-1_5

factor analysis. Second, we analyze longitudinal changes in Europe across regions and countries. Third, we relate these changes to the political and institutional idiosyncrasies of European countries. More precisely, we investigate the relationship between electoral volatility (as an indicator for the decline of party government) and career profiles. Moreover, we discuss the impact of institutional variables, such as parliamentary and semi-presidential systems, as well as presidential and prime ministerial powers on prime ministers' career profiles. We also examine the conditional role that party families and gender plays on the development of the two career profiles. Finally, we summarize and discuss these findings from a comparative perspective.

Dimensions of the Analysis

Similar to our definition of career experiences, we suggest that prime ministers' career profiles result from professional accomplishments. Moreover, we claim that career positions align with specific career profile types. The construction of the party-agent and the party-principal profiles is theory-driven and based on the classification of career positions that prime ministers held prior to entering office. As shown in Chaps. 2 and 4, some prime ministers held a parliamentary seat for longer periods before being appointed, but did not accumulate experience as cabinet ministers. Some prime ministers never spent time in parliament and entered office when they were relatively young, while others were appointed at a later stage in their career, for example, after having managed ministerial portfolios. About one-third of all prime ministers, however, held all three key political positions (member of parliament, cabinet member, head of the national party) before investiture. The way in which prime ministers combine different career features determines their career profile.

We trace prime ministers' career profiles back to two analytical dimensions. First, we examine the extent to which political parties delegate offices within political institutions to the prime ministers in their previous political career. Second, we investigate the scope of national and international leadership roles that prime ministers held before being invested. These two dimensions indicate the acquisition of two different types of skills sets and, most importantly, they underline different relationships between the prime ministers and their parties prior to investiture. In the following sections, we define and measure both types of career profiles.

Defining Career Profiles

In Chap. 3, we argued that, due to the erosion of stable political support and increasing electoral challenges, party organizations have become weaker over the past decades. At the same time, we observe an internationalization of politics, an increasing complexity of national policy-making, and an emphasis on individual candidates, rather than political parties, in electoral campaigns. These trends have made national executive leaders more independent from their parties and strengthened their position in government. As a result, parties rely more on publicly appealing leaders for achieving governmental and electoral success. Prime ministers, in turn, benefit from receiving more room for political maneuver during their time in office. In a nutshell, this is the core of the presidentialization thesis as suggested by Poguntke and Webb (2005a).

We accept this argument and, in developing it one step further, claim that this process forces prime ministers to develop a different set of skills if they want to be successful while in office. In other words, as gate-keepers in the selection of prime ministers, political parties look for candidates with new career profiles, who offer more leadership skills and international expertise, and deliver the expected policy performance for their party once being appointed. Put differently, as long as party government was the dominant model of government, parties selected trustworthy party-agents, responsive to party interests and capable of implementing the party agenda. However, in times of presidentialization, parties have changed their priorities by focusing on a different set of qualities, such as leadership skills, public recognition, and policy expertise. Parties' selection criteria have become more flexible, and they consider a wider range of candidates as potential heads of government. During this selection process, political parties use a candidate's career experiences as informational signals for understanding whether or not she is fit to govern.

Moreover, presidentialization has increased the likelihood that political entrepreneurs will be successful in founding their own political party to reach the office of the prime minister. These political entrepreneurs further break with the dominant selection model of trustworthy party-agents through party-elites because entrepreneurs themselves set the party agenda and define the interests of their newly founded party.

We therefore expect the party-agent profile to be more common in earlier decades, while the party-principal profile has become more prominent in recent years. It is, however, worth stressing that this expectation does not imply any conclusion about the actual influence of prime ministers on governmental policy, or their electoral success while being in office.[1] Neither should one assume that even the most accurate selection of prime ministers will rule out the perils of moral hazard (Strøm 2000, p. 270f), meaning that prime ministers will take actions which do not align with the interests of their party. However, what we expect to find is an increase in the ratio of prime ministers with a party-principal profile compared to the ratio of prime ministers with a party-agent profile over time.

Which career steps signal that a prime minister will effectively personify the goals of the party and reliably keep its interests in mind while running the government? We assume that prime ministers establish a trusting relationship with their party during the course of their career (Müller 2000, p. 327ff.), as the party can evaluate the motivations of the prime ministerial candidates and their commitment to party goals (Mansbridge 2009, p. 381ff.). This applies especially when potential prime ministers occupy political positions that place them in an 'agent' position relative to the 'principal' party. The two most important positions in that context are member of parliament and cabinet minister. When politicians hold one of these two posts, they work under the direction of their parliamentary party group leader, the party leadership in general, and often under their own party's prime minister. Moreover, as cabinet minister, a politician is endowed with executive power and can prove her commitment to the implementation of the party's agenda. We argue that the longer a politician serves in one (or both) of these two positions, the higher the likelihood that political parties know the full range of their preferences and competences, as well as their loyalty; consequently, parties are more likely to avoid the adverse selection of unsuitable prime ministers when they have a substantial track record on which to base their decisions (Strøm 2000, p. 270). Thus, party-agents are characterized by longer tenures in parliament and cabinet before entering the prime ministerial office. Since party-agents need to spend more time in these institutions to prove their credentials to the party, we also claim that—when entering office for the first time—a party-agent is on average older than a party-principal, who usually does not need to prove her party loyalty to a similar extent (see below).

Prime ministers with a party-principal profile, in turn, spent most of their career in leadership positions, determining party agenda (rather than following it) and securing others' commitment to common party goals.

Two positions are particularly suited to fulfilling these functions: national party head and opposition leader of a parliamentary party group.[2] Rather than merely executing party guidelines, politicians in these two positions are used to defining party goals and shaping party strategies. Moreover, they possess considerable public recognition among the electorate. Thus, prime ministers who enter office after acquiring experience as party heads and/or opposition leaders have a different profile than party-agents. They have acted as principals to other party members who have not had substantial opportunities to exercise political leadership within the party. Yet, to hold the position of opposition leader of a parliamentary party group means also occupying a parliamentary seat. For this reason, even party-principals could have spent a considerable portion of their career as members of parliament, similar to party-agents.

Moreover, prime ministers with a party-principal career profile might have acquired career experience at the international level to perform in office. According to the presidentialization thesis, the ability to manage summits has become a salient skill for prime ministers in recent decades. This applies particularly to EU member states, whose heads of political executives regularly meet in the European Council to discuss policies that affect their national polities. A typical party-principal might have held important positions in NATO, UN organizations, or supranational banking and financial institutions. Previously holding a position in one (or more) of these makes chief executives' profiles more independent from their party organizations, in that they have partially developed their previous career outside national party politics. For example, in 2004 Marek Belka was appointed as Polish prime minister for the Democratic Left Alliance after having worked for the World Bank in the 1990s. Another example is the Norwegian Prime Minister Erna Solberg who acted as leader of the Norwegian delegation to the NATO Parliamentary Assembly (2009–2013) prior to entering office in 2013. This type of experience may well have informed her positive inclination toward transatlantic relationships, which were acknowledged when she won the Atlantic Council's Global Citizen Award in 2018.

In sum, different career positions should cluster into two broad types of prime ministers: party-agent and party-principal. Those with a party-agent profile should have held ministerial positions in cabinet and/or a seat in national parliament. Those with a party-principal profile, in contrast, should have gained more experience as a party leader and/or as an opposition leader in a parliamentary party group and/or as a member of international organizations (see Table 5.1).

The two career profiles are ideal-types. Therefore, several prime ministers' careers will resemble a mixture of traits and features of both party-agent and party-principal profiles. It should be noted in this context that both party-agents and party-principals hold political experiences, although their individual experiences may differ.

Measuring Career Profiles

To assess whether and to what extent our theoretical conceptualization of the two career profiles is supported by empirical evidence, we run an exploratory factor analysis. As shown in Table 5.1, we expect that party-agent and party-principal profiles will be characterized by different career attributes, the various combinations of which place prime ministers into different types of relationships *vis-à-vis* their own party. Our conjecture is that prime ministers from either career profile could hold seats in parliament; however, we expect to see divergence across the other four career attributes. We gage the career attributes of (national) party heads and members of parliament by their duration in office. The position of opposition leader is measured as a binary variable, taking the value one if the prime minister held this position before entering office for the first time and zero otherwise. Moreover, the ministerial career attribute is split into two variables: total duration as minister (irrespective of any interruption) and number of ministerial portfolios held. Finally, we include a dummy variable (yes/no) to capture possible membership of an international organization, plus a calculation in years of the age of the prime minister at the first investiture.

Table 5.1 Expected relationship between individual career attributes and career profiles

Career attribute	Party-agent profile	Party-principal profile
Held leadership position in party or parliament	−	+
Held position in parliament	+	+
Held position in cabinet	+	−
Held position in international organization	0	+
Age	+	0

Note: Positive correlation (+); Negative correlation (-); No correlation (0)

Therefore, the factor analysis consists of seven parameters, including duration as member of parliament, as cabinet minister, and as party head; being leader of a parliamentary party group in opposition; number of ministerial portfolios; being member of an international organization; and age. Since our analysis includes continuous as well as dichotomous variables, we estimate correlations between continuous variables using the traditional Pearson correlation and then look for correlations for dichotomous variables using a polychoric matrix (Dolan 1994; Holgado-Tello et al. 2010).[3] Table 5.2 provides the results of our factor analysis.

As hypothesized, the empirical data confirm the existence of two main career profiles (factors) with eigenvalues above one among European prime ministers, while all of the additional factors have an eigenvalue of zero or close to zero (see Fig. A1 in the Appendix). The party-agent factor accounts for 73 percent of the variance, whereas the party-principal factor accounts for 51 percent. The higher variance of the party-agent career profile confirms the assumption that this profile represents the traditional political career of prime ministers.

The number of ministerial portfolios and, in particular, the duration as cabinet ministers are the most highly correlated attributes with the

Table 5.2 Correlation of career profile factors with career attributes (principal factor method)

Career attribute	Factor 1: Party-agent profile	Factor 2: Party-principal profile
Duration as party head, prior to investiture	-0.01	**0.55**
Opposition leader of parliamentary party group	-0.20	**0.65**
Duration MP, years	**0.50**	**0.52**
Duration ministerial posts, years	**0.81**	0.02
Number of ministerial portfolios	**0.76**	-0.12
Age	0.26	0.05
Member of international organization	0.01	**0.32**
Eigenvalue of factors	*1.60*	*1.11*
Variance	*1.59*	*1.25*
Proportion of variance	*0.73*	*0.51*

Note: Rotated factor loadings, orthogonal varimax, $N = 338$ (the N results from the list-wise deletion of 12 prime ministers with at least one missing value in the data). Based on Pearson and polychoric (for variables with less than ten categories) correlation matrices party-agent profile. Moreover, being an opposition leader of a parliamentary party group shows the strongest negative relation with this profile. Finally, prime ministers with a party-agent profile are also older than prime ministers with a party-principal profile at the time of their first investiture. These data suggest that party-agents develop longer careers, in which they prove to be trustworthy party actors, before being selected by their political parties for the prime ministership.

In contrast, both leadership experiences as party head and opposition leader in parliament clearly define the party-principal profile. While we find that party-principals may still hold some ministerial experience, they are unlikely to have held more than one ministerial portfolio before entering office. Finally, experience in an international organization characterizes only party-principals. This reveals that, relative to party-agents, party-principals not only develop different political skills at the national level but also acquire some experience outside national party politics.

Variations of Career Profiles Across Europe

After having confirmed the existence of two distinct career profiles, the results of the factor analysis are used to investigate variations among European prime ministers. In doing so, we opt for a regression method scoring based on the varimax rotated factors (Thomson 1951). This allows us to create a continuous party-agent and a continuous party-principal score for each individual prime minister in our dataset. The two factors' scores have a mean of zero and a standard deviation of about 0.8. Figure 5.1 shows the scores of each prime minister's career profile on both dimensions in the three European regions and across Europe.

Overall, the scores in Fig. 5.1 show more variation among prime ministers with a party-agent than a party-principal profile. This is in particular true for prime ministers in Western Europe. Their counterparts in Southern Europe have similar scores on the party-principal dimension, but none of them score as high on the party-agent dimension as some of their colleagues in Western Europe. Finally, the distribution of prime ministers in Central-Eastern Europe is relatively concentrated on both dimensions: in the 'new' democracies of this region, a low incidence of the party-agent profile is paired with a predominant variation on the party-principal dimension, making some prime ministers approaching the party-principal ideal-type, but no prime minister representing the ideal party-agent as found in Western Europe.

5 CHANGING CAREER PROFILES: FROM PARTY-AGENTS TO PARTY-PRINCIPALS   143

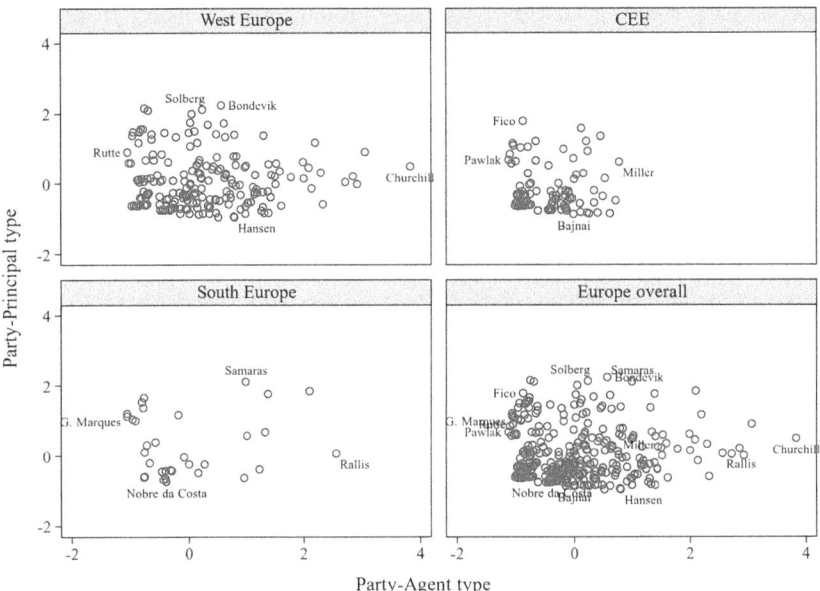

Fig. 5.1 Party-agent and party-principal factor scores of individual prime ministers across Europe. (Note: Prime ministers with the highest and lowest score for each career profile type are named for each region)

Despite these aggregated findings in the three European regions, we have identified some typical cases of prime ministers who exemplify one or the other profile as well as both profiles at the same time. One example for an ideal-type of party-agent is Winston Churchill, who was prime minister from 1940 to 1945 and from 1951 to 1955. As already mentioned in previous chapters, Churchill became head of government in the United Kingdom for the first time in 1940, when he was 65 years old. At that time, he had already experienced a long political career, consisting of 38 years of parliamentary service and 18 years as cabinet minister. In cabinet, he managed/controlled prestigious portfolios, such as finance, internal affairs, and other ministries linked to issues such as colonial administration and war. Furthermore, Churchill had never held any leadership position in his parties (the Conservative Party, but also—from 1904 to 1924—the Liberal Party), and he was only selected as head of the Conservative Party a few months after his investiture as prime minister. Another example of a typical party-agent is Georgios Rallis, prime minister of Greece from 1980 to 1981. He was first elected into the Hellenic parliament in 1950 and was appointed cabinet minister only four years later. During his career, he held positions in the ministries of economy, foreign affairs, interior, as well as several other less prestigious portfolios. When he was appointed chief executive on May 10, 1980, at the age of 61, Rallis had already accumulated 23 years of experience as member of the national parliament and eight years of ministerial experience.

In contrast, the career profiles of some other prime ministers follow the party-principal ideal-type. The Slovak Prime Minister, Robert Fico (in office from 2006 and 2010 and from 2012 to 2018), stands as a good example. Fico entered prime ministerial office for the first time at a relatively young age of 41, though he had already acquired international experience as Slovakia's legal counsel at the European Court of Human Rights for six years and as member of parliament for 14 years. Before entering office, he also acted as party leader for seven years and as opposition leader for the Direction-Social Democracy's parliamentary party group, but he never served in the cabinet until his first investiture. A second example is the Norwegian Prime Minister Erna Solberg (in office from 2013 to 2021), who was 52-year-old when she was appointed for the first time. Solberg acted nine years as national head of the Conservative Party and was opposition leader of her parliamentary group before becoming head of government. Moreover, she worked four years as cabinet minister.

Yet, not all prime ministers can be as easily classified in one of the two profiles. There are, for instance, prime ministers who do not show either a party-agent or a party-principal profile. Prime ministers like Mark Rutte from the Netherlands (2010–in office 2020) and Gordon Bajnai from Hungary (2009–2010) are cases in point. Because Rutte has led the People's Party for Freedom and Democracy since 2006 and served as opposition leader in parliament, he scores negatively on the party-agent dimension, and also low on the party-principal dimension because he had no international experience and spent only four years in national parliament. Another case is Gordon Bajnai, who was an entrepreneur with no previous parliamentary and only limited ministerial experience. He scored about zero as party-agent and negative on the party-principal dimension.

Other prime ministers show both a party-agent and a party-principal career profile. Examples are the Norwegian Prime Minister Kjell Magne Bondevik (in office from 1997 to 2000, and from 2001 to 2005), as well as his colleague Antonis Samaras from Greece (in office from 2012 to

2015). Bondevik became prime minister when he was 50, after being member of parliament for 20 years, minister for four years, and party leader for 12 years. Moreover, he was part of several Norwegian delegations to international organizations, such as the International Parliamentary Delegation and the Nordic Council. Prime Minister Samaras from Greece held a parliamentary seat for 24 years, multiple ministerial portfolios for three years, and his own party's leadership for more than 13 years, before being invested as head of government at the age of 61. Both Bondevik and Samaras occupied the position as opposition leader of their own parliamentary party group.

Overall, the findings in Fig. 5.1 confirm our general argument, which states that the party-agent career profile is more developed in 'old' West European democracies than in regions with newer democratic regimes. Three major reasons explain this observation: first, in Western Europe established mass parties have governed for most of the time over the past 70 years and have usually selected prime ministers from pools of experienced party politicians. Second, in Southern and Central-Eastern Europe the presidentialization of politics has developed faster than in Western Europe due to the initially weak institutionalization of party systems (Chiaramonte and Emanuele 2017). This led, among others, to an increasing (self-)nomination of political entrepreneurs with hardly any political experience for the prime minister's office. Third, in countries that democratized at a later stage, political parties could not rely on a stable support for their prime ministerial candidates by a clearly defined electorate with strong party identification (Mair 1996; Casal Bértoa and Mair 2012). Therefore, the effects of the presidentialization of politics are especially pronounced in Central-Eastern Europe, where voters' alignment is lower and electoral campaigns are leader-centered (Weßels and Klingemann 2006; Berz 2019).

Although these findings are generally in line with our argument, there are some caveats regarding the distribution of the factor scores (Fig. 5.2). In Western Europe, for instance, the median scores for both party-agent and party-principal profiles are very close to the mean score of zero, which reveals that about half of West European prime ministers fit with one of the two career profiles. In Central-Eastern Europe, the score is instead well below the mean for both types. In Southern Europe, the median party-agent score is likewise below average, while it ranges close to zero on the party-principal dimension. However, the data in Fig. 5.2 also confirm the general conjecture that the party-principal type is more prevalent

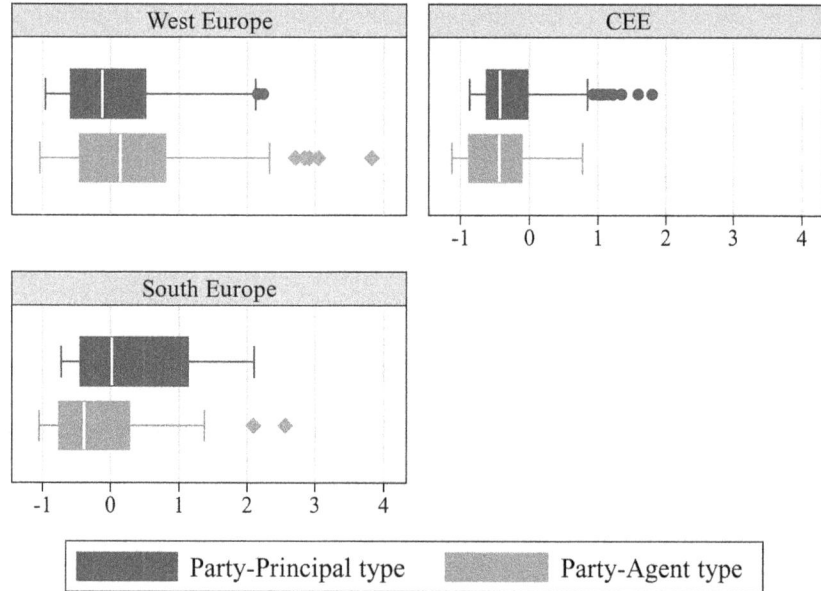

Fig. 5.2 Distribution of factor score coefficients in the three regions. (Note: Boxplots show the median (*white line*) and the lower (25th) and upper (75th) quartiles. Whiskers represent 1.5 times IQR (interquartile range) and individual dots indicate outliers)

in 'new' rather than in 'old' European democracies. Moreover, we observe that fewer prime ministers in 'new' democracies are characterized by a clear political career profile.

Longitudinal Trends Among Career Profiles

Have the career profiles of European prime ministers changed over time? Are party-principals replacing party-agents? As pointed out in the theoretical framework (Chap. 3), due to an increasing presidentialization of politics and a demand for a leader-centered government, we expect an overall rise of prime ministers with a party-principal career profile compared to those with a party-agent profile. This change took place parallel to the decline of party government. We argue that parties have responded to these changes by adopting new selection criteria for their prime ministerial candidates. Selecting prime ministers with a party-principal career profile became more prominent compared to choosing heads of governments with a traditional party-agent career profile.

In order to prove this theoretical argument, we examine the trends of changing career profiles among prime ministers in Europe on three levels: European, regional, and country level.

Trends on European Level

The longitudinal development of both career profiles in Europe is shown in Fig. 5.3. The upper part of the figure includes the linear trends of prime ministers' party-agent and party-principal career profiles from 1940 to 2020. The lower part of the figure provides information about the net incidence of both career profiles, measured as the difference between party-principal and party-agent scores. Positive values indicate that the prime minister's net career profile can be classified as a party-principal profile, whereas negative values indicate that the prime minister has a party-agent profile.

The results in the upper panel of Fig. 5.3 match our expectation. Until the 1980s, the party-agent profile was the dominant career profile, displaying above average scores. However, the party-agent scores sank to below average values between the 1980s and the 1990s, whereas the party-principal scores remained at the average level for the entirety of period under investigation. The combination of the declining trend of party-agent scores and the stable level of party-principal scores implies that, in more recent decades, the party-principal profile has become relatively stronger, overcoming the party-agent profile as the typical career profile of European prime ministers. The lower panel of Fig. 5.3 shows that this change in prime ministers' profiles is statistically significant ($p < 0.001$). We can therefore conclude that the party-principal profile among European prime ministers has increased due to the reduction of the party-agent profile.

Trends on Regional Level

Has this development toward a relative increase of party-principals been equally present in Western, Southern, and Central-Eastern Europe or do we find differences in the trend between the regions? The evidence provided in Chap. 4 shows that, at the aggregate level, career experiences

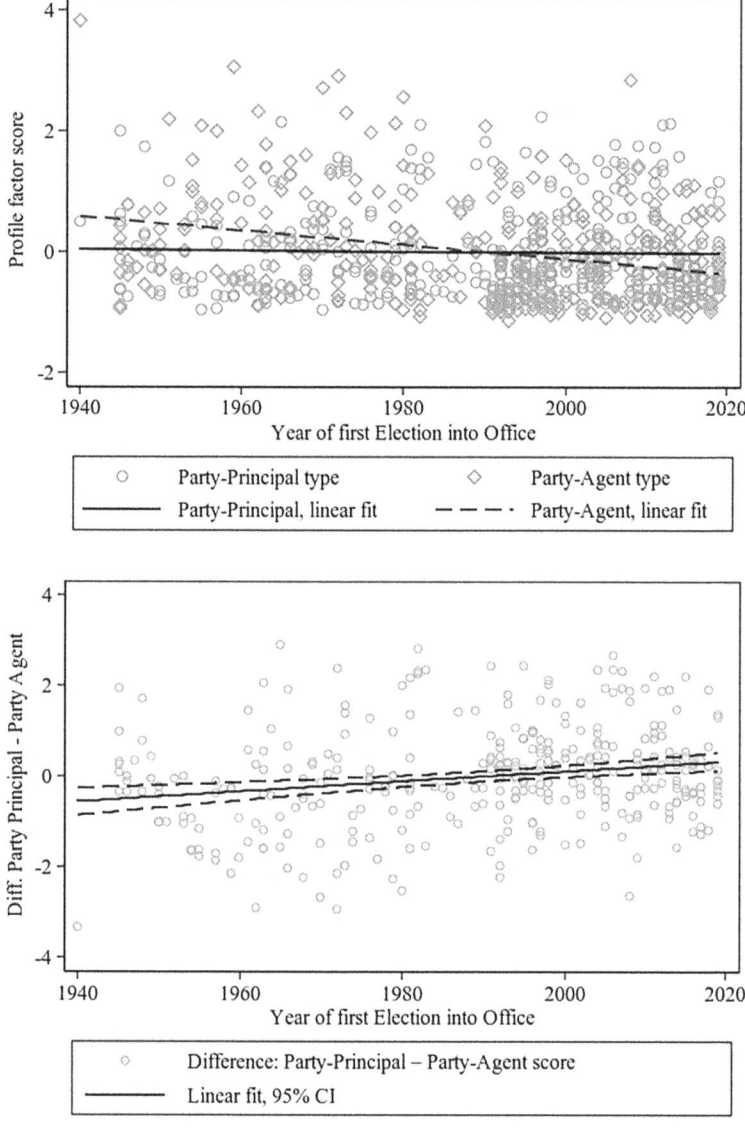

Fig. 5.3 Longitudinal developments of prime ministers' career profiles on European level. (Note: The upper panel shows the raw party-principal and party-agent values. The lower panel shows the difference between party-principal and party-agent scores as a direct test of our hypothesis ($p < 0.001$). Removing the outlier case of Prime Minister Winston Churchill leaves the results and the p-value level unchanged)

5 CHANGING CAREER PROFILES: FROM PARTY-AGENTS TO PARTY-PRINCIPALS

differ considerably between the three European regions. Regarding the change of career profiles, we expect a similar trend (from party-agent toward party-principal profiles) across the three regions over time, but also a more pronounced shift in Southern and Central-Eastern Europe. In both regions, the first appointed prime ministers entered office when the presidentialization of politics was making inroads, and thereby making prime ministers with a party-agent profile less salient for political parties and their voters. Figure 5.4 shows the development of both prime ministers' career profiles for each of the three regions.

The overall findings on prime ministers' career profiles in the three European regions are striking. First, the selection of prime ministers in Western Europe follows the same trend that has been observed in Europe as a whole: party-agent scores decline over time, whereas party-principal scores slightly increase. Moreover, in Western Europe the increasing pace of the party-principal scores is slightly above the average European trend.

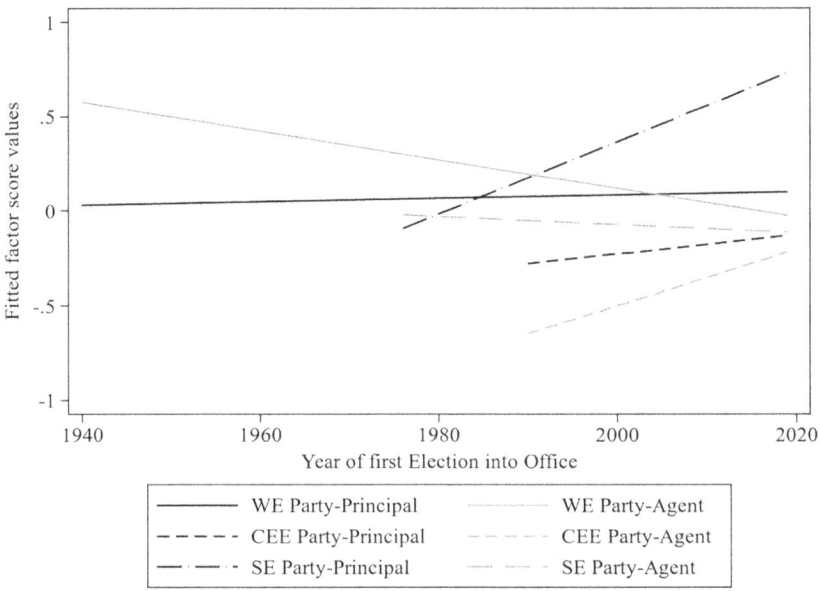

Fig. 5.4 Linear longitudinal change of prime ministers' career profiles by region. (Note: Linear fit between career profile scores and time in the three regions. Western Europe (WE); Central-Eastern Europe (CEE); Southern Europe (SE))

However, as expected, the party-agent profile remained the dominant career profile for many decades—only in the early 2000s we see more party-principals than party-agents in Western Europe. In the other two regions, party-principals clearly increased over time—in particular in Southern Europe—since the very beginning of the democratic regime.

Southern and Central-Eastern Europe also show differences in their party-agent scores over time. In Southern Europe, the party-agent type decreased moderately, while in Central-Eastern Europe, it grew moderately. Furthermore, we find negative party-agent scores in both regions across all periods. The increase in party-agent profiles in Central-Eastern Europe might be due to the democratic transition in this region in the 1990s, which led to the appointment of prime ministers with no political experiences in former autocratic regimes.

To conclude, each region has its own trend, but in correspondence with our general argument, the party-principal profile has become dominant in all regions. Western Europe is marked by the change in the ratio between party-agents and party-principals, whereby the relative increase of party-principals was driven by the reduction of party-agents over the past 70 years. The career profiles in Southern Europe are diverging: while party-principals are rapidly increasing, the party-agent type is slowly decreasing. In Central-Eastern Europe, the career profiles are converging, as both types are increasing over time, although the party-principals grew to a larger extent on average than the party-agents. In Southern and Central-Eastern Europe the party-agent scores tend to converge toward the West European level over time (with slightly downward trajectory in Southern Europe and an upward trajectory in Central-Eastern Europe).

Trends on Country Level

After having examined the change in prime ministers' career profiles at the European level and in the three European regions, we now seek to understand whether all countries share these regional trends equally. Do all countries within the three regions present similar patterns of changes in the prime ministers' career profiles? To what extent do we observe intraregional variation? In order to find appropriate answers to these questions, we disaggregate the data and observe trends in single countries for each region.

The longitudinal developments of party-agent and party-principal scores for each country are documented in Figs. 5.5, 5.6, and 5.7. It is not

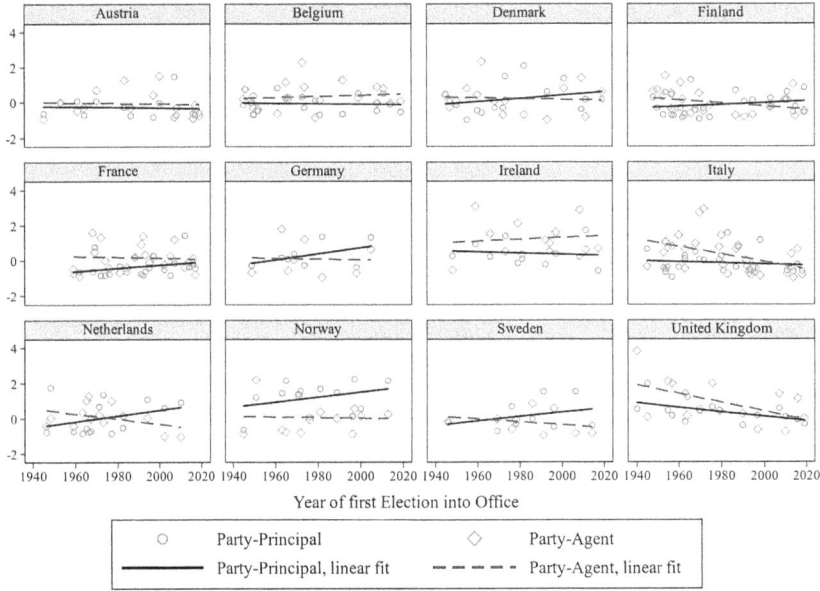

Fig. 5.5 Longitudinal development of prime ministers' career profiles in Western Europe by country

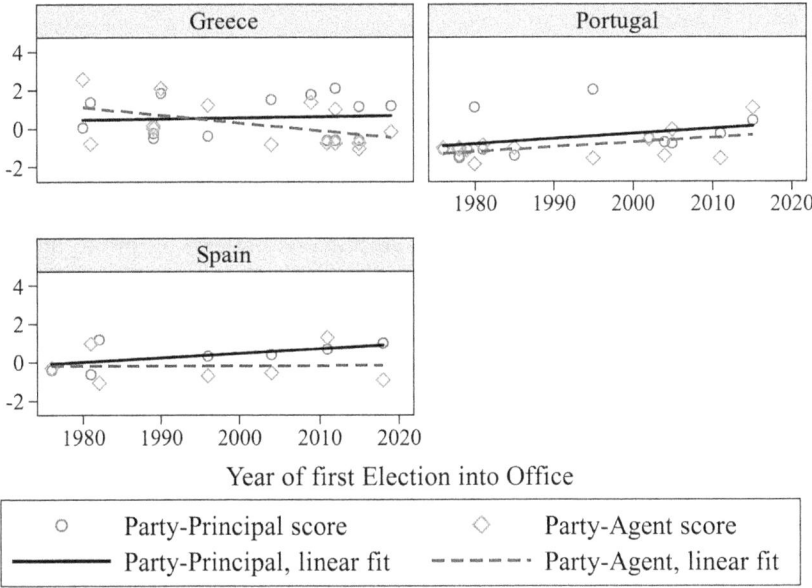

Fig. 5.6 Longitudinal development of prime ministers' career profiles in Southern Europe by country

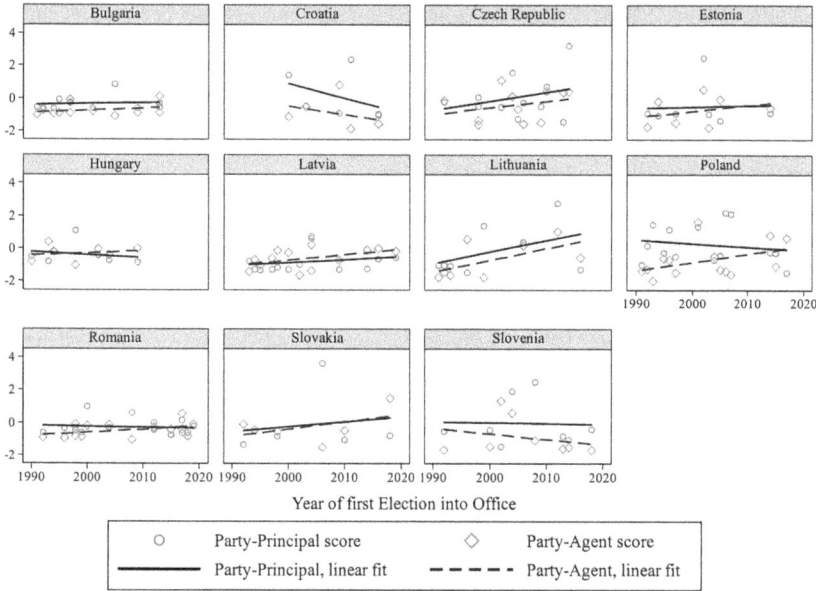

Fig. 5.7 Longitudinal development of prime ministers' career profiles in Central-Eastern Europe by country

surprising that the career profiles of prime ministers in most countries follow the overall European trend. There are, however, some considerable variations across the countries. Before starting with the detailed interpretation of the data, we should note that the number of prime ministers is fairly low in several European countries, particularly in Southern and Central-Eastern Europe, leading to ambiguous patterns in prime ministers' career profiles.

Of the 12 West European countries, 7 show a clear increase in the party-principal profile, only 1 decreases, and 4 exhibit relatively little change over time (see Fig. 5.5). In six countries (Denmark, Finland, Germany, Italy, the Netherlands, and Sweden), we observe party-principals overtaking party-agents as the dominant type while prime ministers in Norway always held a party-principal profile. In Denmark and Finland, the transition from party-agents to party-principals took place in the 1980s and 1990s, while in Germany, the Netherlands, and Sweden, the party-principal career profile increased between the 1960s and especially the

1970s. In Italy, this change occurred in the 2010s. Overall, the most pronounced shifts took place in Germany, the Netherlands, and Sweden.

France represents an interesting case because, although party-agent scores are decreasing and party-principal scores are increasing, party-agents still remain the dominant career profile. This might be due to the French type of semi-presidential system, where a strong president usually suggests prime ministerial candidates with a strong agent profile in order to receive parliamentary support for governmental policy-making (see below about the effects of presidential powers). The empirical findings also indicate that in Austria, Belgium, and Ireland, party-principal scores remain flat across all time periods. In these countries, the party-agent profile always prevailed, and in two countries (Belgium and Ireland), it is actually increasing relative to the party-principal profile. Finally, the United Kingdom is another deviant case because both the party-agent and the party-principal scores declined over time. However, the latter declined at a lower rate compared to the former. As a result, both career profiles reached the same level in the last decade. This indicates that, in most recent years, the selection of British prime ministers has followed neither a party-agent nor a party-principal logic.[4]

In two Southern countries (Portugal and Spain) prime ministers match the overall regional trend, with dominant party-principal scores across all decades. Yet, in Greece, prime ministers' profiles developed differently: party-agent scores declined while party-principal scores increased over time (see Fig. 5.6). One explanation for this trend is that prime ministers in Greece had gained political experience already in a democratic system prior to the coup of 1967. After the democratic breakthrough in 1974, Greek parties selected prime ministers whose career profile had been shaped when the party government model was still dominant in Europe. Greek Prime Minister Andreas Papandreou, for example, was appointed for the first time in 1981 and had been seated in the national parliament for the first time in 1964. Overall, the data show that party-principal scores follow an upward trajectory in all three South European countries.

In Central-Eastern Europe, we find a more heterogeneous picture (see Fig. 5.7). In five countries (Bulgaria, Czech Republic, Latvia, Lithuania, and Slovakia) there is no clear trend toward the decline of either type of career profile. In three countries, the party-principal scores increased remarkably (Czech Republic, Lithuania, and Slovakia), while their growth remained moderate in Estonia and Latvia. On the other hand, we find a decreasing trend among prime ministers with a party-principal profile in

Poland and Hungary, while in three countries we observe hardly any change in the party-principal scores over time (Bulgaria, Romania, and Slovenia). Interestingly enough, the party-agent scores increased in all countries of the region over time, except for Croatia and Slovenia. This latter finding indicates a unique trend in Central-Eastern countries toward more prime ministers acquiring experience in key political institutions, such as the parliament and the cabinet. That said, 7 out of 11 countries in Central-Eastern Europe were characterized by party-principal profile scores above or equal to party-agent scores in the last decade.

In sum, our results provide empirical evidence that the career profiles of European prime ministers have changed over the past seven decades, but this change varied considerably across the three regions and between single countries. Yet, despite regional and country-specific variations, we find a general trend toward an increase of the party-principal type of prime ministers in the majority of all European countries. Deviations of single countries from this general pattern might be due to differences in the pace of the presidentialization of politics and its impact on national politics as well as by institutional idiosyncrasies, which make some countries more susceptible than others to changes in prime ministers' career profiles. We explore these aspects in the following sections.

Electoral Volatility and Career Profiles

In the previous section, we have shown that the career profiles of prime ministers changed as a function of time. In this section, we examine the relationship between electoral volatility and changing career profiles. We argue that an increase in electoral volatility signals the weakening of social cleavages, which the literature has identified as a critical factor in triggering the decline of party government and an increase in the presidentialization of politics (Dalton et al. 2000; Fieldhouse et al. 2020). Therefore, increasing electoral volatility stands as one proxy of those conditions that increase the salience of party-principals relative to party-agents. Aside from this theoretical argument, there are also methodological reasons for applying volatility in our analysis. Compared to other measures of the decline of party government, the data on electoral volatility are precise, consistent, and easily accessible for all European countries. Thus, they provide us with reliable and systematic cross-national, as well as longitudinal, information on party system change.

Previous research has shown that electoral volatility has progressed in all European countries over the past decades, except for Croatia and Spain (Chiaramonte and Emanuele 2017, see also Fig. A2 in the Appendix). There are, however, significant variations between countries. In the following analysis, we use data from Casal Bértoa (2021), which are based on the classic Pedersen Index (1979), to pair the electoral volatility at the most recent parliamentary election with each prime minister. This index of electoral volatility measures the sum of changes in vote share of political parties from the preceding parliamentary elections, divided by the number of parties, and it illustrates the extent to which voters are aligned, or de-aligned, with political parties over subsequent elections (Dalton et al. 2011, p. 10). In our study, electoral volatility ranges from 0.5, when nearly all parties from the last election win the same vote percentages in the next election, to a maximum of 55.8, indicating that over 50 percent of votes are redirected to other parties.

Figure 5.8 shows that prime ministers' career profiles indeed correlate with electoral volatility. The left-hand panel reveals that party-agent scores are above average when electoral volatility is less than 18. However, as

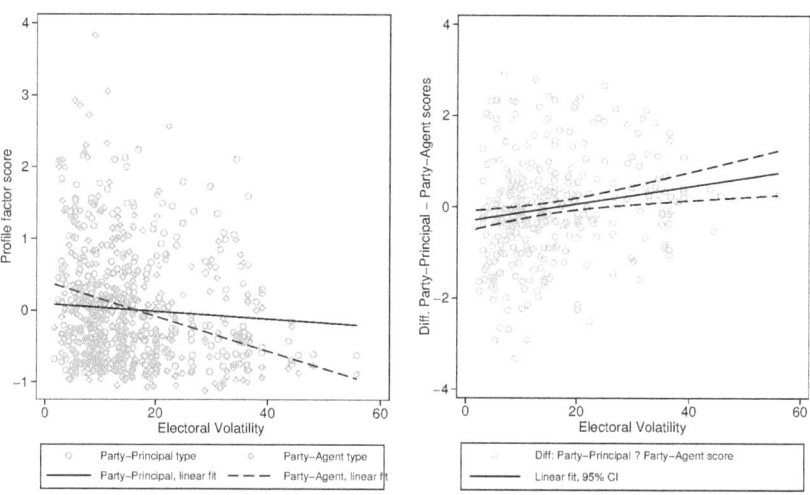

Fig. 5.8 Electoral volatility and prime ministers' career profiles. (Note: The left-hand panel shows the raw party-principal and party-agent scores by electoral volatility. The right-hand panel shows the difference between party-principal and party-agent scores by electoral volatility as a direct test of our hypothesis ($p < 0.01$))

electoral volatility increases, party-agent scores decrease considerably. This matches our expectation: when voters' attachment to political parties is low (and the elections are more personalized), parties will be less focused on selecting prime ministers with a traditional party-agent profile. In contrast, party-principals do not necessarily increase with higher electoral volatility. The positive slope in the right-hand panel of this graph indicates that prime ministers with party-principal profiles are selected more frequently than those with party-agent profiles in times of high electoral volatility, but party-principal values are relatively stable across all levels of volatility. The relative trend toward party-principals is statistically significant ($p < 0.01$). These findings support our theoretical argument: when faced with electoral volatility, party gate-keepers prefer to select prime ministers with a party-principal career profile rather than prime ministers with a party-agent profile.

Institutional Setting and Career Profiles

What impact do institutional settings have on the career profiles of prime ministers? As noted above, political parties are the major political actors that select prime ministers. However, these decisions take place under various institutional conditions. In this section, we examine whether parliamentary or semi-presidential systems affect career profiles. Moreover, we analyze the relationship between the institutional power of prime ministers and presidents on the one hand and prime ministers career profiles on the other.

Career Profiles in Parliamentary and Semi-presidential Systems

Do governmental systems have a measurable impact on prime ministers' career profiles? Unlike parliamentary systems, semi-presidential systems divide executive power between the prime minister and a directly elected president. The different forms of power-sharing in both systems affect the political background and the role of prime minister. First, the skill sets of prime ministers in semi-presidential countries usually differ from their counterparts in parliamentary countries. Prime ministers in semi-presidential countries are less likely to acquire political experience when compared to prime ministers in parliamentary countries (Samuels and Shugart 2010). Second, in semi-presidential systems, prime ministers have a smaller role as catalysts of votes and presidential candidates are often the leading figures for a party during elections. Moreover, presidents are potential key players in government formation (Schleiter and Morgan-Jones 2010). Under semi-presidentialism, parties can thus continue selecting party-agents for the prime ministerial office, even in times of presidentialization, at least as long as presidents are central in government, in the party, and in the electoral campaigns (Poguntke and Webb 2005b, p. 5ff). Moreover, the international role of some presidents in semi-presidential countries can overshadow the prime minister. In this case, the interest of political parties in selecting prime ministers with an international background (which is typical of party-principals) is limited, since the president (and not the prime minister) represents the country in major international summits. Put differently, in semi-presidential systems, presidentialization is less likely to have changed prime ministers' career profiles toward party-principal profiles. Thus, irrespective of the general increase of presidentialization in European political systems, we expect more prime ministers with a party-agent career profile in semi-presidential than in parliamentary countries.

Before testing this expectation, we need to define the notion of semi-presidentialism. Following Robert Elgie's (2018) definition, a semi-presidential political system is one in which a directly elected president coexists with a prime minister and a collective cabinet that is accountable to the parliament. If we apply this definition in the European context, about half of all prime ministers (54 percent) have ruled in a parliamentary system, while the other half (46 percent) have governed in a semi-presidential system.[5]

Do we find major differences in the career profiles of those prime ministers who have served in parliamentary and semi-presidential systems? Figure 5.9 shows the aggregated distribution of all party-agent and party-principal prime ministers in both systems. Overall, the picture is very similar. First, in semi-presidential systems, the median values of both career profiles are below zero. Second, there is no evidence that in semi-presidential systems the distribution is skewed toward the party-agent profile.[6] However, we find that both career profiles score lower in semi-presidential systems than in parliamentary systems, which indicates that prime ministers' careers are more varied and do not adhere as strongly as expected to the ideal-types of party-agent and party-principal career profiles.

While the proportion of both prime ministers' career profiles is, on average, similar in parliamentary and semi-presidential systems, it may very

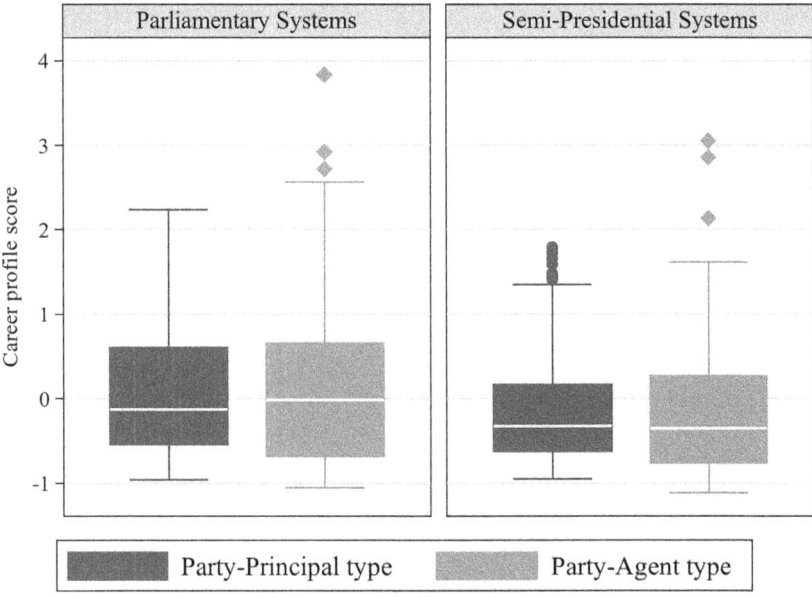

Fig. 5.9 Prime ministers' career profiles in parliamentary and semi-presidential systems. (Note: Boxplots show the median (*white line*) and the lower (25th) and upper (75th) quartiles. Whiskers represent 1.5 times IQR and individual dots reveal outliers)

well vary over time, as predicted by the declining party government and the increasing presidentialization hypothesis. The trend of prime ministers' career profiles goes, however, in the same directions in both governmental systems, that is, the party-agent career profile decreases, and the party-principal profile increases slightly (see Fig. 5.10). There are only minor differences between both career profiles in the two governmental systems. While the party-principal career profile became dominant in parliamentary countries in the 1980s, it took another 20 years before this trend was reached in the semi-presidential systems. Finally, the data suggest that the shift toward party-principals has been slightly stronger in parliamentary systems than in semi-presidential systems.

In sum, the development of prime ministers' career profiles follows the same general trajectory, irrespective of the governmental system. Therefore, we may conclude that the presence of a directly elected president *in itself* has only a minor impact on the overall development of prime ministers' career profiles.

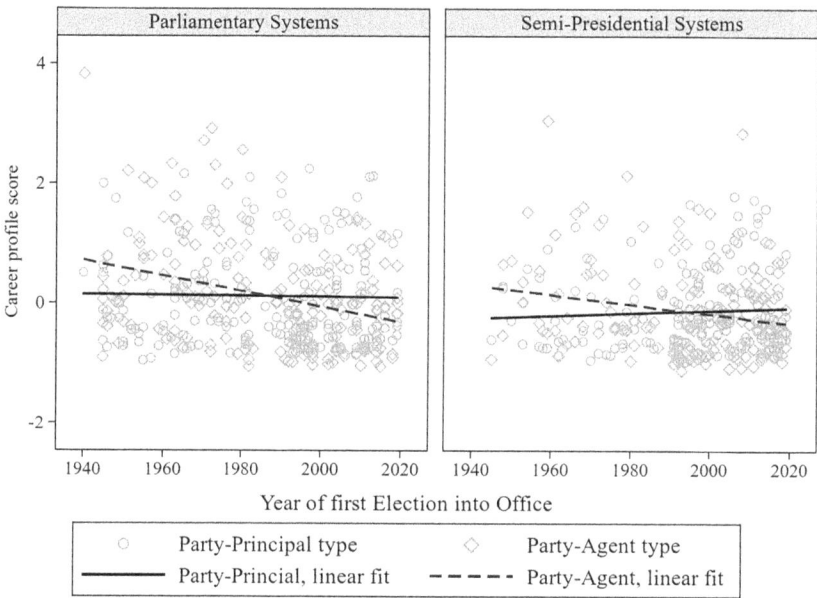

Fig. 5.10 Longitudinal development of prime ministers' career profiles by form of government

Prime Ministerial Powers and Prime Ministers' Career Profiles

Another factor that might determine the selection of prime ministers by political parties is their institutional power. If prime ministers have more institutional powers, they may find it easier to deviate from their own party's policy, since their ability to dismiss cabinet ministers and to set the cabinet agenda according to their own policy preferences is greater. Thus, powerful prime ministers can potentially be more damaging to the party's policy agenda than weak prime ministers. Consequently, political parties should select reliable party-agents in a political system with institutionally strong prime ministers. In contrast, weak prime ministers may be constrained more easily by their political party, cabinet, or president, making the choice for a reliable party-agent less salient. We therefore expect a positive relationship between the extent of prime ministers' institutional powers and the scores in the party-agent career profile as well as a negative relationship with party-principal scores.

The concept of prime ministerial power is multidimensional and difficult to measure (Doyle 2020). For the following analysis, we apply an index of prime ministerial power suggested by Bergman et al. (2003, 2019). According to them, the ranking of prime ministerial power is based on the prime minister's influence within the cabinet, which is measured by seven indicators: (I) appointment of ministers; (II) dismissal of ministers; (III) determination of ministries' jurisdiction; (IV) steering or coordination rights *vis-à-vis* cabinet ministers; (V) full control of the cabinet agenda; (VI) ministers' parliamentary accountability via prime minister; (VII) the presence of a permanent administrative structure supervised by the prime minister and designed to monitor departmental affairs. With the exception of the Italian case, where the reform of the prime minister's office in 1988 increased the influence of the head of government, these formally defined political powers of prime ministers have remained remarkably stable in European countries over the past decades.

Table 5.3 provides a comparative overview of prime ministers' institutional power in Europe from 1945 to 2020. The indicators are operationalized as a dummy variable (1 = yes; 0 = no). The prime ministerial power index is calculated by summing the indicator scores and then dividing the total by seven, which produces the mean of the unweighted scores. An index score of 1.00 indicates that a prime minister has reached the highest level of power within the cabinet.

The overall distribution of institutional power among prime ministers in Europe is straightforward. First, we find prime ministers with the highest institutional power in only five countries (Bulgaria, Germany, Portugal, Spain, and the United Kingdom). Second, the level of prime ministerial power is not directly related to one or the other type of governmental system (correlation 0.1). We find high and low institutional powers of prime ministers in semi-presidential and parliamentary systems. Third, while the formal political power of prime ministers in Southern Europe is comparatively high (ranging from 0.71 to 1.00), we observe considerable variation in the other two European regions (ranging from 0.14 to 1.00). Fourth, prime ministers' institutional power is particularly low in Belgium and Slovakia (0.28), Finland, the Netherlands, and Slovenia (0.14). Fifth, on average the power index of prime ministers is lowest in Western Europe (0.58), medium in Central-Eastern Europe (0.65), and comparatively high in Southern Europe (0.90). Thus, prime ministers in Western Europe have—on average—less institutional power than their counterparts in Central-Eastern and Southern Europe.

Table 5.3 Prime ministerial powers within the cabinet in Europe, 1945–2020

Country	Indicator of power							Total score	Index of prime ministerial power
	I	II	III	IV	V	VI	VII		
Western Europe									
Germany	1	1	1	1	1	1	1	7	1.00
United Kingdom	1	1	1	1	1	1	1	7	1.00
Ireland	1	1	1	1	1	0	1	6	0.85
France	1	1	1	1	0	1	1	6	0.85
Denmark	1	1	1	0	1	0	1	5	0.71
Austria	1	1	0	1	0	0	1	4	0.57
Italy	1	0	0	1	1	0	1	4	0.57
Norway	1	1	0	0	0	0	1	3	0.42
Sweden	1	1	0	0	0	0	1	3	0.42
Belgium	0	0	0	1	0	0	1	2	0.28
Finland	0	0	0	0	0	0	1	1	0.14
Netherlands	0	0	0	0	0	0	1	1	0.14
Southern Europe									
Portugal	1	1	1	1	1	1	1	7	1.00
Spain	1	1	1	1	1	1	1	7	1.00
Greece	1	1	1	1	0	0	1	5	0.71
Central-Eastern Europe									
Bulgaria	1	1	1	1	1	1	1	7	1.00
Czech Republic	1	1	1	1	1	0	1	6	0.85
Poland	1	1	1	1	1	0	1	6	0.85
Romania	1	1	0	1	1	1	1	6	0.85
Hungary	1	1	0	1	1	0	1	5	0.71
Lithuania	1	1	0	1	1	0	1	5	0.71
Estonia	1	1	0	0	1	0	1	4	0.57
Latvia	1	1	0	1	0	0	1	4	0.57
Slovakia	1	1	0	0	0	0	0	2	0.28
Slovenia	0	0	0	1	0	0	0	1	0.14
Croatia	Not available								

Source: own calculation based on information from Bergman et al. (2003, pp. 186–188, 2019, p. 535)

In a second step, we relate the prime ministerial power index to the distribution of party-agent and party-principal scores across Europe (Fig. 5.11). Overall, we find no support of our expectation that weak institutional power of prime ministers relates to a party-principal profile and vice versa. Instead, the levels of prime ministerial power have no effect on

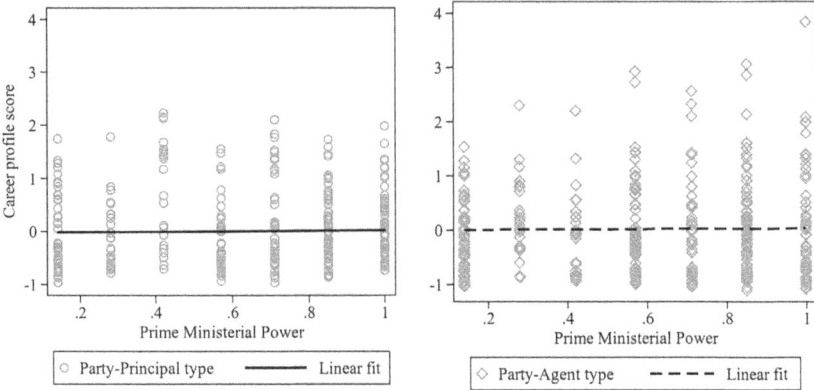

Fig. 5.11 The relationship between prime ministerial powers and prime ministers' career profiles

the scores of either party-agents or party-principals and exhibit roughly the same variation across all levels of prime ministerial power.

Some variation exists, however, when analyzing specific indicators, such as the prime ministers' power to define specific governmental policy. While prime ministers hold the formal power to appoint or dismiss the cabinet ministers in almost all European countries, they control the cabinet agenda in 14 out of 25 (see column V in Table 5.3). We argue that the power to set the cabinet agenda endows prime ministers with substantial control over government policies. Therefore, we concentrate specifically on the prime ministers' control over the cabinet agenda as the most influential power of chief executives. We expect that in those countries where prime ministers have cabinet agenda-setting power, the party-agent career profile should be more common than the party-principal profile.

The findings presented in Fig. 5.12 do not support this expectation either. In line with the general European trend, party-agent scores decrease over time and prime ministers with party-principal profiles become more common in comparison to party-agents, irrespective of the prime ministerial power to control the cabinet agenda. Although Fig. 5.12 shows that prime ministers who lack formal control of their cabinet's agenda have slightly lower party-agent scores compared to prime ministers who have control over the cabinet agenda, the difference in career profiles between the two scenarios is negligible. Thus, there is hardly any direct connection between prime ministers' strength of institutional power and their career profiles.

5 CHANGING CAREER PROFILES: FROM PARTY-AGENTS TO PARTY-PRINCIPALS

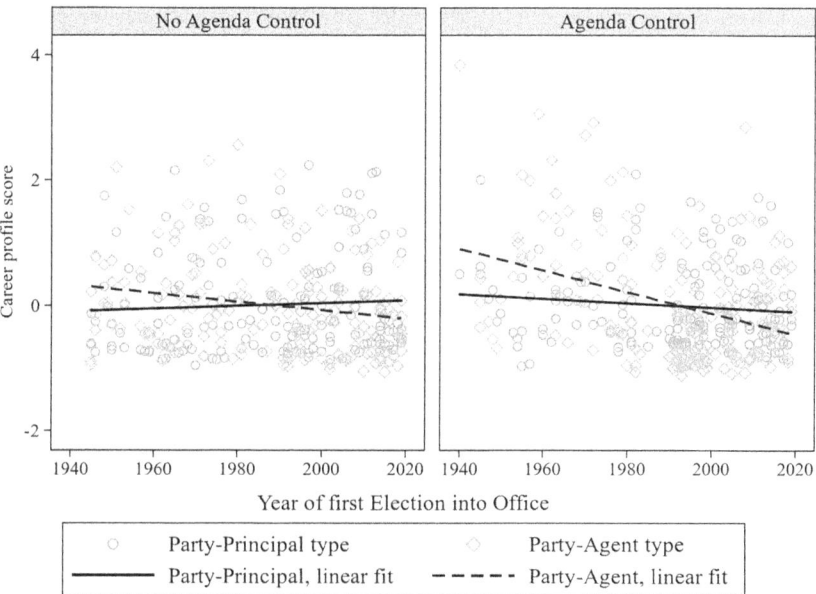

Fig. 5.12 Longitudinal development of prime ministers' career profiles by power of cabinet agenda control

Presidential Powers and Prime Ministers' Career Profiles

It is widely known and empirically proven that not all presidents share equal power across the globe (Blondel 2015). Among semi-presidential countries, the French president, for example, is usually considered as one of the most powerful. In contrast, Austrian politics traditionally works according to a parliamentary logic, although the Austrian president is elected by voters and has the formal power to dismiss the cabinet. Similar to France, Finland was a fully-fledged example of West European semi-presidentialism until the constitutional reform of 2000, when presidential powers were restricted. A similar change affected Portugal after the constitutional reform of 1982. Moreover, while the directly elected president of Ireland has little say in national politics, the presidents of Lithuania and Romania, both semi-presidential systems, are relatively powerful (Raunio and Sedelius 2020). In the following, we focus on presidential powers in both parliamentary and semi-presidential systems.

Given that some presidents are more powerful than others, we expect that prime ministers should be more likely to have a traditional party-agent profile in systems with politically powerful presidents because in these systems presidentialization will increase the autonomy and influence of presidents rather than that of prime ministers. However, this 'presidential effect' might be weaker in those systems where the prime ministers themselves display a high level of political power relative to the president. Building on these conjectures, we first examine the relationship between presidential powers and prime ministers' career profiles, and, second, the combined influence of presidential *and* prime ministerial power on prime ministers' career profiles.

The degree of presidential power in European democracies is measured using the *Prespow2* index suggested by Doyle and Elgie (2014). This index provides presidential power scores for almost all countries in our study and uses a principal component analysis to aggregate 28 previous presidential indices, measuring various formal constitutional powers of presidents, that is, legislative veto powers, appointment of cabinet ministers, and emergency decrees (Doyle and Elgie 2015). In contrast to the measure of institutional prime ministerial powers, as outlined above, the presidential index varies over time and takes a minimum value of 0.07 and a maximum of 0.59.[7] Since presidents do not exist in countries with hereditary heads of state (i.e., monarchies), 27 percent of the prime ministers in our dataset are excluded in the following analysis.[8] The total sample therefore covers only 256 prime ministers. Within this sample, the Portuguese head of state, who was in office from 1976 to 1982, was the most powerful, while his Latvian colleague was the weakest of all presidents in Europe.

Figure 5.13 shows the overall relationship between presidents' powers and prime ministers' career profiles. As expected, party-agent scores relate positively with presidential powers, whereas party-principal scores decrease as presidential powers increase. However, the differences are very minor. Party-agent scores range slightly below the average when presidents yield limited power, but they rise to the average as presidential powers become greater. Although these findings underline our general expectation, the relationship between presidential powers and prime ministers' career profiles is fairly weak.

Presidential powers may condition prime ministers' career profiles only when prime ministers are relatively weak compared to presidents. It might very well be that, in the presence of strong presidents and weak prime

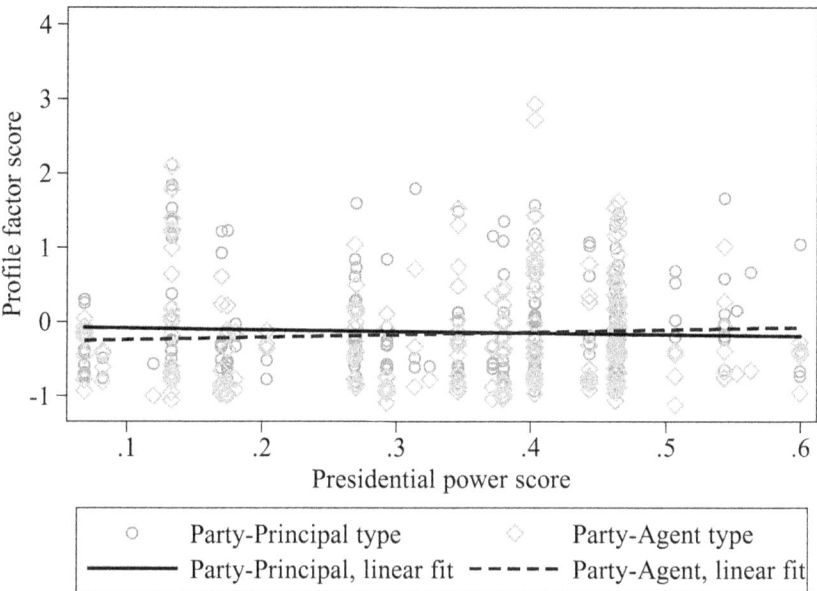

Fig. 5.13 Relationship between presidential powers and prime ministers' career profiles

ministers, political parties face fewer pressures from presidentialization because politics already follows a 'presidential' logic. In this case, political parties favor appointing prime ministers with a party-agent profile as a preferable strategy for ensuring a trustworthy prime minister to pursue party goals in government. In contrast, when presidents are weak and prime ministers are strong, political parties face increasing pressures to select prime ministers with a party-principal profile to meet the demands of presidentialization. Thus, we expect to find more party-agents in an institutional setting with strong presidents and weak prime ministers.

In the following analysis, we test the combined effect of presidential and prime ministerial powers. In particular, we observe how career profiles change under different sets of presidential powers, while distinguishing between countries where prime ministers have (and do not have) the institutional power to set the cabinet agenda. We argue that under strong presidents the appointment of party-agents will be more common than the appointment of party-principals in situations when prime ministers do not have the power to control the cabinet agenda. Figure 5.14 shows the relationship between presidential powers and prime ministers' career profiles, conditional on the prime ministers' agenda-setting power.

Overall, the findings are in line with our theoretical expectation. The left-hand panel of Fig. 5.14 shows that, without control over the cabinet agenda, party-principal scores and presidential power are negatively correlated, while party-agent scores and presidential power are positively linked. These relationships underline our general argument about the correlations between presidential power and career profiles (see above). The right-hand panel of Fig. 5.14 illustrates that the relation between presidential power and prime ministers' career profiles does not change in governmental systems which give prime ministers the power to formally control the cabinet agenda. The scores of both career profiles remain essentially constant over the whole range of presidential power. Finally, the data show that the career profile scores are lower under the 'no agenda control' scenario than under the 'agenda control' scenario. This indicates

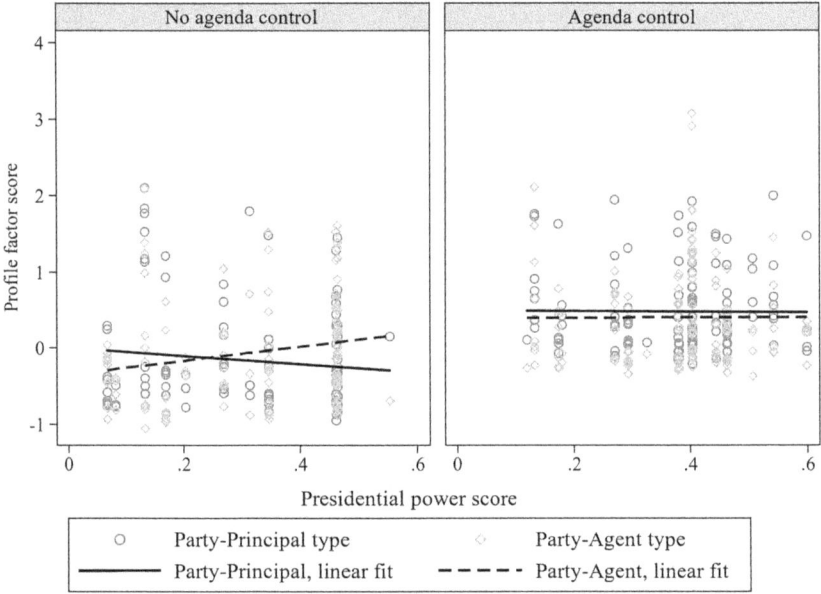

Fig. 5.14 Presidential powers and prime ministers' career profiles by prime ministerial agenda control

that, under a non-hereditary head of state, the selection of prime ministers with a party-agent or a party-principal profile is less salient if the prime ministers' institutional power is relatively weak. In other words, in republican systems where prime ministers do not formally control the cabinet agenda, political parties appear to be more likely to select prime ministers for reasons other than their career profile. One explanation for this behavior of political parties could be that the cost of selecting prime ministers without one or the other career profiles is relatively low when parties can more effectively control the executive via a president.

In sum, we find that institutional factors do not affect prime ministers' career profiles very much. We observe that party-agent and party-principal profiles are equally common in parliamentary and semi-presidential systems and not directly linked to the strength of presidential or prime ministerial institutional powers.

THE IMPACT OF PARTY FAMILIES ON PRIME MINISTERS' CAREER PROFILES

Why would party families have an impact on prime ministers' career profiles? Do different party families select prime ministers with different career profiles? Has the selection of different prime ministers' career profiles among party families changed over time? As noted in Chap. 2, prime ministers have been politically and ideologically socialized within various European party families. Nearly half of all European prime ministers (46 percent) are members of the center, center-left, and left-wing party families (i.e., the Socialists and Social Democrats, the Liberals, and the Agrarians) while the center-right and right-wing party families (i.e., Christian Democrats, Conservatives, and right-wing nationalists) have sent 148 prime ministers into office (42 percent). The remaining 42 prime ministers did not belong to any party family (12 percent).

According to our general assumptions, we expect that parties from all party families will increasingly select prime ministers with a party-principal profile. Although single political parties within these party families often differ from each other in terms of their membership size, their organizational structures, their ideological program, and their mobilization strategies, they all face the universal pressures of presidentialization and the decline of party government, which have changed the demands about prime ministers' career profiles among all political parties. From this expectation we exclude prime ministers without party families because they have not pursued an established political career and developed a clear career profile.

That said, one can additionally expect variations in the absolute preference for either party-agents or party-principals between party families for two main reasons: first, the changes in the organizational structure between party families may lead to differences in prime ministers' career profiles. On the one hand, both Socialist and Social Democratic as well as Christian Democratic parties belong to the type of 'traditional' mass parties that shifted electoral strategies in order to appeal to a wider cross-section of voters (Kirchheimer 1966). Yet they were still shaped by their origin in terms of larger membership numbers and organizational complexity (Panebianco 1988) which informs their preference for prime ministers who are able to accommodate the interests of various party factions and leaders. Therefore, we expect both mass party families to be more likely to select prime ministers with a party-agent profile.

In contrast, smaller, non-mass-based parties lack organizational complexity. Therefore, it should be much easier for gate-keepers in these parties to accept prime ministerial candidates who have held the office as party leader or other external positions. Thus, the proportion of prime ministers with party-principal career profiles should be higher among non-mass-based party families.

Second, the differences in the timing of prime ministerial investitures matters for the career profile of prime ministers from the Social Democratic and the Christian Democratic party families. The total number of Social Democratic prime ministers was fairly low between 1960 and 1990 and increased only in the last three decades. Overall, more than 60 percent of all Social Democratic prime ministers entered office after 1990. The reverse is true for the Christian Democratic party family which selected about 70 percent of its prime ministers before 1990. Thus, we expect that the proportion of party-agents is higher among the Christian Democratic party family since the presidentialization of politics started to develop only in the 1980s.

Changes Within and Between Party Families Over Time

If the presidentialization thesis holds true, we should expect an increasing trend toward the selection of prime ministers with a party-principal career profile within all party families, which is precisely what we find. Prime ministers with a party-principal career profile did indeed increase in almost all European party families over time (Fig. 5.15). The most evident shift from party-agents to party-principals is visible in the Conservative party family, where the dominant party-agent career profile of the earlier decades underwent remarkable changes toward the party-principal profile. Although less pronounced, the trend toward increasing numbers of prime ministers with a party-principal profile also took place within the Social Democrats, the Liberals,[9] and the Christian Democrats. The Agrarian party family experienced a similar change, although the low number of prime ministers and the high variation in the career profiles' scores makes it difficult to draw a clear conclusion. Finally, we observe a relatively flat trend in the right-wing and nationalist party family, which exhibits high levels of variation in the career profiles of its prime ministers.

Over time, all major party families have increased their selection of prime ministers with a party-principal profile, but does this also mean that preferences for party-agents and party-principals do not differ between party families? Figure 5.16 shows that, despite a general trend toward the

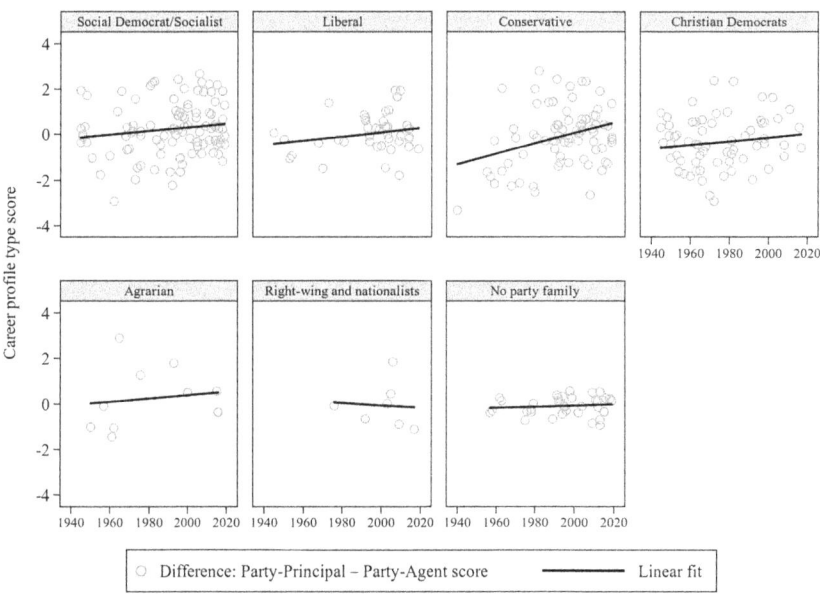

Fig. 5.15 Longitudinal developments of prime ministers' career profiles by party family

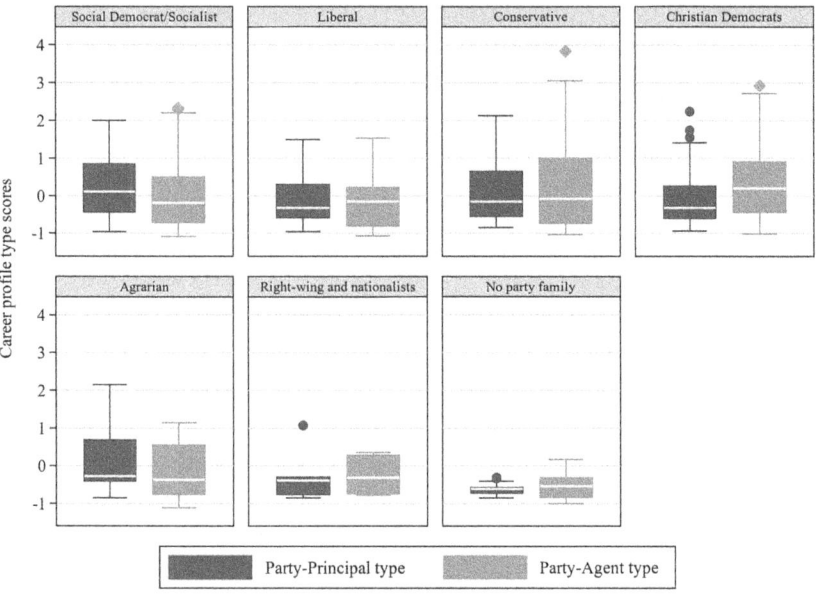

Fig. 5.16 Party-agents and party-principals in different party families. (Note: Boxplots show the median (*white line*) and the lower (25th) and upper (75th) quartiles. Whiskers represent 1.5 times IQR and individual dots reveal outliers)

party-principal profile, substantial differences in the overall distribution of career profiles exist between party families. The positive difference values indicate that Social Democrats and Socialists clearly favor party-principals over party-agents. Furthermore, we find a similar preference among Agrarian parties. The Christian Democratic party family, on the other hand, demonstrates a preference for party-agent profiles, although some prime ministers have also held a pronounced party-principal profile. Career profile scores in the Conservative parties are likewise higher with reference to the party-agent profile relative to the party-principal profile. Yet, in contrast to the Social Democrats and the Christian Democrats, the distribution between party-agents and party-principals is more balanced among Conservatives parties, with a median score slightly below the average (see Fig. 5.16). Among prime ministers from the Liberal party family, the median values of party-agent and party-principal scores are about the same, revealing a balanced selection of prime ministers. Furthermore, liberal prime ministers' career profile scores are, on average, slightly lower than the overall scores of Social Democrats, Conservatives, and Christian Democrats. This highlights that in Liberal parties, prime ministers are selected less clearly along party-agent and party-principal lines. Similarly, prime ministers from the right-wing and nationalist party family score very low on both the party-agent and the party-principal career profile. Overall, we observe the most prevalent difference in prime ministers' career profiles between Social Democratic parties, which favor the party-principals, and Christian Democratic parties, which favor the party-agents.

Our findings indicate that the Christian Democratic party family still belongs more to the old type of 'traditional' mass party than the Social Democrats who display a preference for party-principal profiles. The dominance of party-agent profiles among Christian Democratic parties also matches our expectation that the Christian Democratic party family faced less pressure from the presidentialization of politics. In contrast, the larger presence of prime ministers with a party-principal profile among the Social Democrats corresponds with the increasing presidentialization in the last decades. Yet, we do not have any strong counterfactual evidence about what type of prime ministers Social and Christian Democrats would have selected in times without the impact of presidentialization.

In summary, we find that the presidentialization of politics affected the type of prime ministers' career profile within all major European party families (Socialist and Social Democrats, Liberals, Conservatives, and Christian Democrats) in that these profiles have shifted toward the party-principal type over time.

GENDER AND PRIME MINISTERS' CAREER PROFILES

Does gender matter for the career profiles of prime ministers? We know that women are more likely to reach the prime ministerial office after acquiring extensive experience in parliament and as cabinet ministers (Müller-Rommel and Vercesi 2017). Moreover, women have increasingly held ministerial portfolios that have been considered traditionally 'masculine' (O'Brien et al. 2015; Barnes and O'Brien 2018; Goddard 2019). For these reasons, we first expect women's career profiles to align more with the party-agent than with the party-principal career type. Second, we expect that the party-agent career profile remains fairly stable among women prime ministers, while it has become less salient over time among their male counterparts (relative to the party-principal profile).[10]

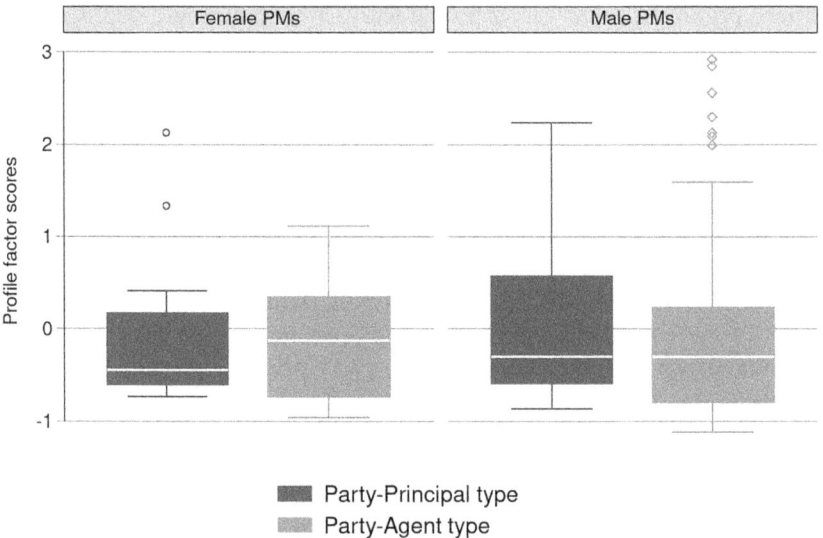

Fig. 5.17 Distribution of party-agent and party-principal factor score coefficients between women and men. (Note: Boxplots show the median (*white line*) and the lower (25th) and upper (75th) quartiles. Whiskers represent 1.5 times IQR and individual dots reveal outliers)

As Fig. 5.17 shows there are several differences between women and men's career profiles.[11] First, the median scores of the two career profiles are fairly similar among men prime minister, while women indeed score higher with reference to the party-agent profile. Second, the party-principal career profile is less salient among female prime ministers than among their male colleagues. Although the overwhelming majority of women prime minister have entered office in the most recent decades when presidentialization already had its effect on the career profiles of prime ministers, the number of female prime ministers with a party-agent profile was higher than the ones with a party-principal profile. Third, no woman prime minister displays a party-principal score higher than 0.5 (excluding the two outlier profiles of Angela Merkel and Erna Solberg) while 25 percent of all male prime ministers ranged above this level. However, these differences may eventually decline, as the number of women prime minister with experience as former party leaders increases, thus breaking the glass ceiling in Europe (Jalalzai 2018).

5 CHANGING CAREER PROFILES: FROM PARTY-AGENTS TO PARTY-PRINCIPALS 173

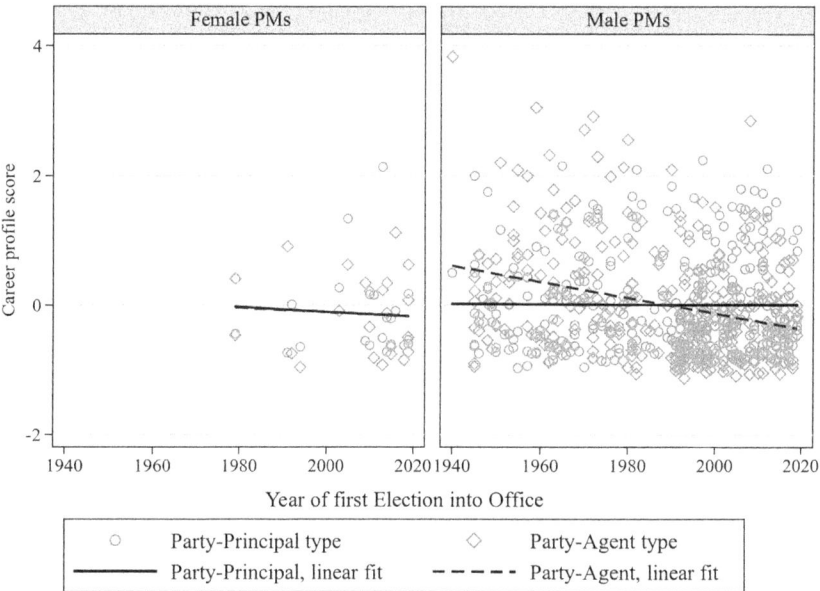

Fig. 5.18 Development of party-agent and party-principal factor score coefficients among women and men. (Note: The linear development of party-principal and party-agent profile scores among women prime ministers is visually indistinguishable)

Our data further reveals that the party-agent and party-principal profile scores of women prime ministers declined with the same linear trend. The trends of both profiles are nearly the same for female prime ministers and therefore indistinguishable in Fig. 5.18. This suggests that, in recent years, more women entered the prime ministerial office through non-traditional or 'outsider' careers. In contrast, career profiles among men follow the general European pattern, in that party-agents decrease over time and party-principals become relatively more salient.

Conclusion

This chapter has examined the distribution of different prime ministerial career profiles over time and across the three European regions. We have theoretically derived two ideal-types of career profiles that build on previous career experience of prime ministers: the party-agent and the party-principal profiles. While the former is defined by former experience in parliament, in cabinet, and an entry into office at an older age, the latter is characterized by former leadership position (i.e., as party head and opposition leadership of the parliamentary party group) and by previous experience in international organizations. A factor analysis supports the empirical viability of both career profiles.

Our empirical findings have confirmed that the rate of prime ministers with a party-agent career profile has decreased over time, while the rate of prime ministers with a party-principal profile remained relatively constant. However, the party-principal profile has become the dominant profile since the 1990s, since the number of prime ministers with a party-agent profile decreased. Thus, we observe the emergence of a new type of prime minister, whose career experience differs from the career experience of her predecessors. For decades, European prime ministers have been characterized by the typical profile of a reliable party-agent, who was dependent upon the decisions of her political party. In more recent times, the typical prime minister has become a principal of her party which implies that political parties are more dependent upon their own prime ministers than in the past. Put differently, prime ministers with a party-principal career profile are more likely to control the government as well as their political party.

Interestingly, this new type of prime minister is more common in the 'new' democracies, where the presidentialization of politics has been underway from the very beginning of the democratization process. In particular, after a transitional period of self-adaptation to new democratic rules, South and Central-East European countries have witnessed the most pronounced trend toward the party-principal career profile among their prime ministers. The analysis has also shown that substantial intra-regional variations exist between European countries. Some of them do, indeed, follow the general trend, whereas others appear more resistant to change.

Cross-country variations provide an interesting basis for further research and suggest that, in addition to the presidentialization of politics, several other factors might have an impact on prime ministers' career profiles and may explain some of the observed variation in career profiles between countries. Among them are, first, the institutional setting of the country. Although parliamentary and semi-presidential forms of government only have a minor effect on the different career types, our analysis shows that prime ministerial and presidential powers affect career profiles when they interact in a specific way. More precisely, the data show that party-agents are selected more frequently under strong presidents and in situations where (weak) prime ministers lack formal control over the cabinet agenda. Second, in all major European party families (Socialists, Social Democrats, Liberals, Christian Democrats and Conservatives), we observe a general trend toward the selection of more prime ministers with a party-principal career profile. Finally, contrary to this overall trend, we still find more party-agents among woman prime ministers. This result underlines that gender differences still exist in the political careers of women and men prime minister. Future studies may investigate additional factors that could impact on prime ministers' career profiles in addition to presidentialization, such as the electoral system or party regulations about the selection of party heads.

Are these observed trends toward the party-principal career profile of prime ministers likely to continue in European democracies? Our long-term investigation suggests that this may very well be the case. We also anticipate that prime ministers' career profiles will continue to converge between European regions, so that differences between 'old' and 'new' Europe will decrease. Finally, we expect that the change of career profiles will probably be conducive to a significant change in the behavior and performance of European chief executives in office. These aspects are discussed in the concluding chapter of this book.

Notes

1. The terms party-agent and party-principal refer to the relationship between prime ministers and their party *before* being appointed. See Chap. 6 for a discussion on the relationship between career profiles and behavior in office.
2. Unlike heads of parliamentary parties in government, leaders of parliamentary party groups in opposition fulfill a role of major importance within the party by acting as counterparts to the incumbent prime minister in parliament.
3. For this purpose, we use the *polychoric* package implemented for Stata (Kolenikov & Angeles, 2004).
4. The Italian case similarly reveals low levels of party-agents and party-principals in recent years. This may be explained by the presence of 'outsider' prime ministers in recent decades, who score low in both career profiles.

5. See Chap. 1 for the classification of the 26 countries according to their form of government. Slovakia turned from being a parliamentary country to a semi-presidential country in 1998. Despite this change, we decided to consider it as a semi-presidential country for the whole period, since only the first president (Michal Kováč) was elected by parliament for one term in office. Soon after the termination of his mandate, a constitutional change introduced the direct election of the president.
6. The aggregated data cover prime ministers career profiles in the semi-presidential countries of Austria, Bulgaria, Croatia, Czech Republic since 2013, Finland, France, Ireland, Lithuania, Poland, Portugal, Romania, Slovakia, and Slovenia.
7. The presidents in republican countries rank as follows from the strongest to the weakest (Doyle and Elgie 2015): Portugal (1976–1982); Finland (1995–1999); Portugal (1983–); Poland (1993–1996); France (1963–2008); Romania (1992–); Finland (1957–1994); Poland (1997–); Italy (1948–); Hungary (1991–2011); Lithuania (1993–); Croatia (2001–); Austria (1945–); Poland (1990–1992); Slovakia (2002–); Bulgaria (1992–); Ireland (1938–); Czech Republic (2001–2011); Finland (2000–2011); Slovakia (1993–1998); Slovakia (1999–2001); Czech Republic (1993–2000); Estonia (1992–); Slovenia (1992–); Germany (1946–); Greece (1986–); Bulgaria (1990–1991); Latvia (1992–1997); Latvia (1998–).
8. Prime ministers have governed in several democratic monarchies. These include: Belgium (20 prime ministers), Denmark (15 prime ministers), the Netherlands (14 prime ministers), Norway (14 prime ministers), Spain (seven prime ministers), Sweden (nine prime ministers), and United Kingdom (15 prime ministers).
9. The only Green prime minister (Indulis Emsis from Latvia) is included in the 'Liberal' category. When appointed in 2004, Emsis had been already member of parliament, cabinet minister, and party leader since the 1990s. The choice of including this Green prime minister among the Liberals is due to the common sharing of libertarian values, in terms of civil rights, between Green and Liberals and, most importantly, the fact the Latvian Green Party is conservative in economic terms.
10. One major problem when it comes to comparing career profiles of both women and men over time is that no woman was appointed before 1979. This implies that it is not possible to fully assess the long-term effects of presidentialization on the selection of women prime ministers as much as it is possible with men.
11. Since Margret Thatcher was the first woman to become prime minister in the United Kingdom in 1979, our sample in Fig. 5.17 only includes those European prime ministers who entered office for the first time in the 1970s.

References

Barnes, T. D., & O'Brien, D. Z. (2018). Defending the Realm: The Appointment of Female Defense Ministers Worldwide. *American Journal of Political Science*, 62(2), 355–368.

Bergman, T., Illonszki, G., & Müller, W. C. (2019). The Coalition Life-Cycle in Central Eastern Europe. In T. Bergman, G. Illonszki, & W. C. Müller (Eds.), *Coalition Governance in Central Eastern Europe* (pp. 522–576). Oxford University Press.

Bergman, T., Müller, W. C., Strøm, K., & Blomgren, M. (2003). Democratic Delegation and Accountability: A Cross National Pattern. In K. Strøm, W. C. Müller, & T. Bergman (Eds.), *Delegation and Accountability in Parliamentary Democracies* (pp. 109–220). Oxford University Press.

Berz, J. (2019). Potent Executives: The Electoral Strength of Prime Ministers in Central Eastern Europe. *East European Politics*, 35(4), 517–537.

Blondel, J. (2015). *The Presidential Republic*. Palgrave Macmillan.

Casal Bértoa, F. (2021). *Database on WHO GOVERNS in Europe and Beyond*. PSGo. whogoverns.eu

Casal Bértoa, F., & Mair, P. (2012). Party System Institutionalization across Time in Post-Communist Europe. In H. Keman & F. Müller-Rommel (Eds.), *Party Government in the New Europe* (pp. 85–112). Routledge.

Chiaramonte, A., & Emanuele, V. (2017). Party System Volatility, Regeneration and De-Institutionalization in Western Europe (1945–2015). *Party Politics*, 23(4), 376–388.

Dalton, R. J., Farrell, D., & McAllister, I. (2011). *Political Parties & Democratic Linkage. How Parties Organize Democracy*. Oxford University Press.

Dalton, R. J., McAllister, I., & Wattenberg, M. P. (2000). The Consequences of Partisan Dealignment. In R. J. Dalton & M. P. Wattenberg (Eds.), *Parties Without Partisans: Political Change in Advanced Industrial Democracies* (pp. 37–63). Oxford University Press.

Dolan, C. V. (1994). Factor Analysis of Variables with 2, 3, 5 and 7 Response Categories: A Comparison of Categorical Variable Estimators Using Simulated Data. *British Journal of Mathematical and Statistical Psychology*, 47(2), 309–326.

Doyle, D. (2020). Measuring Presidential and Prime Ministerial Power. In R. B. Andeweg, R. Elgie, L. Helms, J. Kaarbo, & F. Müller-Rommel (Eds.), *The Oxford Handbook of Political Executives* (pp. 382–401). Oxford University Press.

Doyle, D., & Elgie, R. (2014). Maximizing the Reliability of Cross-National Measures of Presidential Power. *British Journal of Political Science*, 46(4), 731–741.

Doyle, D., & Elgie, R. (2015). Maximizing the Reliability of Cross-National Measures of Presidential Power. https://doi.org/10.7910/DVN/28939. Harvard Dataverse, V2.

Elgie, R. (2018, April 3). Semi-Presidentialism, Premier-Presidentialism and President-Parliamentarism—A New Country-Years Dataset. *Blog Post*. http://presidential-power.com/?p=7869.

Fieldhouse, E., Green, J., Evans, G., Mellon, J., Prosser, C., Schmitt, H., & van der Eijk, C. (2020). *Electoral Shocks: The Volatile Voter in a Turbulent World*. Oxford University Press.

Goddard, D. (2019). Entering the Men's Domain? Gender and Portfolio Allocation in European Governments. *European Journal of Political Research, 58*(2), 631–655.

Holgado-Tello, F. P., Chacón-Moscoso, S., Barbero-García, I., & Vila-Abad, E. (2010). Polychoric versus Pearson Correlations in Exploratory and Confirmatory Factor Analysis of Ordinal Variables. *Quality & Quantity, 44*(1), 153–166.

Jalalzai, F. (2018). Women Heads of State and Government. In A. C. Alexander, C. Bolzendahl, & F. Jalalzai (Eds.), *Measuring Women's Political Empowerment across the Globe Strategies, Challenges and Future Research* (pp. 257–282). Palgrave Macmillan.

Kirchheimer, O. (1966). The Transformation of the Western European Party Systems. In J. La Palombara & M. Weiner (Eds.), *Political Parties and Political Development* (pp. 177–200). Princeton University Press.

Kolenikov, S., & Angeles, G. (2004). *The Use of Discrete Data in Principal Component Analysis with Applications to Socio-Economic Indices*. MEASURE/Evaluation Project Working Paper WP-04-85. Chapel Hill: Carolina Population Center, University of North Carolina.

Mair, P. (1996). Party Systems and Structures of Competition. In L. LeDuc, R. G. Niemi, & P. Norris (Eds.), *Comparing Democracies: Elections and Voting in Global Perspectives* (pp. 83–106). SAGE.

Mansbridge, J. (2009). A 'Selection Model' of Political Representation. *Journal of Political Philosophy, 17*(4), 369–398.

Müller, W. C. (2000). Political Parties in Parliamentary Democracies: Making Delegation and Accountability Work. *European Journal of Political Research, 37*(3), 309–333.

Müller-Rommel, F., & Vercesi, M. (2017). Prime Ministerial Careers in the European Union: Does Gender Make a Difference?'. *European Politics and Society, 18*(2), 245–262.

O'Brien, D. Z., Mendez, M., Carr Peterson, J., & Shin, J. (2015). Letting Down the Ladder or Shutting the Door: Female Prime Ministers, Party Leaders, and Cabinet Ministers. *Politics & Gender, 11*(4), 689–717.

Panebianco, A. (1988). *Political Parties: Organization and Power*. Cambridge University Press.

Pedersen, M. N. (1979). The Dynamics of European Party Systems: Changing Patterns of Electoral Volatility. *European Journal of Political Research, 7*(1), 1–26.

Poguntke, T., & Webb, P. (Eds.). (2005a). *The Presidentialization of Politics. A Comparative Study of Modern Democracies.* Oxford University Press.

Poguntke, T., & Webb, P. (2005b). The Presidentialization of Politics in Democratic Societies: A Framework for Analysis. In T. Poguntke & P. Webb (Eds.), *The Presidentialization of Politics. A Comparative Study of Modern Democracies* (pp. 1–25). Oxford University Press.

Raunio, T., & Sedelius, T. (2020). *Semi-Presidential Policy-Making in Europe. Executive Coordination and Political Leadership.* Palgrave Macmillan.

Samuels, D. J., & Shugart, M. S. (2010). *Presidents, Parties, and Prime Ministers. How the Separation of Powers Affects Party Organization and Behavior.* Cambridge University Press.

Schleiter, P., & Morgan-Jones, E. (2010). Who's in Charge? Presidents, Assemblies, and the Political Control of Semipresidential Cabinets. *Comparative Political Studies, 43*(11), 1415–1441.

Strøm, K. (2000). Delegation and Accountability in Parliamentary Democracies. *European Journal of Political Research, 37*(3), 261–290.

Thomson, G. H. (1951). *The Factorial Analysis of Human Ability. Fifth Edition.* University of London Press.

Weßels, B., & Klingemann, H.-D. (2006). Parties and Voters-Representative Consolidation in Central and Eastern Europe? *International Journal of Sociology, 36*(2), 11–44.

CHAPTER 6

Conclusion: What Have We Learned and What Needs to Be Done?

Prime ministers are universal in all parliamentary and semi-presidential liberal democracies. They set the tone of the government, whose political success depends to a large extent on the performance of prime ministers in office. Yet, all political activities of prime ministers are embedded in the shape and the format of party governments. Previous research confirms, however, that party governments in Europe have changed over the past seven decades (Keman & Müller-Rommel, 2012). Our novel argument is that the careers of prime ministers who ran these party governments have changed accordingly over time. Thus, the question of how the decline of party government has changed the careers of European prime ministers stands at the core of this book.

Since the 1970s the notion of party government worked as an effective heuristic concept for explaining the functioning of democratic delegation and accountability. Moreover, it served as benchmark normative concept for assessing the quality of democratic representation. In its ideal form, party government requires that cohesive parties which are electorally supported by citizens formulate public policy and operate as the prime organizations for recruiting, controlling, and holding government officials accountable. However, the ideal-type of the party government model has never fully matched with the real world. This has become most evident since the 1980s and 1990s when exogenous pressures such as the rising importance of international governance, as well as the personalization and the mediatization of politics, have gradually challenged the ideal forms of party government.

In particular, traditional parties in government have met increasing difficulties in fulfilling the contradictory demands of being both responsive toward the political preferences of their voters and responsible toward the overall demands of the state (Mair, 2009; Bardi et al., 2014). The tension between party responsiveness and party responsibility has led to a higher demand for populist and technocratic forms of representation and to the development of a so-called presidentialization of politics. Parallel to these developments, we observe that individual political leaders became the gravitational centers of electoral campaigns. Put differently, the political success of parties became less dependent on the formulation of responsive public policies by the party, but rather on the personal appeal of party leaders to the public.

We claim that these trends have three major effects on the development of careers of prime ministers: first, a decrease in prime ministers' political experiences prior to entering office; second, an increase in their technical experiences, and third, a general shift of prime ministers' career profiles from the ideal-type of 'party-agent' (defined by party reliability and apprenticeship within political institutions), to the ideal-type of 'party-principal' (defined by strong personal leadership skills and public visibility). We also suggest that these changes among the careers of prime ministers have major implications on the democratic representation and the democratic governance in contemporary European democracies.

The main contribution of this book is therefore two-fold: first, we propose a new theoretical argument that relates the decline of party government to changes in the career experiences and profiles of prime ministers in parliamentary and semi-presidential democracies. Second, we provide systematic empirical evidence to support our argument by studying the careers of 350 prime ministers in 26 European countries from 1945 to 2020.

Conclusions are not the place to be nuanced. We therefore summarize only the major results of this book and then speculate about the implication of changing prime ministers' career patterns on the processes of democratic representation and democratic governance in liberal democracies. Finally, we present some avenues for future research on prime ministers in contemporary party governments.

Key Findings

The professional career of all prime ministers is determined by their experiences acquired during lifetime. In very general terms, prime ministers are considered to hold either political or technical experiences or a combination of both. Thus, theoretically, the experience that prime ministers bring into office should vary substantially. Our empirical findings strongly support this expectation.

In a first step, we have distinguished between experiences that prime ministers gather inside or outside of politics. Our results confirm that insider prime ministers, who gathered political experiences in parliament, cabinet, or as head of the party, are by far the most dominant type compared to outsiders. However, there is also ample evidence that the number of prime ministers who entered offices with no direct political experiences has increased: overall, 8 percent of all prime ministers in Europe have been outsiders at the time of their investiture. While the number of political outsiders was almost zero before 1970, it increased to one out of five by 2010. Several of these outsiders have been prime ministers in caretaker governments, particularly in Southern Europe or in the first (founding) governments in Central and Eastern Europe in the early 1990s.

The increase of political outsiders over time is coherent with the second empirical finding in this book: the longitudinal decline of prime ministers' political experiences and the growing relative importance in prime ministers' technical experience. Our analysis shows that the majority of prime ministers have gained political experiences as members of parliament, as cabinet members, and as heads of political parties. However, their proportion decreases over time while the number of prime ministers who have gathered technical experiences—for instance in private enterprises, interest groups, state bureaucracy, or international organizations—remains stable in absolute terms. We therefore find a proportional increase in technical experiences compared to the decreasing political experiences in the careers of prime ministers. These results confirm our general expectation that the career experiences of prime ministers become relatively 'less political' and 'more technical'.

So far, both categories were examined dichotomously. However, prime ministers may have gathered political as well as technical experiences on their pathway to office. We therefore provide a classification of prime ministers' experiences on two dimensions (political and technical experiences), which consists of four types: *political veterans, technopols, technicians, and novices*. Our findings show that, particularly in Western Europe, the number of political veterans (defined by high political and low technical experience) and of *technopols* (defined by high/medium political and low/medium technical experience) decreased. This development benefitted technicians (defined by high technical and low political experiences) and novice prime ministers (defined by zero or low levels of both types of experience); the number of these two career types increased over time. We have also observed that the number of *technopols* and novices remain in the minority, while the majority of all prime ministers belong to the type of political veterans and technicians. Finally, our results show that the decrease of political veterans began in the early 1990s, slightly after the start of the decline of party government and at the beginning of the transformation of former communist countries into democratic regimes.

Around the same time, we find that the career profiles of prime ministers changed. In this book, we have differentiated between the party-agent career profile (defined by membership in parliament and/or cabinet before entering the prime ministers' office) and the party-principal profile (defined by previous leadership skills as head of the national party or as opposition leader of a parliamentary party group, and/or by former experience in international organizations). Admittedly, these are ideal-types. They nevertheless provide a first attempt to specify career profiles of prime ministers that build on previous career experiences.

Our results show that the rate of prime ministers with a party-agent career profile has decreased over time, while the rate of prime ministers with a party-principal profile remained relatively constant. Thus, we observe a relative increase of the party-principal compared to the party-agent career profile and suggest that several factors might explain the variations in these career profiles within single European countries. Among them are increasing electoral volatility between elections; different institutional setting of parliamentary versus semi-presidential systems; differences in the selection of prime ministers among the various party families; and different experiences between women and men on their way to the prime ministerial office.

Overall, our analysis shows that the party-agent type relates to low electoral volatility. As the volatility increases, the party-agent scores decrease considerably. Second, we find that institutional factors do not affect prime ministers' career profiles very much. Both career profiles are equally common in parliamentary and semi-presidential systems and not directly linked to the strength or presidential or prime ministerial constitutional powers.

Third, there is no relation between changes in both career profiles and the type of party family. All major parties have increased their selection of prime ministers with a party-principal profile over the past years. Finally, contrary to the overall trend, we find more party-agent career profiles among women than among men prime ministers.

This book started with a comparative exploration of prime ministers' individual background characteristics prior to entering office. Although that chapter is not directly linked to the overall theoretical framework about the relationship between party government and prime ministers' career experiences and career profiles, it offers valid answers to the important question of who these chief executives are. In a nutshell, our findings show that prime ministers are not an internally homogeneous group of politicians, neither socially nor politically. Rather, we find substantial differences between prime ministers in the three European regions related to their age, their gender, their education, and their occupation.

In sum, our robust empirical findings on the differences between the social background of prime ministers, their changes in the political and technical experiences as well as their career profiles over the past decades indicate that a new type of prime minister is emerging. The individual and political characteristics and experiences of this prime minister differ substantially from the ones of their predecessors.

IMPLICATIONS ON DEMOCRATIC REPRESENTATION AND DEMOCRATIC GOVERNANCE

What impact do these changes in prime ministers' career experiences and career profiles have on citizens' interest representation in European democracies? As noted in Chap. 3, political parties have been the key agents in ensuring the democratic representation of citizens over many decades. Democratic systems assure that those who rule may act in a way that matches the interests of citizens. Strong party government claims to be the best possible model to ensure a direct connection between promises made by political parties during electoral campaigns, the mandate given by voters to the party in parliament, and the resulting governmental policies (*mandate representation*). Political parties' control over the executive and their policy-making in government, together with a coherent party brand supported by electoral promises to voters, allow voters to reward and punish parties for the quality of representation.

Yet, with the decline of the traditional party government model in contemporary Europe, prime ministers have become key actors in delivering democratic representation in their own right and in addition to (if not as substitutes of) political parties. The trend toward the presidentialization of politics has fostered the executive strength of prime ministers to the detriment of political parties, who have lost much of their electoral support. The decline of social cleavages, the dealignment of voters from political parties, and the increasing amount of decision-making at the international level have made it easier for prime ministers to govern against some of the interests of their own party (Johansson & Tallberg, 2010). In this sense, prime ministers, as heads of government, have become the major players for representing the interests of the citizens to the state (responsibility role). However, prime ministers also have to represent the interests of the state to the citizens (responsive role). The balance between responsiveness and responsibility echoes the balance between democracy and efficiency (Mair, 2009, p. 7). Therefore, prime ministers determine the quality of democratic representation by acting either as responsive or responsible heads of government toward the demands of the citizens.

This book reveals that the decline of the party government model has led to an alteration in the career experiences and the career profiles of prime ministers. These changes will, in turn, lead to changing developments in democratic representation and democratic governance. This is because the shifting professional background of prime ministers is likely to affect their behavior and their role within the democratic chain of delegation and accountability, that is, as agents of political parties to principals of their cabinet government. In a nutshell, we identify four areas where changes have taken place in the democratic representation and/or in democratic governance.

First, the descriptive representation of voters by politicians with similar socio-demographic characteristics is an important element for inclusive democratic representation, in that descriptive representation increases the likelihood of responsiveness to the interests of respective social groups (Wängnerud, 2009; Dingler et al., 2019). However, as in most other democratic regimes, the socio-demographic background of European prime ministers deviates strongly from the societies which they govern. Prime ministers differ in terms of education and occupation from the majority of their voters. In other words, the general 'law of increasing disproportionality' among political elites is also valid for chief executives in European parliamentary and semi-presidential systems (Putnam, 1976, p. 33).

Yet, the changing trends in the descriptive representation of age groups and gender in prime ministers' offices signal a new phenomenon. According to our data, the share of relatively young prime ministers has increased significantly in more recent decades, particularly in smaller countries, although the average of citizens in most European countries becomes older over the same time. Similarly, the descriptive representation of women among prime ministers has improved over time. Although gender equality in appointments to the prime ministerial office has increased, our findings also show that much progress is still needed for genuine equal representation. Given that women often bring into office more extensive political experience (in particular as cabinet minister) than men, the profound differences in the levels of descriptive representation between women and men are likely to derive from discriminatory factors on the demand side of woman prime ministers rather than a shortage on the supply side. This may also explain why we observe that women prime ministers have occupied political leadership positions (e.g., the position as party head) less frequently than their male peers, leading them to be classified as party-agents rather than party-principals. Together with the pronounced party-agent profile of women prime ministers, the lower descriptive representation of women in the prime ministerial office can be interpreted as an indicator that prime ministerial paths to power remain gendered, although some parties have made efforts to introduce party quotas (Krook & Mackay, 2011). Overall, prime ministers' careers are likely to be affected by gender stereotypes and 'customized' for specific male profiles, which explains the observed differences between women and men. Therefore, inequalities between the sexes are likely to persist, which implies that prime ministers' career paths will not become 'de-gendered' any time soon. In other words, the representation of women prime ministers will remain relatively low compared to their male counterparts.

Second, the observed changes in prime ministers' political and technical experiences affect democratic governance and democratic representation. The different types of experiences that prime ministers bring with them is crucial for determining how they approach their job, which policies they pursue, how they negotiate policy compromises among actors in cabinet, and how often they delegate policy responsibilities to their ministers. Most importantly, the varying experiences of the four different types of prime ministers (*political veterans*, *technicians*, *technopols*, and *novices*) results in different balances of responsive and responsible government.

Political veterans, who are politically experienced but lack technical experience, are expected to behave more responsively to the interests of citizens in their policy-making. They have been socialized within political parties, whose aim is to maximize votes and to win elections by proposing and fulfilling policy pledges. Political veterans should therefore be more likely to reject claims from experts that run counter to public sentiment. Even if the re-election chances of politically experienced prime ministers are low, or if they have announced their pending retirement from active politics, they will be concerned about their political legacy and therefore likely to stay responsive to the interests of citizens in the remainder of their term in office. In that way, they can also leave office as popular chief executives.

In contrast, *technicians*, who are technically experienced but lack substantial political experience, are likely to be attentive to long-term needs and pursue responsible governmental policy. Technically experienced prime ministers have a mind-set attuned to the logic and arguments of other experts. Furthermore, they rely on their personal expertise, which allows them to advocate more extensively and convincingly for publicly unpopular policies.

In turn, *technopols*, being both politically and technically experienced, are most likely capable of balancing the demands of responsive and responsible government, depending on the circumstances. The balanced presence of political and technical experience among *technopols* means that for their behavior in cabinet decision-making, contextual factors are highly decisive. One of these contextual factors is, for instance, the limitation of financial public resources during the legislative term, which requires responsible governance. In contrast, upcoming parliamentary election will foster responsive policy-making, which is assumed to be more rewarding during elections.

The governmental outputs of *novice* prime ministers, who possess neither political nor technical experience, should be even more affected by contextual factors, since novices possess no major experiences of their own and are more dependent for their political success on public appeal, government advisers, and experienced party colleagues. Moreover, because they lack strong party ties or expertise, novices are more likely to change their (loose) political positions on the ideological spectrum and are therefore characterized by 'political waffling' (Castaldo & Verzichelli, 2020, p. 492). Novice prime ministers are symbols of the porosity of the political elite. In times of declining party organizations, private resources and networks become more important for prime ministers to perform successfully. Thus, in governments led by novice prime ministers, the void left by parties will be filled by those private interest groups that are strongly connected to individual politicians. Therefore, the quality of democratic representation is at risk when the novice type holds the prime ministerial office.

Third, the observed decline in the political experience among European prime ministers, in particular a decline in previous ministerial experience, affects the composition and the stability of the cabinet and thereby the sustainability of democratic governance. As the literature indicates, political career experience helps performing successfully in executive office (Alexiadou, 2015; Bright et al., 2015; Grotz et al., 2021). It is very well known that politically inexperienced prime ministers usually manage their cabinets less successfully because they have gained less experience in reaching policy compromises and in delegating tasks to other political actors. Prime ministers with little to no first-hand experience of intra-cabinet politics most often find it hard to manage and scrutinize their ministerial teams. Our observed trend of decreasing political experience among prime ministers is therefore expected to lead to increasing ministerial conflicts in cabinet decision-making. In this situation, cabinet ministers could easily deviate from the prime ministers' agenda and therefore end up by a dismissal of these ministers from cabinet. Thus, the decline of political experiences among prime ministers has an implication on the (in-)stability of cabinet government.

A continuing decline in prime ministers' political experience is also likely to further tip democratic representation in Europe toward responsible governance which leads to less government responsiveness of citizens' interests. In particular, the decline of prime ministers with direct experience in the management of cabinet government increases the likelihood that individual cabinet ministers will deviate from electoral mandates that have been secured by the government parties.

Fourth, the change in prime ministers' career profiles from the party-agent to the party-principal type leads to informal changes in the relationship between prime ministers and their parliamentary party, which affects major characteristics of democratic representation. In parliamentary and semi-presidential systems, prime ministers are expected to govern as agents 'on behalf' of their party by implementing its agenda in government. Yet, the observed increase of European prime ministers with a strong party-principal profile, who pursued an extensive career in leadership positions within their political party, gives prime ministers greater opportunities to shape the agenda of their political party prior to their investiture into office. Moreover, since party-principals are incentivized to develop an own political agenda and to build up their electoral base, they deviate from their party's agenda by seeking to increase personal publicity around popular policies that are not necessarily part of its program. Thus, our findings about the changes of prime ministers' profiles from party-agent to party-principal suggest that the probability of prime ministers to veer from the party agenda and thereby damage party mandate representation will increase over time.

In this context, it is also worth noting that one of the most effective instruments parties use to keep prime ministers accountable to the party program is the threat of a 'vote of no confidence' in parliament, which allows political parties to replace prime ministers who stray too far from the party agenda (Laver & Shepsle, 1996). Yet, if the number of prime ministers with party-principal career profiles is relatively increasing—as shown in our data—the effectiveness of this political instrument is undermined because the blackmail potential of no confidence motions is based on the credibility of finding a viable and reliable alternative prime minister. The pool of candidates with a party-principal profile is by definition limited and, therefore, the increasing demand of party-principals reduces the supply side of suitable candidates. Prime ministers with a party-principal profile have primarily developed their professional background in two political offices (party head and opposition leader), whose availability is restricted among the top political offices, while party-agents have mostly built their career profile in more accessible positions, such as members of parliament or cabinet ministers. A party-agent can therefore be more easily replaced by an equally qualified prime minister than a party-principal. This will give incumbent party-principals more room to maneuver to drifting away from the party line, without suffering significant losses of support from their political party.

In sum, the observed changes in the biographical background, the political experiences, and the career profiles of European prime ministers over the past seven decades will have major implications on the future of democratic representation and democratic governance. Thus, there are good reasons for being concerned when facing the combination of party government decline and the changes of prime ministers' careers.

Avenue for Future Research

This book carries out the first descriptive comparative analysis of prime ministers' careers in European democracies. We acknowledge that two main avenues warrant further investigation. First, future research should move from description to explanation. Scholars who study the careers of prime ministers should develop more comprehensive theories for explaining the variation of prime ministers' careers across and within parliamentary and semi-presidential systems. Second, researchers should refine and expand the empirical knowledge about prime ministers' careers.

We see a vibrant research agenda for explaining both the causes of different prime ministers' careers and the effects that these careers have on executive politics in various countries. While this book has mapped variation in individual background characteristics, political and technical experience, and career profiles of prime ministers, the empirical findings have raised several questions about why and under which circumstances prime ministers enter office. It is, for instance, still unclear to what extent psychological explanations matter for prime ministers' careers. Studies on personality traits are still dismissed as being too idiosyncratic, conceptually vague, and difficult to measure. We do, however, need more work on the personality characteristics of prime ministers since they are likely to affect both their ambition to enter a political career and their behavior in the chief executive office. It is, for instance, important to know whether personality characteristics outperform the established characteristics of prime ministers such as their political experiences and their occupational and social background as explanatory factors for prime ministers' careers.

Additionally, new insights about party gate-keepers' strategies in nominating candidates with a typical party profile *vis-à-vis* a personalized profile would enhance the ongoing debate about prime ministers' career trajectories. How do we explain that political parties increasingly select prime ministers with a party-principal profile although they cannot control them as much as those with a party-agent profile? What explains the change of prime ministerial recruitment over time and across regions in the career attributes and the career profiles that we have shown in our analysis?

Further research also needs to continue investigating the effect of institutional conditions on the careers of prime ministers. It is, for instance, important to examine how institutional settings mediate between psychological factors and different opportunity structures in parliamentary and semi-presidential systems. Do different personality traits, different degrees of party system institutionalization, or different electoral rules affect prime ministers' career profiles? In light of a an ongoing 'institutional backlash' within some Central-East European countries, future research should also address the direct or indirect nexus between certain prime ministerial career trajectories and 'defected' democracies.

Future studies should also develop more conceptual and empirical work on the effect of prime ministers' career experience and their career profile on cabinet management and governmental stability. It would, for instance, be theoretically and empirically interesting to see whether there is a systematic relationship between prime ministers' duration in office and their political and/or technical experience. Similarly, personal experiences of prime ministers might also be related to their interruption in office and their final resignation from the post. Why do some prime ministers come back after a period away from office, while others end their career after resigning?

Ultimately, one major aim of studying prime ministers' careers should also be to explain how individual trajectories are linked to the political behavior and the political success of prime ministers in office. More systematic, cross-national research is, for instance, needed for examining the effect of prime ministers' careers on their governmental performance. It would, for instance, be most valuable to examine the impact of the observed decline in prime ministers' ministerial experience on their management style in government, including the decision-making processes in cabinet. Do prime ministers with a strong party-principal profile (i.e., with developed leadership experiences in the party and parliament) treat cabinet affairs more independently from the influence of their political party? Finally, but also in this context, we propose a more normative question: what kind of prime ministerial career type do we favor in our liberal democracies? Do we want *political veterans* with high political and low technical experience, *technopols* with a high level of both, *technicians* with mostly technical and hardly any political experience, or *novice* outsiders with hardly any political and technical experiences?

The second research avenue should concentrate on the creation of an encompassing dataset on prime ministers' careers. Despite its rich dataset on the careers of all European prime ministers over seven decades, the present analysis could not cover the careers of their counterparts in parliamentary and semi-presidential systems outside of Europe. One avenue for further research would, therefore, lie in the expansion of the geographical scope, from the European-centered approach presented in this study, to a worldwide collection of data on prime ministers' careers in parliamentary and semi-presidential liberal democracies. There is still a dearth of comparative data on prime ministers' careers outside Europe. Admittedly, there are some empirical studies on the political careers of prime ministers in Japan, but hardly any comprehensive information exists on their careers in the parliamentary and semi-presidential systems of Africa, Latin America and the Caribbean, Asia, or Oceania. Thus, the limited empirical research on prime ministers in Europe hampers our ability to develop generalizable propositions about prime ministers' careers across various institutional and geographical contexts. Based on a worldwide dataset on prime ministers' careers, we need to answer questions such as: what features of prime ministers' careers are unique to European countries or shared with other parliamentary and semi-presidential democracies in other continents? What are the various career attributes and trajectories of prime ministers outside Europe and how have these features changed over time? Does the type of democracy—consensus or majoritarian—has an impact on the different prime ministerial career experiences and profiles?

Moreover, future research should not only concentrate on the single career steps but also on the length and the sequencing of the career positions occupied by prime ministers before entering office. Applying sequence analysis would allow scholars to track individual prime ministers' careers more comprehensively than simply measuring their duration in certain political positions. It would also provide new insights into the type of institutions that determines prime ministers' careers. Which pre-parliamentary, parliamentary, and governmental career paths are most common in which party family? Under which institutional conditions, and in which countries, are prime ministers more likely to engage earlier in politics? Does the order with which politicians become parliamentarians and cabinet ministers' matters for their performance in office? Does starting a professional career in the private sector and entering politics at a later stage affect the way prime ministers understand their job in office?

Furthermore, while our analysis relied primarily on the career paths of prime ministers at the national level, we have arguably only just begun to scratch the surface regarding their political experiences at the subnational and supranational levels. As indicated in Chap. 4, it might very well be that previous experiences at the local, regional, and supranational levels may influence prime ministers' behavior in government. This applies especially to prime ministers of EU member states because the 'multi-level-governance' setting provides them with more opportunities to gain experiences on their pathway to the prime ministers' office. It would, therefore, be important to refine the measurement of a prime minister's career by adding experiences at these different levels of governance.

Finally, it is not only relevant to know which positions a prime minister held outside of party politics or at the subnational and supranational levels. More importantly, we need to know how long prime ministers have served in technical positions outside the political party and in posts at the local, regional, and international levels prior to entering office. It will be extremely difficult to find cross-national data in this field of research, but it is absolutely essential to start collecting this information. Any comprehensive analysis which aims to explain the impact of prime ministers' careers on governmental politics needs these data.

The overall take-home message for future research is that scholars need to collect additional data, not only on the individual characteristics of prime ministers worldwide, but also on the institutional conditions that determine their political careers. So far, theoretical concepts as well as existing empirical studies on the origins and the impact of prime ministers' careers remain far from being comprehensive. Researchers therefore need to generate a theoretically rigorous set of propositions about the implication of prime ministers' careers on representative democracies, which should then be tested systematically by combing cross-national and longitudinal individual data on prime ministers with aggregated institutional data in single countries. This conceptual and empirical innovation would contribute substantially to our general understanding about the dynamics and the implications of prime ministers' careers in parliamentary and semi-presidential democracies. Our book is a first step in this direction.

References

Alexiadou, D. (2015). Ideologues, Partisans, and Loyalists: Cabinet Ministers and Social Welfare Reform in Parliamentary Democracies. *Comparative Political Studies, 48*(8), 1051–1086.

Bardi, L., Bartolini, S., & Trechsel, A. H. (Eds.). (2014). *Responsive and Responsible? The Role of Parties in Twenty-First Century Politics.* London: Routledge (Special Issue of *West European Politics, 37*(2)).

Bright, J., Döring, H., & Little, C. (2015). Ministerial Importance and Survival in Government: Tough at the Top? *West European Politics, 38*(3), 441–464.

Castaldo, A., & Verzichelli, L. (2020). Technocratic Populism in Italy after Berlusconi: The Trendsetter and his Disciples. *Politics and Governance, 8*(4), 485–495.

Dingler, S., Kroeber, C., & Fortin-Rittberger, J. (2019). Do Parliaments Underrepresent Women's Policy Preferences? Exploring Gender Equality in Policy Congruence in 21 European Democracies. *Journal of European Public Policy, 26*(2), 302–321.

Grotz, F., Müller-Rommel, F., Berz, J., Kroeber, C., & Kukec, M. (2021). How Political Careers affect Prime-Ministerial Performance: Evidence from Central and Eastern Europe. *Comparative Political Studies, 54*(11), 1907–1938.

Johansson, K. M., & Tallberg, J. (2010). Explaining Chief Executive Empowerment: EU Summitry and Domestic Institutional Change. *West European Politics, 33*(2), 208–236.

Keman, H., & Müller-Rommel, F. (Eds.). (2012). *Party Government in the New Europe*. Routledge.

Krook, M. L., & Mackay, F. (Eds.). (2011). *Gender, Politics and Institutions. Towards a Feminist Institutionalism*. Palgrave Macmillan.

Laver, M., & Shepsle, K. A. (1996). *Making and Breaking Governments. Cabinets and Legislatures in Parliamentary Democracies*. Cambridge University Press.

Mair, P. (2009). *Representative versus Responsible Government*. MPIfG Working Paper 09/8. Cologne: Max Planck Institute for the Study of Societies.

Putnam, R. D. (1976). *The Comparative Study of Political Elites*. Prentice Hall.

Wängnerud, L. (2009). Women in Parliaments: Descriptive and Substantive Representation. *The Annual Review of Political Science, 12*, 51–69.

Correction to: Studying Prime Ministers' Careers: An Introduction

Correction to:

Chapter 1 in: F. Müller-Rommel et al., Prime Ministers in Europe, https://doi.org/10.1007/978-3-030-90891-1_1

The original version of this chapter was revised; "the chapter numbers have been included under the section "Outline of the Book"". The book has been updated with the change.

The updated version of this chapter can be found at
https://doi.org/10.1007/978-3-030-90891-1_1

© The Author(s), under exclusive license to Springer Nature Switzerland AG 2022
F. Müller-Rommel et al., *Prime Ministers in Europe*, Palgrave Studies in Political Leadership,
https://doi.org/10.1007/978-3-030-90891-1_7

Appendix

Country Selection: Democracy Scores and Population

For country selection, we used the sample of the European Representative Democracy Data Archive (ERDDA) (Andersson, S., Bergman, T., & Ersson, S. [2014]. *The European Representative Democracy Data Archive, Release 3*. Main sponsor: Riksbankens Jubileumsfond (In 2007-0149:1-E). [www.erdda.se].), adding Croatia as the only missing member state of the European Union as of 2019.

As specified in Chap. 2, we slimmed down the resulting list according to three criteria: (1) having a parliamentary or a semi-presidential system of government; (2) being democratic—operationalized as scoring 5 or more on the Polity V scale (see notes below the list of countries)—without interruptions; and (3) having more than one-million inhabitants in 2019.

Below, we provide details about the level of democracy for the observed periods and the population of the resulting 26 countries.

Level of Democracy in 26 European Countries

Country	Democratic score
Austria, 1945	5[a]
Austria, 1946–2018	10
Belgium, 1945–1969	9
Belgium, 1970–2006	10
Belgium, 2007–2018	8
Bulgaria, 1991	7
Bulgaria, 1992–2000	8
Bulgaria, 2001–2018	9
Croatia, 2000–2004	8
Croatia, 2005–2018	9
Czech Republic, 1993–2005	10
Czech Republic, 2006–2018	9
Denmark, 1945–2018	10
Estonia, 1992–1998	7
Estonia, 1999	8
Estonia, 2000–2018	9
Finland, 1946–2018	10
France, 1959–1964	5
France, 1965–1968	7
France, 1969–1985	9
France, 1986–2018	10
Germany, 1949–2018 (Germany West, 1949–1990)	10
Greece, 1980–1985	8
Greece, 1986–2018	10
Hungary, 1990–2018	10
Ireland, 1945–1951	8
Ireland, 1952–2018	10
Italy, 1946	5[a]
Italy, 1947	8[a]
Italy, 1948–2018	10
Latvia, 1993–2018	8
Lithuania, 1991–2018	10
Netherlands, 1945–2018	10
Norway, 1945–2018	10
Poland, 1991–1994	8
Poland, 1995–2001	9
Poland, 2002–2018	10
Portugal, 1976–1981	9
Portugal, 1982–2018	10
Romania, 1992–1995	5
Romania, 1996–2003	8

(*continued*)

(continued)

Country	Democratic score
Romania, 2004–2018	9
Slovakia, 1993–1997	7
Slovakia, 1998–2005	9
Slovakia, 2006–2018	10
Slovenia, 1992–2018	10
Spain, 1977	5[a]
Spain, 1978–1981	9
Spain, 1982–2018	10
Sweden, 1945–2018	10
United Kingdom, 1945–2015	10
United Kingdom, 2016–2018	8

Notes: democratic scores are based on the composite 'democ' index from the *POLITY5: Political Regime Characteristics and Transitions, 1800–2018* dataset (Marshall, M. G., Gurr, T. R., & Jaggers, K. [2018]. *POLITY IV Project: Political Regime Characteristics and Transitions, 1800–2018. Dataset and User's Manual*. Vienna: Center for Systemic Peace). The index is based on the assessment of four aspects of the polity: the competitiveness of executive recruitment; the openness of executive recruitment; the constraint on chief executive; and the competitiveness of political participation. The index is an additive 11-point scale from 0 to 10, whereby 10 is the highest democratic level possible. Data are available until 2018

[a]These scores are based on the 'Polity2' index, which is a combined score resulting from the subtraction of autocratic scores ('autoc' index in the dataset) from the 'democ' scores, whereby –10 means fully autocratic and 10 means fully democratic. The 'Polity2' index measures the level of democracy during political transitions, for which values of the 'democ' index are not available

POPULATION IN 26 COUNTRIES, FROM THE MOST TO THE LEAST POPULATED (2019)

Country	Population (thousands)
Germany	83,132.80
France	67,059.89
United Kingdom	66,834.40
Italy	60,297.40
Spain	47,076.78
Poland	37,970.87
Romania	19,356.54
Netherlands	17,332.85
Belgium	11,484.06
Greece	10,716.32
Czech Republic	10,669.71
Sweden	10,285.45
Portugal	10,269.42
Hungary	9769.95

(continued)

(continued)

Country	Population (thousands)
Austria	8877.07
Bulgaria	6975.76
Denmark	5818.55
Finland	5520.31
Slovakia	5454.07
Norway	5347.90
Ireland	4941.44
Croatia	4067.50
Lithuania	2786.84
Slovenia	2087.95
Latvia	1912.79
Estonia	1326.59

Source: World Bank (https://data.worldbank.org/)

DATA SOURCES

The information collected to build the dataset about the background characteristics and careers of prime ministers in Europe were drawn from the following sources.

- List and types of cabinets and prime ministerial terms:
  - Annual volumes of the *European Journal of Political Research Political Data Yearbook*
  - Döring, H., & Manow, P. (2020). *Parliaments and Governments Database (ParlGov): Information on Parties, Elections and Cabinets in Modern Democracies*. Development version
  - Müller-Rommel, F., Schultze, H., Harfst, P., & Fettelschoss, K. (2008). Parteienregierungen in Mittel- und Osteuropa: Empirische Befunde im Ländervergleich (1990–2008). *Zeitschrift für Parlamentsfragen*, 39(4), 810–831
  - Woldendorp, J., Keman, H., & Budge, I. (2011). *Party Government in 40 Democracies 1945–2008. Composition-Duration-Personnel*.
- Socio-demographic background and career variables:
  - Biografías Líderes Políticos of the Barcelona Centre for International Affairs (www.cidob.org)
  - Bundeskanzler Konrad Adenauer Stiftung (www.willy-brandt.de)

- Cook, B. A. (2001). *Europe Since 1945: An Encyclopedia*. 2 volumes. Abingdon: Routledge.
- Enciclopedia Treccani (www.treccani.it)
- Encyclopedia Britannica (www.britannica.com)
- European Commission (ec.europa.eu)
- European Parliament (www.europarl.europa.eu)
- Haus der Geschichte der Bundesrepublik Deutschland Stiftung (www.hdg.de)
- Heidar, K., & Koole, R. (Eds.) (2000). *Parliamentary Party Groups in European Democracies. Political Parties Behind Closed Doors*. London: Routledge.
- Jeffries, I. (2004). *The Countries of the Former Soviet Union at the Turn of the Twenty-First Century: The Baltic and European States in Transition*. Abingdon: Routledge.
- Jensen, J. S. (2008). *Women Political Leaders. Breaking the Highest Glass Ceiling*. Basingstoke: Palgrave Macmillan.
- Kolumbus.fi
- Konrad Adenauer (www.konrad.adenauer.de)
- Konrad Adenauer Stiftung (www.kas.de)
- Lentz, H. M. (Ed.) (1994). *Heads of State and Governments. A Worldwide Encyclopedia of Over 2,300 Leaders, 1945 through 1992*. Abingdon: Routledge.
- Munzinger. Wissen, das zählt (www.munzinger.de)
- National Biography of Finland (kansallisbiografia.fi/)
- Novinite news provider (www.novinite.com)
- Odis database (www.odis.be)
- Official government, presidential, and prime ministerial websites
- Official parliamentary websites
- Official personal websites of former and incumbent prime ministers
- Official websites of political parties
- Virtual Centre for Knowledge about Europe (CVCE) (www.cvce.eu)
- Wikipedia (www.wikipedia.org) (for cross-checking).
- Zárate's Political Collections: World Political Leaders (zarate.eu/countries.htm)

List of Prime Ministers in 26 European Countries (1945–2019)

To find the names of the prime ministers, we first listed in chronological order all democratic cabinets between 1945 and 31 December 2019 in the 26 selected countries. Second, we counted all prime ministers who entered office in at least one of these cabinets, excluding acting prime ministers. Overall, we counted 354 names. For each prime minister, we searched the year of the first appointment, regardless of whether or not this year falls within the investigated period for each country or it is antecedent. For example, Winston Churchill entered office as British prime minister for the first time in 1940 (and again in 1951) and Alcide De Gasperi ruled as Italian head of government in the last months of the Reign of Italy, before the birth of the Republic in June 1946. Overall, we decided to take into account only prime ministers who were invested not earlier than 1940 and only when no democratic break occurred after their first investiture.

Accordingly, we excluded from the analysis four prime ministers: Juho Kusti Paasikivi from Finland, in office in 1918 and from 1944 to 1946; Éamon de Valera from Ireland, in office from 1932 to 1948, from 1951 to 1954, and from 1957 to 1959; Paul-Henri Spaak from Belgium, in office from 1938 to 1939, in 1946, and from 1947 to 1949; Konstantinos Karamanlis from Greece, in office from 1955 to 1958, from 1958 to 1961, from 1961 to 1963, and from 1974 to 1980.

The following list includes the resulting 350 prime ministers of the dataset. Prime ministers are clustered by country and ordered by year of first appointment, from the oldest to the newest. The 26 countries are listed in alphabetical order. Prime ministers are listed as follows: surname, given name.

Prime minister	Country	Sex	First appointment	Years (continuous) in office
Figl, Leopold	Austria	Male	1945	1945–1953
Raab, Julius	Austria	Male	1953	1953–1961
Gorbach, Alfons	Austria	Male	1961	1961–1964
Klaus, Josef	Austria	Male	1964	1964–1970
Kreisky, Bruno	Austria	Male	1970	1970–1983
Sinowatz, Fred	Austria	Male	1983	1983–1986
Vranitzky, Franz	Austria	Male	1986	1986–1997
Klima, Viktor	Austria	Male	1997	1997–2000
Schüssel, Wolfgang	Austria	Male	2000	2000–2007

(continued)

(continued)

Prime minister	Country	Sex	First appointment	Years (continuous) in office
Gusenbauer, Alfred	Austria	Male	2007	2007–2008
Faymann, Werner	Austria	Male	2008	2008–2016
Kern, Christian	Austria	Male	2016	2016–2017
Kurz, Sebastian	Austria	Male	2017	2017–2019
Bierlein, Brigitte	Austria	Female	2019	2019–
Van Acker, Achille	Belgium	Male	1945	1945–1946; 1946; 1954–1958
Huysmans, Camille	Belgium	Male	1946	1946–1947
Eyskens, Gaston	Belgium	Male	1949	1949–1950; 1958–1961; 1968–1973
Duvieusart, Jean	Belgium	Male	1950	1950
Pholien, Joseph	Belgium	Male	1950	1950–1952
Van Houtte, Jean	Belgium	Male	1952	1952–1954
Lefèvre, Théo	Belgium	Male	1961	1961–1965
Harmel, Pierre	Belgium	Male	1965	1965–1966
Vanden Boeynants, Paul	Belgium	Male	1966	1966–1968; 1978–1979
Leburton, Edmond	Belgium	Male	1973	1973–1974
Tindemans, Leo	Belgium	Male	1974	1974–1978
Martens, Wilfried	Belgium	Male	1979	1979–1981; 1981–1992
Eyskens, Mark	Belgium	Male	1981	1981
Dehaene, Jean-Luc	Belgium	Male	1992	1992–1999
Verhofstadt, Guy	Belgium	Male	1999	1999–2008
Leterme, Yves	Belgium	Male	2008	2008; 2009–2011
Van Rompuy, Herman	Belgium	Male	2008	2008–2009
Di Rupo, Elio	Belgium	Male	2011	2011–2014
Michel, Charles	Belgium	Male	2014	2014–2019
Wilmès, Sophie	Belgium	Female	2019	2019–
Dimitrov, Philip	Bulgaria	Male	1991	1991–1992
Berov, Lyuben	Bulgaria	Male	1992	1992–1994
Indzhova, Reneta	Bulgaria	Female	1994	1994–1995
Videnov, Zhan	Bulgaria	Male	1995	1995–1997
Sofiyanski, Stefan	Bulgaria	Male	1997	1997
Kostov, Ivan	Bulgaria	Male	1997	1997–2001
Saxe-Coburg-Gotha, Simeon	Bulgaria	Male	2001	2001–2005
Stanishev, Sergei	Bulgaria	Male	2005	2005–2009
Borisov, Boyko	Bulgaria	Male	2009	2009–2013;2014–2017;2017–
Raykov, Marin	Bulgaria	Male	2013	2013
Oresharski, Plamen	Bulgaria	Male	2013	2013–2014

(continued)

(continued)

Prime minister	Country	Sex	First appointment	Years (continuous) in office
Bliznashki, Georgi	Bulgaria	Male	2014	2014
Račan, Ivica	Croatia	Male	2000	2000–2003
Sanader, Ivo	Croatia	Male	2003	2003–2009
Kosor, Jadranka	Croatia	Female	2009	2009–2011
Milanović, Zoran	Croatia	Male	2011	2011–2016
Orešković, Tihomir	Croatia	Male	2016	2016
Plenković, Andrej	Croatia	Male	2016	2016–
Klaus, Václav	Czech Republic	Male	1992	1992–1998
Tošovský, Josef	Czech Republic	Male	1998	1998
Zeman, Miloš	Czech Republic	Male	1998	1998–2002
Špidla, Vladimír	Czech Republic	Male	2002	2002–2004
Gross, Stanislav	Czech Republic	Male	2004	2004–2005
Paroubek, Jiří	Czech Republic	Male	2005	2005–2006
Topolánek, Mirek	Czech Republic	Male	2006	2006–2009
Fischer, Jan	Czech Republic	Male	2009	2009–2010
Nečas, Petr	Czech Republic	Male	2010	2010–2013
Rusnok, Jiří	Czech Republic	Male	2013	2013–2014
Sobotka, Bohuslav	Czech Republic	Male	2014	2014–2017
Babiš, Andrej	Czech Republic	Male	2017	2017–
Kristensen, Knud	Denmark	Male	1945	1945–1947
Hedtoft, Hans	Denmark	Male	1947	1947–1950; 1953–1955
Eriksen, Erik	Denmark	Male	1950	1950–1953
Hansen, Hans Christian	Denmark	Male	1955	1955–1960
Kampmann, Viggo	Denmark	Male	1960	1960–1962
Krag, Jens Otto	Denmark	Male	1962	1962–1968; 1971–1972
Baunsgaard, Hilmar	Denmark	Male	1968	1968–1971
Jørgensen, Anker	Denmark	Male	1972	1972–1973; 1975–1982
Hartling, Poul	Denmark	Male	1973	1973–1975
Schlüter, Poul	Denmark	Male	1982	1982–1993

(continued)

(continued)

Prime minister	Country	Sex	First appointment	Years (continuous) in office
Rasmussen, Poul Nyrup	Denmark	Male	1993	1993–2001
Rasmussen, Anders Fogh	Denmark	Male	2001	2001–2009
Rasmussen, Lars Løkke	Denmark	Male	2009	2009–2011; 2015–2019
Thorning-Schmidt, Helle	Denmark	Female	2011	2011–2015
Frederiksen, Mette	Denmark	Female	2019	2019–
Vähi, Tiit	Estonia	Male	1992	1992; 1995–1997
Laar, Mart	Estonia	Male	1992	1992–1994; 1999–2002
Tarand, Andres	Estonia	Male	1994	1994–1995
Siimann, Mart	Estonia	Male	1997	1997–1999
Kallas, Siim	Estonia	Male	2002	2002–2003
Parts, Juhan	Estonia	Male	2003	2003–2005
Ansip, Andrus	Estonia	Male	2005	2005–2014
Rõivas, Taavi	Estonia	Male	2014	2014–2016
Ratas, Jüri	Estonia	Male	2016	2016–
Pekkala, Mauno	Finland	Male	1946	1946–1948
Fagerholm, Karl-August	Finland	Male	1948	1948–1950; 1956–1957; 1958–1959
Kekkonen, Urho	Finland	Male	1950	1950–1953; 1954–1956
Tuomioja, Sakari	Finland	Male	1953	1953–1954
Törngren, Ralf	Finland	Male	1954	1954
Sukselainen, Vieno Johannes	Finland	Male	1957	1957; 1959–1961
von Fieandt, Rainer	Finland	Male	1957	1957–1958
Kuuskoski, Reino	Finland	Male	1958	1958
Miettunen, Martti	Finland	Male	1961	1961–1962; 1975–1977
Karjalainen, Ahti	Finland	Male	1962	1962–1963; 1970–1971
Lehto, Reino Ragnar	Finland	Male	1963	1963–1964
Virolainen, Johannes	Finland	Male	1964	1964–1966
Paasio, Rafael	Finland	Male	1966	1966–1968; 1972
Koivisto, Mauno	Finland	Male	1968	1968–1970; 1979–1982
Aura, Teuvo	Finland	Male	1970	1970; 1971–1972
Sorsa, Kalevi	Finland	Male	1972	1972–1975; 1977–1979; 1982–1987
Liinamaa, Keijo	Finland	Male	1975	1975
Holkeri, Harri	Finland	Male	1987	1987–1991
Aho, Esko	Finland	Male	1991	1991–1995
Lipponen, Paavo	Finland	Male	1995	1995–2003
Jäätteenmäki, Anneli	Finland	Female	2003	2003

(continued)

(continued)

Prime minister	Country	Sex	First appointment	Years (continuous) in office
Vanhanen, Matti	Finland	Male	2003	2003–2010
Kiviniemi, Mari	Finland	Female	2010	2010–2011
Katainen, Jyrki	Finland	Male	2011	2011–2014
Stubb, Alexander	Finland	Male	2014	2014–2015
Sipilä, Juha	Finland	Male	2015	2015–2019
Rinne, Antti	Finland	Male	2019	2019
Marin, Sanna	Finland	Female	2019	2019–2020
Debré, Michel	France	Male	1959	1959–1962
Pompidou, Georges	France	Male	1962	1962–1968
Couve de Murville, Maurice	France	Male	1968	1968–1969
Chaban-Delmas, Jaques	France	Male	1969	1969–1972
Messmer, Pierre	France	Male	1972	1972–1974
Chirac, Jaques	France	Male	1974	1974–1976; 1986–1988
Barre, Raymond	France	Male	1976	1976–1981
Mauroy, Pierre	France	Male	1981	1981–1984
Fabius, Laurent	France	Male	1984	1984–1986
Rocard, Michel	France	Male	1988	1988–1991
Cresson, Édith	France	Female	1991	1991–1992
Bérégovoy, Pierre	France	Male	1992	1992–1993
Balladur, Édouard	France	Male	1993	1993–1995
Juppé, Alain	France	Male	1995	1995–1997
Jospin, Lionel	France	Male	1997	1997–2002
Raffarin, Jean-Pierre	France	Male	2002	2002–2005
de Villepin, Dominique	France	Male	2005	2005–2007
Fillon, François	France	Male	2007	2007–2012
Ayrault, Jean-Marc	France	Male	2012	2012–2014
Valls, Manuel	France	Male	2014	2014–2016
Cazeneuve, Bernard	France	Male	2016	2016–2017
Philippe, Édouard	France	Male	2017	2017–
Adenauer, Konrad	Germany	Male	1949	1949–1963
Erhard, Ludwig	Germany	Male	1963	1963–1966
Kiesinger, Kurt Georg	Germany	Male	1966	1966–1969
Brandt, Willy	Germany	Male	1969	1969–1974
Schmidt, Helmut	Germany	Male	1974	1974–1982
Kohl, Helmut	Germany	Male	1982	1982–1998
Schröder, Gerhard	Germany	Male	1998	1998–2005
Merkel, Angela	Germany	Female	2005	2005–
Rallis, Georgios	Greece	Male	1980	1980–1981

(continued)

(continued)

Prime minister	Country	Sex	First appointment	Years (continuous) in office
Papandreou, Andreas	Greece	Male	1981	1981–1989; 1993–1996
Tzannetakis, Tzannis	Greece	Male	1989	1989
Grivas, Ioannis	Greece	Male	1989	1989
Zolotas, Xenophon	Greece	Male	1989	1989–1990
Mitsotakis, Konstantinos	Greece	Male	1990	1990–1993
Simitis, Costas	Greece	Male	1996	1996–2004
Karamanlis, Kostas	Greece	Male	2004	2004–2009
Papandreou, George	Greece	Male	2009	2009–2011
Papademos, Lucas	Greece	Male	2011	2011–2012
Pikrammenos, Panagiotis	Greece	Male	2012	2012
Samaras, Antonis	Greece	Male	2012	2012–2015
Tsipras, Alexis	Greece	Male	2015	2015; 2015–2019
Thanou-Christophilou, Vassiliki	Greece	Female	2015	2015
Mitsotakis, Kyriakos	Greece	Male	2019	2019–
Antall, József	Hungary	Male	1990	1990–1993
Boross, Péter	Hungary	Male	1993	1993–1994
Horn, Gyula	Hungary	Male	1994	1994–1998
Orbán, Viktor	Hungary	Male	1998	1998–2002; 2010–
Medgyessy, Péter	Hungary	Male	2002	2002–2004
Gyurcsány, Ferenc	Hungary	Male	2004	2004–2009
Bajnai, Gordon	Hungary	Male	2009	2009–2010
Costello, John A.	Ireland	Male	1948	1948–1951; 1954–1957
Lemass, Seán	Ireland	Male	1959	1959–1966
Lynch, John M. (known as Jack)	Ireland	Male	1966	1966–1973; 1977–1979
Cosgrave, Liam	Ireland	Male	1973	1973–1977
Haughey, Charles	Ireland	Male	1979	1979–1981; 1982; 1987–1992
FitzGerald, Garret	Ireland	Male	1981	1981–1982; 1982–1987
Reynolds, Albert	Ireland	Male	1992	1992–1994
Bruton, John	Ireland	Male	1994	1994–1997
Ahern, Bertie	Ireland	Male	1997	1997–2008
Cowen, Brian	Ireland	Male	2008	2008–2011
Kenny, Enda	Ireland	Male	2011	2011–2017
Varadkar, Leo	Ireland	Male	2017	2017–
De Gasperi, Alcide	Italy	Male	1945	1945–1953
Pella, Giuseppe	Italy	Male	1953	1953–1954

(continued)

(continued)

Prime minister	Country	Sex	First appointment	Years (continuous) in office
Fanfani, Amintore	Italy	Male	1954	1954; 1958–1959; 1960–1963; 1982–1983; 1987
Scelba, Mario	Italy	Male	1954	1954–1955
Segni, Antonio	Italy	Male	1955	1955–1957; 1959–1960
Zoli, Adone	Italy	Male	1957	1957–1958
Tambroni, Fernando	Italy	Male	1960	1960
Leone, Giovanni	Italy	Male	1963	1963; 1968
Moro, Aldo	Italy	Male	1963	1963–1968; 1974–1976
Rumor, Mariano	Italy	Male	1968	1968–1970; 1973–1974
Colombo, Emilio	Italy	Male	1970	1970–1972
Andreotti, Giulio	Italy	Male	1972	1972–1973; 1976–1979; 1989–1992
Cossiga, Francesco	Italy	Male	1979	1979–1980
Forlani, Arnaldo	Italy	Male	1980	1980–1981
Spadolini, Giovanni	Italy	Male	1981	1981–1982
Craxi, Bettino	Italy	Male	1983	1983–1987
Goria, Giovanni	Italy	Male	1987	1987–1988
De Mita, Ciriaco	Italy	Male	1988	1988–1989
Amato, Giuliano	Italy	Male	1992	1992–1993; 2000–2001
Ciampi, Carlo Azeglio	Italy	Male	1993	1993–1994
Berlusconi, Silvio	Italy	Male	1994	1994–1995; 2001–2006; 2008–2011
Dini, Lamberto	Italy	Male	1995	1995–1996
Prodi, Romano	Italy	Male	1996	1996–1998; 2006–2008
D'Alema, Massimo	Italy	Male	1998	1998–2000
Monti, Mario	Italy	Male	2011	2011–2013
Letta, Enrico	Italy	Male	2013	2013–2014
Renzi, Matteo	Italy	Male	2014	2014–2016
Gentiloni, Paolo	Italy	Male	2016	2016–2018
Conte, Giuseppe	Italy	Male	2018	2018–
Godmanis, Ivars	Latvia	Male	1990	1990–1993; 2007–2009
Birkavs, Valdis	Latvia	Male	1993	1993–1994
Gailis, Māris	Latvia	Male	1994	1994–1995
Šķēle, Andris	Latvia	Male	1995	1995–1997; 1999–2000
Krasts, Guntars	Latvia	Male	1997	1997–1998
Krištopans, Vilis	Latvia	Male	1998	1998–1999
Bērziņš, Andris	Latvia	Male	2000	2000–2002
Repše, Einars	Latvia	Male	2002	2002–2004
Emsis, Indulis	Latvia	Male	2004	2004
Kalvītis, Aigars	Latvia	Male	2004	2004–2007

(continued)

(continued)

Prime minister	Country	Sex	First appointment	Years (continuous) in office
Dombrovskis, Valdis	Latvia	Male	2009	2009–2014
Straujuma, Laimdota	Latvia	Female	2014	2014–2016
Kučinskis, Māris	Latvia	Male	2016	2016–2019
Kariņš, Arturs Krišjānis	Latvia	Male	2019	2019–
Vagnorius, Gediminas	Lithuania	Male	1991	1991–1992; 1996–1999
Lubys, Bronislovas	Lithuania	Male	1992	1992–1993
Šleževičius, Adolfas	Lithuania	Male	1993	1993–1996
Stankevičius, Laurynas	Lithuania	Male	1996	1996
Paksas, Rolandas	Lithuania	Male	1999	1999; 2000–2001
Kubilius, Andrius	Lithuania	Male	1999	1999–2000; 2008–2012
Brazauskas, Algirdas	Lithuania	Male	2001	2001–2006
Kirkilas, Gediminas	Lithuania	Male	2006	2006–2008
Butkevičius, Algirdas	Lithuania	Male	2012	2012–2016
Skvernelis, Saulius	Lithuania	Male	2016	2016–
Beel, Louis	Netherlands	Male	1946	1946–1948; 1958–1959
Drees, Willem	Netherlands	Male	1948	1948–1958
de Quay, Jan	Netherlands	Male	1959	1959–1963
Marijnen, Victor	Netherlands	Male	1963	1963–1965
Cals, Jo	Netherlands	Male	1965	1965–1966
Zijlstra, Jelle	Netherlands	Male	1966	1966–1967
de Jong, Piet	Netherlands	Male	1967	1967–1971
Biesheuvel, Barend	Netherlands	Male	1971	1971–1973
den Uyl, Joop	Netherlands	Male	1973	1973–1977
van Agt, Dries	Netherlands	Male	1977	1977–1982
Lubbers, Ruud	Netherlands	Male	1982	1982–1994
Kok, Wim	Netherlands	Male	1994	1994–2002
Balkenende, Jan Pieter	Netherlands	Male	2002	2002–2010
Rutte, Mark	Netherlands	Male	2010	2010–
Gerhardsen, Einar	Norway	Male	1945	1945–1951; 1955–1963; 1963–1965
Torp, Oscar	Norway	Male	1951	1951–1955
Lyng, John	Norway	Male	1963	1963
Borten, Per	Norway	Male	1965	1965–1971
Bratteli, Trygve	Norway	Male	1971	1971–1972; 1973–1976
Korvald, Lars	Norway	Male	1972	1972–1973
Nordli, Odvar	Norway	Male	1976	1976–1981
Harlem Brundtland, Gro	Norway	Female	1981	1981; 1986–1989; 1990–1996

(continued)

(continued)

Prime minister	Country	Sex	First appointment	Years (continuous) in office
Willoch, Kåre	Norway	Male	1981	1981–1986
Syse, Jan P.	Norway	Male	1989	1989–1990
Jagland, Thorbjørn	Norway	Male	1996	1996–1997
Bondevik, Kjell Magne	Norway	Male	1997	1997–2000; 2001–2005
Stoltenberg, Jens	Norway	Male	2000	2000–2001; 2005–2013
Solberg, Erna	Norway	Female	2013	2013–
Olszewski, Jan	Poland	Male	1991	1991–1992
Suchocka, Hanna	Poland	Female	1992	1992–1993
Pawlak, Waldemar	Poland	Male	1993	1993–1995
Oleksy, József	Poland	Male	1995	1995–1996
Cimoszewicz, Włodzimierz	Poland	Male	1996	1996–1997
Buzek, Jerzy	Poland	Male	1997	1997–2001
Miller, Leszek	Poland	Male	2001	2001–2004
Belka, Marek	Poland	Male	2004	2004–2005
Marcinkiewicz, Kazimierz	Poland	Male	2005	2005–2006
Kaczyński, Jarosław	Poland	Male	2006	2006–2007
Tusk, Donald	Poland	Male	2007	2007–2014
Kopacz, Ewa	Poland	Female	2014	2014–2015
Szydło, Beata	Poland	Female	2015	2015–2017
Morawiecki, Mateusz	Poland	Male	2017	2017–
Soares, Mário	Portugal	Male	1976	1976–1978; 1983–1985
Nobre da Costa, Alfredo	Portugal	Male	1978	1978
Mota Pinto, Carlos	Portugal	Male	1978	1978–1979
Pintasilgo, Maria de Lourdes	Portugal	Female	1979	1979–1980
de Sá Carneiro, Francisco	Portugal	Male	1980	1980
Pinto Balsemão, Francisco	Portugal	Male	1981	1981–1983
Cavaco Silva, Aníbal	Portugal	Male	1985	1985–1995
Guterres, António	Portugal	Male	1995	1995–1902
Barroso, José Manuel	Portugal	Male	2002	2002–2004
Santana Lopes, Pedro	Portugal	Male	2004	2004–2005
Sócrates, José	Portugal	Male	2005	2005–2011
Passos Coelho, Pedro	Portugal	Male	2011	2011–2015
Costa, António	Portugal	Male	2015	2015–

(continued)

(continued)

Prime minister	Country	Sex	First appointment	Years (continuous) in office
Văcăroiu, Nicolae	Romania	Male	1992	1992–1996
Ciorbea, Victor	Romania	Male	1996	1996–1998
Dejeu, Gavril	Romania	Male	1998	1998
Vasile, Radu	Romania	Male	1998	1998–1999
Athanasiu, Alexandru	Romania	Male	1999	1999
Isărescu, Mugur	Romania	Male	1999	1999–2000
Năstase, Adrian	Romania	Male	2000	2000–2004
Popescu-Tăriceanu, Călin	Romania	Male	2004	2004–2008
Boc, Emil	Romania	Male	2008	2008–2012
Ungureanu, Mihai Răzvan	Romania	Male	2012	2012
Ponta, Victor	Romania	Male	2012	2012–2015
Cîmpeanu, Sorin	Romania	Male	2015	2015
Cioloş, Dacian	Romania	Male	2015	2015–2017
Grindeanu, Sorin	Romania	Male	2017	2017
Tudose, Mihai	Romania	Male	2017	2017–2018
Dăncilă, Viorica	Romania	Female	2018	2018–2019
Orban, Ludovic	Romania	Male	2019	2019–
Mečiar, Vladimír	Slovakia	Male	1992	1992–1994; 1994–1998
Moravčík, Jozef	Slovakia	Male	1994	1994
Dzurinda, Mikuláš	Slovakia	Male	1998	1998–2006
Fico, Robert	Slovakia	Male	2006	2006–2010; 2012–2018
Radičová, Iveta	Slovakia	Female	2010	2010–2012
Pellegrini, Peter	Slovakia	Male	2018	2018–
Drnovšek, Janez	Slovenia	Male	1992	1992–2000; 2000–2002
Bajuk, Andrej	Slovenia	Male	2000	2000
Rop, Anton	Slovenia	Male	2002	2002–2004
Janša, Janez	Slovenia	Male	2004	2004–2008; 2012–2013
Pahor, Borut	Slovenia	Male	2008	2008–2012
Bratušek, Alenka	Slovenia	Female	2013	2013–2014
Cerar, Miro	Slovenia	Male	2014	2014–2018
Šarec, Marjan	Slovenia	Male	2018	2018–
Suárez, Adolfo	Spain	Male	1976	1976–1981
Calvo-Sotelo, Leopoldo	Spain	Male	1981	1981–1982
González, Felipe	Spain	Male	1982	1982–1996
Aznar, José María	Spain	Male	1996	1996–2004
Rodríguez Zapatero, José Luis	Spain	Male	2004	2004–2011
Rajoy, Mariano	Spain	Male	2011	2011–2018
Sánchez, Pedro	Spain	Male	2018	2018–

(continued)

(continued)

Prime minister	Country	Sex	First appointment	Years (continuous) in office
Erlander, Tage	Sweden	Male	1946	1946–1969
Palme, Olof	Sweden	Male	1969	1969–1976; 1982–1986
Fälldin, Thorbjörn	Sweden	Male	1976	1976–1978; 1979–1982
Ullsten, Ola	Sweden	Male	1978	1978–1979
Carlsson, Ingvar	Sweden	Male	1986	1986–1991; 1994–1996
Bildt, Carl	Sweden	Male	1991	1991–1994
Persson, Göran	Sweden	Male	1996	1996–2006
Reinfeldt, Fredrik	Sweden	Male	2006	2006–2014
Löfven, Stefan	Sweden	Male	2014	2014–
Churchill, Winston	United Kingdom	Male	1940	1940–1945; 1951–1955
Attlee, Clement	United Kingdom	Male	1945	1945–1951
Eden, Anthony	United Kingdom	Male	1955	1955–1957
Macmillan, Harold	United Kingdom	Male	1957	1957–1963
Douglas-Home, Alec	United Kingdom	Male	1963	1963–1964
Wilson, Harold	United Kingdom	Male	1964	1964–1970; 1974–1976
Heath, Edward	United Kingdom	Male	1970	1970–1974
Callaghan, James	United Kingdom	Male	1976	1976–1979
Thatcher, Margaret	United Kingdom	Female	1979	1979–1990
Major, John	United Kingdom	Male	1990	1990–1997
Blair, Anthony (known as Tony)	United Kingdom	Male	1997	1997–2007
Brown, Gordon	United Kingdom	Male	2007	2007–2010
Cameron, David	United Kingdom	Male	2010	2010–2016
May, Theresa	United Kingdom	Female	2016	2016–2019
Johnson, Boris	United Kingdom	Male	2019	2019–

Codebook for Identifying Prime Ministerial Background Variables and Career Patterns

DATASET: Prime Ministers in Europe. Changing Career Experiences and Profiles
Authors: Ferdinand Müller-Rommel, Michelangelo Vercesi, Jan Berz
Dataset publicly available on *Harvard Dataverse*, https://doi.org/10.7910/DVN/QX26VI

The dataset includes information about the socio-demographic background, occupations, and political careers of prime ministers in European liberal democracies from 1945 to 31 December 2019. The last update was made on 31 January 2020. The units of observation are individual prime ministers. Prime ministers' terms in office are counted whenever one or more of the following conditions apply: change in the cabinet party composition, change of prime minister, general election, and meaningful resignation.

var1	INDIVIDUAL ID	
	Country ID plus the nth prime minister of the country	
	Annotations: ordered by first observed prime minister since 1945	
var2	PM NAME	
	Surname of prime minister	
var3	COUNTRY	
	(1) Austria	
	(2) Belgium	
	(3) Bulgaria	
	(4) Croatia	
	(5) Czech Republic	
	(6) Denmark	
	(7) Estonia	
	(8) Finland	
	(9) France	
	(10) Germany	
	(11) Greece	
	(12) Hungary	
	(13) Ireland	
	(14) Italy	
	(15) Latvia	
	(16) Lithuania	
	(17) Netherlands	
	(18) Norway	
	(19) Poland	
	(20) Portugal	
	(21) Romania	

(*continued*)

(continued)

	(22) Slovakia
	(23) Slovenia
	(24) Spain
	(25) Sweden
	(26) United Kingdom
var4	SEX
	(1) Female
	(2) Male
var5	AGE WHEN ENTERING OFFICE AS PM FOR THE FIRST TIME (IN YEARS)
var6	FIRST OCCUPATION
	(1) Blue-collar employee (factory worker/operative)
	(2) Cadre/engineer/technician
	(3) Industry/business
	(4) Capital market/banking
	(5) Legal profession (lawyer/judge)
	(6) Journalist/media/artist
	(7) Teacher
	(8) University teacher/professor or equivalent
	(9) Civil servant
	(10) Political consultant
	(11) Full-time politician
	(12) Full-time union official
	(−66) Other
	(−1) Not known
var7	OCCUPATION WHEN ENTERING OFFICE AS PM FOR THE FIRST TIME
	(1) Blue-collar employee (factory worker/operative)
	(2) Cadre/engineer/technician
	(3) Industry/business
	(4) Capital market/banking
	(5) Legal profession (lawyer/judge)
	(6) Journalist/media/artist
	(7) Teacher
	(8) University teacher/professor or equivalent
	(9) Civil servant
	(10) Political consultant
	(11) Full-time politician
	(12) Full-time union official
	(−1) Not known
	(−66) Other
var8	UNIVERSITY DEGREE
	Annotations: mixed title indicates multidisciplinary degrees or cases of two or more obtained degrees. Honoris causa degrees excluded
	(1) Agriculture/forestry
	(2) Medicine/psychology
	(3) Biology/chemistry/biotechnology

(continued)

(continued)

        (4) Mathematics/physics/informatics/geosciences
        (5) Engineering
        (6) Architecture
        (7) Pedagogics/teaching
        (8) Languages/philology/literature/music
        (9) History/philosophy
        (10) Theology
        (11) Political science/sociology
        (12) Journalism
        (13) Economics/business administration/finance
        (14) Law/public administration
        (15) Mixed title
        (−1) Not known
        (−66) Other
        (−88) Not available
        (−99) Not applicable
var9 MEMBER OF POLITICAL ASSEMBLY AND/OR EXECUTIVE—LOCAL/REGIONAL
        (0) No
        (1) Yes, head
        (2) Yes, member
        (3) Yes, both
        (−1) Not known
        (−66) Other
        (−88) Not available
        (−99) Not applicable
var10 MEMBER OF THE NATIONAL PARLIAMENT WHEN ENTERING OFFICE AS PM (FIRST CHAMBER)
        (0) No
        (1) Yes
        (−66) Other
        (−88) Not available
        (−99) Not applicable
var11 DURATION AS MEMBER OF NATIONAL PARLIAMENT PRIOR TO BECOMING PM IN MONTHS (FIRST CHAMBER)
        Annotations: continuous or discontinuous. Where applicable, no days counted during the occupation of another position, which is incompatible with a seat in parliament
        (−88) Not available
var12 PARTY HEAD PRIOR TO BECOMING PM
        (0) No
        (1) Yes (national)
        (−1) Not known
        (−66) Other
        (−88) Not available

(*continued*)

(continued)

var13	OFFICE HELD IN NATIONAL INTEREST GROUPS PRIOR TO BECOMING PM (HEAD) (0) No (1) Yes, in union (2) Yes, in employers' organization (3) Yes, in interest group (others) (4) Yes, in more than one of the above (−1) Not known (−66) Other (−88) Not available
var14	SENIOR CIVIL SERVANT PRIOR TO BECOMING PM (0) No (1) Yes (−1) Not known (−66) Other (−88) Not available
var15	MEMBER OF PUBLIC ENTERPRISE PRIOR TO BECOMING PM *Annotations: only top positions* (0) No (1) Yes (−1) Not known (−66) Other (−88) Not available
var16	MEMBER OF PRIVATE ENTERPRISE PRIOR TO BECOMING PM *Annotations: only top positions* (0) No (1) Yes (−1) Not known (−66) Other (−88) Not available
var17	MEMBER OF INTERNATIONAL ORGANIZATION PRIOR TO BECOMING PM (0) No (1) Yes (−1) Not known (−66) Other (−88) Not available
var18	MEMBER OF EUROPEAN INSTITUTION PRIOR TO BECOMING PM (0) No (1) Yes (−1) Not known (−66) Other (−88) Not available
var19	AMBASSADOR/DIPLOMAT PRIOR TO BECOMING PM (0) No

(*continued*)

(continued)

        (1) Yes, ambassador
        (2) Yes, diplomat (or consul)
        (3) Yes, both
        (−1) Not known
        (−66) Other
        (−88) Not available
        (−99) Not applicable
var20 REASON FOR LEAVING PM POSITION (FIRST PM TERM ONLY)
        (0) End of term: conclusive
        (1) End of term: returning immediately
        (2) End of term: returning at later point
        (3) Other
        (−1) Not known
        (−88) Not available
        (−99) Not applicable
var21 PM DURATION IN OFFICE IN MONTHS (TOTAL)
var22 PM PARTY FAMILY
        (1) Communist
        (2) Social Democrat
        (3) Green
        (4) Liberal
        (5) Conservative
        (6) Christian Democrat
        (7) Agrarian
        (8) Right-wing and nationalist
        (−66) Other
        (−99) Not applicable
var23 MINISTERIAL POST HELD PRIOR TO BECOMING PM (FINANCE/TREASURY)
        (0) No
        (1) Yes
        (−1) Not known
        (−88) Not available
Var24 MINISTERIAL POST HELD PRIOR TO BECOMING PM (ECONOMY)
        (0) No
        (1) Yes
        (−1) Not known
        (−88) Not available
var25 MINISTERIAL POST HELD PRIOR TO BECOMING PM (JUSTICE)
        (0) No
        (1) Yes
        (−1) Not known
        (−88) Not available
var26 MINISTERIAL POST HELD PRIOR TO BECOMING PM (FOREIGN AFFAIRS)

(continued)

(continued)

	(0) No
	(1) Yes
	(−1) Not known
	(−88) Not available
var27	MINISTERIAL POST HELD PRIOR TO BECOMING PM (DEFENCE)
	(0) No
	(1) Yes
	(−1) Not known
	(−88) Not available
var28	MINISTERIAL POST HELD PRIOR TO BECOMING PM (INTERIOR)
	(0) No
	(1) Yes
	(−1) Not known
	(−88) Not available
var29	MINISTERIAL POST HELD PRIOR TO BECOMING PM (LABOR/SOCIAL AFFAIRS)
	(0) No
	(1) Yes
	(−1) Not known
	(−88) Not available
Var30	MINISTERIAL POST HELD PRIOR TO BECOMING PM (EUROPEAN AFFAIRS)
	(0) No
	(1) Yes
	(−1) Not known
	(−88) Not available
var31	MINISTERIAL POST HELD PRIOR TO BECOMING PM (OTHER)
	(0) No
	(1) Yes
	(−1) Not known
	(−88) Not available
var32	TOTAL NUMBER OF MINISTERIAL POSTS HELD PRIOR TO BECOMING PM
	Annotations: based on variables 23–31
var33	TOTAL DURATION OF MINISTERIAL POSTS IN MONTHS
var34	OPPOSITION LEADER OF PARLIAMENTARY PARTY PRIOR TO BECOMING PM (FIRST CHAMBER)
	(0) No
	(1) Yes
	(−1) Not known
	(−88) Not available
var35	PARTY LEADER WHILE BEING PM
	(0) No
	(1) Yes (predominantly)
	(−1) Not known

(*continued*)

(continued)

  (–88) Not available
var36 NUMBER OF TERMS (CABINETS) IN OFFICE AS PM
var37 NUMBER OF SINGLE-PARTY MAJORITY CABINETS THAT PM DIRECTED
var38 NUMBER OF MINIMAL WINNING COALITION CABINETS THAT PM DIRECTED
var39 NUMBER OF SURPLUS COALITION CABINETS THAT PM DIRECTED
var40 NUMBER OF SINGLE-PARTY MINORITY CABINETS THAT PM DIRECTED
var41 NUMBER OF MULTI-PARTY MINORITY CABINETS THAT PM DIRECTED
var42 NUMBER OF CARETAKER CABINETS THAT PM DIRECTED
var43 WESTERN/CENTRAL AND EASTERN EUROPE
  Annotations: Western Europe includes also Greece, Portugal, and Spain
  (1) Western Europe
  (2) Central and Eastern Europe
var44 FIRST OCCUPATION, CATEGORIES
  (1) (University) teacher
  (2) Civil servant
  (3) Full-time politicians
  (4) Legal profession
  (5) Business/banking
  (6) Political consultant
  (7) Other
  (–88) Not available
var45 FULL-TIME POLITICIAN WHEN ENTERING OFFICE AS PM FOR THE FIRST TIME
  (1) Full-time politician
  (2) Other
  (–88) Not available
var46 UNIVERSITY DEGREE, CATEGORIES
  (1) Natural sciences/mechanical engineers
  (2) Other social sciences/humanities
  (3) Economics/law
  (4) Mixed title
var47 MEMBER OF POLITICAL ASSEMBLY
  (0) No
  (1) Yes
var48 TOTAL DURATION AS MEMBER OF PARLIAMENT IN YEARS
var49 OFFICE HELD IN NATIONAL INTEREST GROUPS
  (0) No
  (1) Yes
var50 AMBASSADOR/DIPLOMAT
  (0) No
  (1) Yes

(continued)

(continued)

var51	PM DURATION IN CATEGORIES	

    var51 PM DURATION IN CATEGORIES
           (1) Duration below 1 year
           (2) Duration between 1 and 3 years
           (3) Duration between 3 and 4 years
           (4) Duration between 4 and 6 years
           (5) Duration between 6 and 8 years
           (6) Above 8 years
    var52 TOTAL DURATION OF MINISTERIAL POSTS IN YEARS
    var53 PM POLITICAL EXPERIENCE CAPITAL BY TYPES
           (1) Party head, member of parliament, cabinet member
           (2) Party head, member of parliament
           (3) Party head, cabinet member
           (4) Party head
           (5) Cabinet member
           (6) Member of parliament
           (7) Cabinet member, member of parliament
           (8) None
    var54 PM DURING COUNTRY TRANSITION
           Annotations: transition as 10-year period
           (0) No
           (1) Yes
    var55 REGIME TYPE
           (1) Parliamentary
           (2) Semi-presidential
    var56 PM INSIDER OUTSIDER
           (1) Party head, member of parliament, cabinet member
           (2) Party head, member of parliament
           (3) Party head, cabinet member
           (4) Cabinet member, member of parliament
           (5) Party head
           (6) Member of parliament
           (7) Cabinet member, party member
           (8) Cabinet member, no party member
           (9) None
    var57 PARTY POLITICS INSIDER
           (0) No
           (1) Yes
    var58 TOTAL NUMBER OF INTERRUPTIONS OF BETWEEN TERMS AS PM
    var59 PARTY HEAD PRIOR TO PM OFFICE, BUT NOT WHILE BEING PM
           (0) No
           (1) Yes
           (−88) Not applicable
    var60 YEAR OF FIRST APPOINTMENT AS PM FOR THE FIRST TIME
    var61 DECADE OF PM MAIN ACTIVITY, WESTERN EUROPE
           (1) 1945–1960

(continued)

(continued)

      (2) 1961–1970
      (3) 1971–1980
      (4) 1981–1990
      (5) 1991–2000
      (6) 2001–2010
      (7) 2011–2019
var62 DECADE OF PM MAIN ACTIVITY, SOUTHERN EUROPE
      (1) 1974–1980
      (2) 1981–1990
      (3) 1991–2000
      (4) 2001–2010
      (5) 2011–2019
var63 DECADE OF PM MAIN ACTIVITY, CENTRAL-EASTERN EUROPE
      (1) 1989–2000
      (2) 2001–2010
      (3) 2011–2019
var64 CURRENTLY HOLDING OFFICE
      (0) No
      (1) Yes
var65 DURATION AS PARTY HEAD PRIOR TO BECOMING PM FOR THE FIRST TIME IN MONTHS
      Annotations: continuous or discontinuous. 0 means less than one month, but still party head
      (–88) Not available
      (–99) Not applicable
var66 DECADE WHEN ENTERING OFFICE AS PM FOR THE FIRST TIME
      (1) Before 1960
      (2) 1961–1970
      (3) 1971–1980
      (4) 1981–1990
      (5) 1991–2000
      (6) 2001–2010
      (7) 2011–2020
var67 HELD LOW PRESTIGE MINISTERIAL OFFICE PRIOR TO FIRST INVESTITURE
      (0) No
      (1) Yes
var68 HELD HIGH PRESTIGE MINISTERIAL OFFICE PRIOR TO FIRST INVESTITURE
      (0) No
      (1) Yes
var69 DIRECT PRESIDENTIAL ELECTION/SEMI-PRESIDENTIAL SYSTEM
      (0) Parliamentary system
      (1) Semi-presidential system

(continued)

(continued)

var70	PRIME MINISTERIAL POWER INDEX	
var71	PRIME MINISTER AGENDA SETTING POWER	
	(0) No control over cabinet agenda	
	(1) Control over cabinet agenda	
var72	DURATION AS MEMBER OF THE EUROPEAN PARLIAMENT PRIOR TO ENTERING OFFICE AS PM FOR THE FIRST TIME IN MONTHS	
	Annotations: continuous or discontinuous.	
var73	DURATION AS MEMBER OF THE EUROPEAN COMMISSION PRIOR TO ENTERING OFFICE AS PM FOR THE FIRST TIME IN MONTHS	
	Annotations: continuous or discontinuous.	
var74	PARTY-PRINCIPAL TYPE SCORE	
	Annotations: regression score prediction from factor analysis	
var75	PARTY-AGENT TYPE SCORE	
	Annotations: regression score prediction from factor analysis	
var76	PRESIDENTIAL POWER 1	
	Annotations: Prespow1, mean method (Doyle and Elgie's [2015] measure)	
var77	PRESIDENTIAL POWER 2	
	Annotations: Prespow2, matrix method (Doyle and Elgie's [2015] measure)	
var78	TECHNICAL EXPERIENCE INDEX	
	Annotations: ordinal measure	
var79	TOTAL NATIONAL POLITICAL EXPERIENCE	
	Annotations: sum of standardized duration as party head, member of parliament, cabinet member	
var80	NAME OF EUROPEAN POSITION	
	Annotations: string, name of the position, based on var18	

EIGENVALUES IN THE FACTOR ANALYSIS, ELECTORAL VOLATILITY, AND PARTY FAMILY FINDINGS BY REGION

The factor analysis in Chap. 5 has confirmed the existence of two main types (i.e., factors) of political career profiles (party-agent and party-principal) among European prime ministers. Figure A1 shows the scree plot of the related eigenvalues. The figure provides evidence that only two factors with values higher than one are detectable in the dataset.

In Chap. 5, we have also investigated the relationship between electoral volatility and these two career profiles. Figure A2 provides information about the electoral volatility in the election antecedent to the first appointment of all prime ministers for each country, proving that electoral volatility has increased in most countries over time.

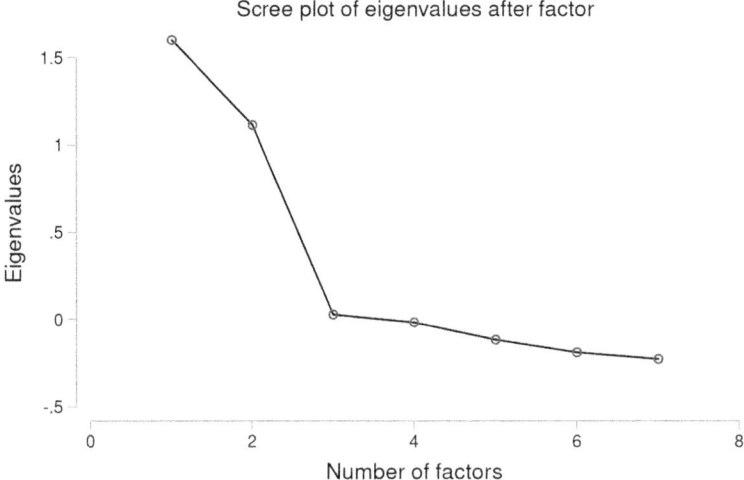

Fig. A1 Eigenvalues of the correlation matrix show only two factors with values above one

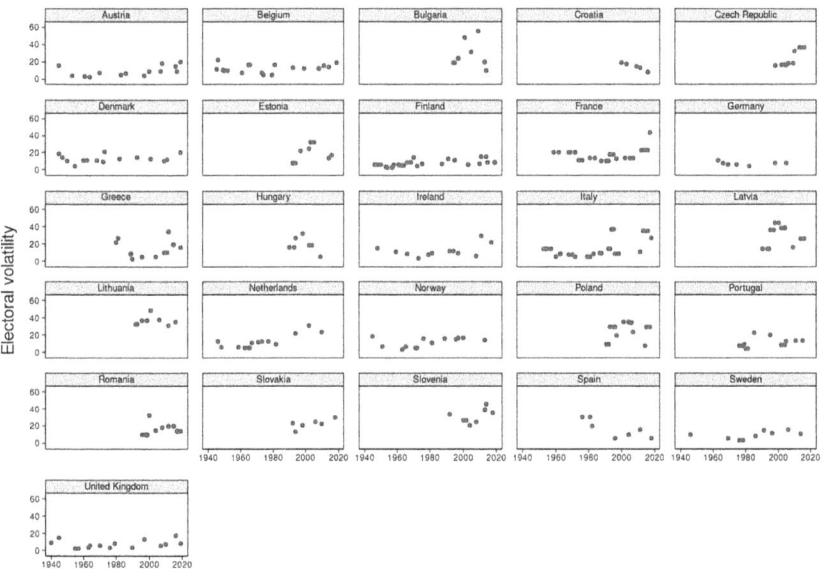

Fig. A2 Electoral volatility at the time of prime ministers' first investiture into office

Index[1]

A
Accountability, 4, 11, 79, 186
Adenauer, Konrad, 34, 89, 117
Agenda-setting power, 5
Agrarians, 167
Aho, Esko, 37
Ambitious politicians, 66
Antall, József, 109, 122
Anti-establishment, 85
Anti-system, 93n5
ATO Parliamentary Assembly, 139
Aznar, José María, 115

B
Babiš, Andrej, 86, 88
Bajnai, Gordon, 144
Barre, Raymond, 51, 119
Barroso, José Manuel, 115
Belka, Marek, 139
Berlusconi, Silvio, 79, 86, 90, 113

Bierlein, Brigitte, 32, 51, 106
Biesheuvel, Barend, 119
Biographies, 9
Blair, Tony, 90
Bondevik, Kjell Magne, 144
Borisov, Boyko, 117
Brandt, Willy, 117
Bratušek, Alenka, 32
Brundtland, Gro Harlem, 32
Buzek, Jerzy, 113

C
Cabinet, 66
  decision-making, 188
  experiences, 102
  government, 67
  members, 183
  ministers, 69, 85, 138, 141
  politics, 66
  portfolio, 49

[1] Note: Page numbers followed by 'n' refer to notes.

Calvo-Sotelo, Leopoldo, 115
Career background, 66
Career experiences, 65, 66,
    75, 84, 101
Career paths, 66, 102
Career politicians, 2
Career profiles, 67, 75, 91, 101, 136
Career types, 14, 127
Caretaker governments, 183
Center of government, 2
Centralization of power, 89
Challenger parties, 67
Chancellor, 106
Chief executives, 82, 87, 114
Christian Democratic, 168
Christian Democratic parties, 82
Churchill, Winston, 34, 85, 89, 113,
    114, 143
Ciampi, Carlo Azeglio, 51, 79
Cioloş, Dacian, 119
Civil servants, 103
Coelho, Pedro Passos, 128
Colombo, Emilio, 114
Conservative and agrarian parties, 82
Conservatives, 167
Conte, Giuseppe, 51, 87, 109, 129
Couve de Murville, Maurice, 113
Cresson, Édith, 32

D
D'Alema, Massimo, 117
Dăncilă, Viorica, 32, 118
Dealignment, 186
Decisional autonomy, 89
Decision-making, 3, 7
Decline of party government, 3, 65
Delegation, 3, 91, 186
Demand side, 72
Democratic governance, 5,
    21, 67, 182
Democratic representation, 21, 182

De-politicization, 75
Descriptive representation, 186
Dimitrov, Philip, 37, 113
Dini, Lamberto, 51
Diplomats, 103, 123
Dombrovskis, Valdis, 37, 77
Draghi, Mario, 80
Duration, 111
Duration in office, 20

E
Election campaigns, 83
Electoral campaigns, 4
Electoral personalization, 81
Electoral system, 175
Electoral volatility, 74, 136
Electronic media, 71
Elite circulation, 58
Empowerment, 2
Emsis, Indulis, 54
Erlander, Tage, 55, 117
Established parties, 84
EU commissioner, 119
European Council, 139
European Court of Human
    Rights, 144
European Parliament, 103
European regions, 101
Executive leaders, 88
Expertise, 79
Experts, 104

F
Factor analysis, 136
Female prime ministers, 13
Fico, Robert, 91, 144
Fieandt, Rainer von, 51
Figl, Leopold, 113
Fischer, Jan, 80
Frederiksen, Mette, 32

G

Gate-keepers, 84, 191
Gender parity, 31
Geographical variation, 41
Global governance, 2
Godmanis, Ivars, 37, 109, 131n1
Governance, 66
Governmental policy, 59, 66
Governments, 65
Grivas, Ioannis, 115
Gross, Stanislav, 37
Guterres, António, 115

H

Head of government, 113
Huysmans, Camille, 113

I

Indzhova, Reneta, 32
Insider experiences, 92, 105
Insiders, 85
Institutional settings, 7
Interest groups, 103
Intergovernmental negotiations, 2
International expertise, 137
Internationalization of politics, 2, 81
International organizations, 103, 123, 140

J

Jäätteenmäki, Anneli, 32, 114
Janša, Janez, 116

K

Kaczyński, Jarosław, 55, 91
Kallas, Siim, 125
Kalvītis, Aigars, 37
Karamanlis, Konstantinos, 115
Kataine, Jyrki, 37
Kenny, Enda, 113
Kern, Christian, 1
Kiesinger, Kurt Georg, 116, 119
Kiviniemi, Mari, 32
Klaus, Václav, 88
Koizumi, Junichiro, 86
Kopacz, Ewa, 32
Kosor, Jadranka, 32, 54
Krasts, Guntars, 37
Kurz, Sebastian, 37, 116
Kuuskoski, Reino, 51

L

Laar, Mart, 37
Leadership autonomy, 83
Leadership skills, 91, 102, 137
Leadership styles, 3
Legitimacy, 71
Lehto, Reino Ragnar, 51
Lemass, Seán, 114
Leterme, Yves, 117
Letta, Enrico, 118
Liberal democracies, 3
Liberals, 167
Liinamaa, Keijo, 51
Local assembly, 118
Löfven, Stefan, 88, 113
Loyalty, 84

M

Managerial skills, 87, 120
Mandate representation, 185, 190
Marcinkiewicz, Kazimierz, 54–55
Marin, Sanna, 32, 37
Mass communication, 3
Mass parties, 168
May, Theresa, 32
Mayors, 117
Mečiar, Vladimír, 55, 90

Mediatization, 66, 182
Member of parliament, 138, 183
Merkel, Angela, 32, 48, 55, 89, 116
Merz, Friedrich, 48
Messmer, Pierre, 113
Michel, Charles, 37
Ministerial, 91
　conflicts, 189
　experiences, 108, 113
Mitsotakis, Kyriakos, 115
Modi, Narendra, 86
Monti, Mario, 51, 80, 109, 119
Moral hazard, 138
Morawiecki, Mateusz, 55, 77
Mota Pinto, Carlos, 115
Municipal councils, 117

N
NATO, 139
New democracies, 37, 109
New parties, 34, 78
Nobre da Costa, Alfredo, 115
Non-majoritarian institutions, 73
Non-partisan cabinet, 80
Non-political, 120
　expertise, 87
　sectors, 104
Nordic Council, 145

O
Occupational background, 66
Occupational composition, 10
Occupational positions, 103
Opposition leader, 12, 139
Orbán, Viktor, 37, 55, 77, 86, 91
Oresharski, Plamen, 131n1
Orešković, Tihomir, 87
Outsider experiences, 92
Outsiders, 78, 86, 87

P
Pahor, Borut, 116
Papademos, Lucas, 80, 109
Papandreou, Andreas, 80, 115, 153
Parliamentarians, 85
Parliamentary democracies, 66
Parliamentary election, 188
Parliamentary experiences, 102
Parliamentary party group, 184
Parliamentary systems, 156
Parliaments, 65, 66
Partisan background, 20
Partisan experiences, 111
Partisan governments, 81
Partisan identification, 81
Partisan prime minister, 1
Parts, Juhan, 37, 77, 113
Party-agents, 2, 3, 65, 67, 91, 135
Party apprenticeships, 84, 89
Party-based, 79, 103
Party-based politics, 67
Party brand, 185
Party careers, 107
Party-centered, 84
Party families, 54, 175
Party governments, 2, 66,
　135, 154
Party head, 102, 139, 187
Party identification, 2
Party leaders, 12, 85, 115, 116
Party leadership, 11, 105
Party loyalty, 135
Party membership, 74
Partyness of government, 69
Party organizations, 67, 137
Party politicians, 78
Party politics, 104
Party-principal, 3, 65, 67, 91, 135
Party representation, 22n1
Party responsibility, 182
Party responsiveness, 182

Party systems, 82
  fragmentation, 2
  institutionalization, 192
Party training, 85
Pathway to power, 107
Pawlak, Waldemar, 37
Pedersen Index, 155
Performance in office, 8
Personal characteristics, 10
Personal governing, 89
Personal government, 80
Personality traits, 191
Personalization, 6
Personalization of politics, 6
Personalized style, 3
Personal leaders, 5
Personal leadership, 68, 91
Personal mandates, 83, 89
Personal parties, 86
Personal power, 67
Personal voting, 89
Pikrammenos, Panagiotis, 109
Pintasilgo, Maria de Lourdes, 32, 115, 123, 128
Plenković, Andrej, 119
Policy coordination, 2
Political arenas, 66
Political behavior, 8
Political career, 9, 67
Political competition, 82
Political elite, 30
Political entrepreneurs, 137
Political executives, 65
Political experiences, 3, 12, 20, 44, 65, 68, 183
Political ideologies, 67
Political influence, 5
Political insiders, 11, 102
Political institutions, 65, 84
Political leaders, 85
Political leadership, 91
Political life, 65
Political outsiders, 45, 102, 183
Political participation, 3
Political parties, 65, 66
Political power, 83
Political professionals, 66
Political recruitment, 31
Political representation, 87
Political skills, 67, 103
Pompidou, Georges, 51
Ponta, Victor, 37
Populism, 65, 84
Populists, 79
  demands, 87
  leaders, 67, 85
  parties, 77
  prime ministers, 86
Portfolios, 91
Presidentialization, 5, 65, 135
Presidentialization of politics, 3, 67
Presidentialized governments, 89
Presidentialized politics, 88
Presidential powers, 163–167
Prime ministerial job, 4, 102
Prime ministerial offices, 30, 31, 86
Prime ministerial performance, 4
Prime ministerial powers, 136, 160
Prime ministers' profiles, 65
Principal-agent approach, 91
Principal-agent theory, 11
Prodi, Romano, 51, 113, 128, 131n1

Q
Quay, Jan de, 116

R
Račan, Ivica, 116
Radičová, Iveta, 32
Rajoy, Mariano, 115

Rallis, Georgios, 115, 144
Ratas, Jüri, 37
Regime transition, 34
Regional, 117
Reliability, 2, 68, 84
Renzi, Matteo, 37, 78, 90
Representation, 66, 76
Representative institutions, 87
Research questions, 15
Responsibility, 5, 69, 70
Responsible, 66, 93n4
Responsible government, 72
Responsive, 66, 77, 93n4
Responsive government, 72
Responsiveness, 70
Rocard, Michel, 78
Rõivas, Taavi, 37
Rupo, Elio Di, 116, 117
Rutte, Mark, 144

S
Samaras, Antonis, 115, 144
Sanader, Ivo, 54
Sánchez, Pedro, 115
Saxe-Coburg-Gotha, Simeon, 86
Schmidt, Helmut, 119
Schröder, Gerhard, 48, 90, 116
Selection and de-selection, 10, 11
Selection of prime ministers, 2, 84
Semi-presidential democracies, 4
Semi-presidential systems, 136, 156
Senior civil servant, 123
Seniority, 36
Šķēle, Andris, 37, 114
Skvernelis, Saulius, 113
Social cleavages, 2, 82, 154
Social Democratic, 168
Social Democrats, 82
Socialists, 167
Sofiyanski, Stefan, 117
Solberg, Erna, 32, 139, 144

Stanishev, Sergei, 37
State bureaucracies, 122
Stoiber, Edmund, 48
Straujuma, Laimdota, 32
Suárez, Adolfo, 115
Subnational, 193
Subnational institution, 118
Suchocka, Hanna, 32
Summit meetings, 103
Supply side, 72
Supranational, 193
Supranational organizations, 79
Szydło, Beata, 32, 77

T
Tarand, 131n1
Technical experiences, 3, 20, 65, 103, 182
Technical expertise, 68
Technical knowledge-based, 103
Technical skills, 104
Technocracy, 65, 84
Technocratic governments, 87
Technocratic populists, 88
Technocratic prime minister, 1, 87
Technocratic traits, 67
Technocrats, 47, 79
Technopopulism, 88
Thanou-Christophilou, Vassiliki, 32, 106, 109
Thatcher, Margaret, 32, 55, 78, 90
Thorning-Schmidt, Helle, 32, 119
Torp, Oscar, 116
Tsipras, Alexis, 86, 106, 115, 122
Tusk, Donald, 91
Tzannetakis, Tzannis, 115

U
Ungureanu, Mihai Răzvan, 61n2
United Nation (UN), 139

V
Vagnorius, Gediminas, 37, 131n1
Vähi, Tiit, 131n1
Vanhanen, Matti, 114
Varadkar, Leo, 37
Videnov, Zhan, 37
Volatility, 2

W
Wilmès, Sophie, 32
World Bank, 139

Z
Zapatero, Rodríguez, 115
Zolotas, Xenophon, 115

GPSR Compliance
The European Union's (EU) General Product Safety Regulation (GPSR) is a set of rules that requires consumer products to be safe and our obligations to ensure this.

If you have any concerns about our products, you can contact us on

ProductSafety@springernature.com

In case Publisher is established outside the EU, the EU authorized representative is:

Springer Nature Customer Service Center GmbH
Europaplatz 3
69115 Heidelberg, Germany

www.ingramcontent.com/pod-product-compliance
Ingram Content Group UK Ltd.
Pitfield, Milton Keynes, MK11 3LW, UK
UKHW021251180426
11946UKWH00004B/76